The Family Portrait

A STRUGGLE TO HAVE A FAMILY

By Carol M. Johnson

Copyright © 2018 by Carol May Johnson

All rights reserved. No part of this book may be reproduced or used in any manner without written permission of the copyright owner except for the use of quotations in a book review. For more information, address: cjohnsonauthor.com

FIRST EDITION

www.carolmayjohnson.com

ISBN-13: 978-1729851814
ISBN-10: 1729851819

WHY I WROTE

"THE FAMILY PORTRAIT"

I started writing "THE FAMILY PORTRAIT" so my son, Cameron would know what it took to bring him into the world. After helping run a support group for people who had lost their babies, I realized that others would also benefit from my story. If my story helps one person know that they are not alone, then my story was worth sharing.

-Carol

HUGS AND THANK YOU'S

My biggest "THANK YOU" goes to my husband and love, Kennie. He has been there from the start and never left my side. I couldn't have gone through this without you. You are my rock. Big hugs!

To my son Cameron who has been my pride and joy. I love you!

Hugs to my mom and dad who has always been there to support my every move in life. Also: thank you to my dad's encouraging words: "Never stop writing your story until you are finished."

In memory of my mother-in-law who encouraged me to continue writing my story.

To the ladies that took the time to read for me and keep me on track: Michelle Garcia, Marisa Treadway, Jessica Garcia, Charlotte Slattum, Sheri Stickley and Liz Le Blanc.

Special thanks to Laura Pawlicki and Laura Dunkel for proof reading.

Huge thank you to my niece Traci Ross who jumped in and helped make my book cover come to life.

A thank you goes out to my niece Jennifer Nelson who helped me rediscover makeup.

Hugs to a very talented family Gina, Victoria and Don Butz for my author photo. Awesome job!

BIG HUGS TO YOU ALL!

Editing by:

Darica Smith
Crimson Turtle

Book Cover by:

Traci Ross

MY THOUGHTS

"I am the mother of six but I have only one living son." -Carol

"Many people don't have any problems having a baby, but there are those of us who do have trouble, downright tragedies. Those that can and choose to continue trying to have a baby, have a rough road ahead, I know, I am one of them." -Carol

NO NAME

"A spouse that loses a partner is called a widow/widower. A child who loses a parent is called an orphan. There is no NAME for a parent who loses their child." -Carol

TIME FOR GREIVING

"There is no time limit for grief, because you never stopped missing the person you lost. You just have to live day-by-day in the memory of them, instead of 'them'." -Carol

SMILES

"It amazes me that we can endure so much in life and still have a smile left in us." -Carol

TABLE OF CONTENTS

CHAPTER ONE: FOR THE LOVE OF KENNIE 9

CHAPTER TWO: STARTING A FAMILY 33

CHAPER THREE: BACK TO THE DRAWING BOARD 48

CHAPTER FOUR: NOT GIVING UP 63

CHAPTER FIVE: ONE MORE TRY 74

CHAPTER SIX: MOMENT BY MOMENT 107

CHAPTER SEVEN: TRYING TO COPE 222

CHAPTER EIGHT: THE COURAGE TO CONTINUE 254

MY STORY

My story is about my struggle to have a family. I was married at 19, my husband was 20, we decided to wait to have babies. Four years into the marriage my husband was paralyzed from the neck down with Guillain-Barre syndrome (GBS). I was told that if he survived, her would be in a wheelchair for the rest of his life. The one thing that got him through this illness was the thought of having a baby and completing "THE FAMILY PORTRAIT".

CHAPTER ONE: FOR THE LOVE OF KENNIE

As I kiss my son goodnight, I begin to look back on the struggle I had trying to have a family.

It's been years since my husband and I said "I do." We were very young when we got married. I was 19 and my husband Kennie was 20. Our plan was to get a financial head start by buying a house, paying off the cars, and then when the time was right, we would try to start a family. We would have two to three children over a period of six years and complete "The Family Portrait".

Kennie and I were married on April 19. The untold road ahead seemed to be paved for us. We were both from strong family backgrounds. My father and mother, Ted and Donna, and Kennie's father and mother, Roger and Ruth, have been married for years and never divorced. They never had any problems having children. I'm the youngest of three girls and Kennie is the youngest with one older brother and two older sisters. Our brothers and sisters, for the most part, never had any problems having children. We figured why should we be any different in our quest to have a family?

After living in an apartment for almost a year (at the ages of 20 and 21) we were ready to buy our first house. In February we closed escrow on a three-bedroom, two bath, one car garage house in a family setting neighborhood – we considered this to be remarkable at our tender young ages. Cars paid off and figuring that we had two years until we started a family, we planned to go on a few small vacations, starting with Disneyland on New Years' eve. We celebrated New Year's Eve in Anaheim, California and New Year's Day we spent playing at Disneyland. We had a blast! There were no worries back then. We still had our innocence and had no idea the tricks life can play on you. We had been married for three years. I was 23 with long, straight, brown hair, five feet six inches, 130 pounds, and ready to spend the rest of my life with Kennie. Kennie was 24 and very outgoing, six feet, also 130 pounds, brown hair, green eyes and the man I chose to be my husband. He drove a truck delivering major appliances for a living. He coached little league for three years, played on an adult softball team, and in his spare time I always had something planned.

A few days after we came home from Disneyland, Kennie moved a refrigerator from our house to my dad's rental house all by himself. It was a full size, side-by-side refrigerator. He loaded it into and out of the back of his lifted pickup truck. I kept telling him he should wait for someone to help him, but knowing that he did this for a living, I finally gave up. I guess it's like stopping to ask for directions, he was going to figure this out for himself. This was the first time I saw how strong Kennie really was and I was impressed! To look at him you would have never known.

It was Friday morning on January 5 and we were getting ready for work. I worked at a car dealership as a Title Clerk. We both left the house around the same time so we would get up and get moving at the same pace. Kennie was sitting on the side of the bed attempting to put his shoes on and it was taking quite a while.

"What's wrong?" I asked

"I don't know. My hands and feet are tingling."

Kennie explained that it was like when your foot falls asleep, but there was no reason for both of his hands and feet to fall asleep.

"You probably pinched a nerve when you moved that refrigerator all by yourself." I replied, hoping that next time he would stop and ask for directions. Figuring that the tingling would eventually go away, we went to work.

I was sitting at my desk, just before lunch when the phone rang. Our insurance had changed as of the first of the year. Kennie wanted to know what doctor and doctor's office I had chosen. Kennie then tells me that the tingling in his hands and feet had spread to his arms and legs. He had been talking to his boss and they both agreed that he should leave work early and go have it checked out, to be on the safe side. Kennie never calls in sick, that's just the type of person he is, and this did sound serious. I hung up the phone still convinced that it had something to do with the refrigerator he moved all by himself a few days earlier.

Several hours later I pulled up to the house and Kennie's truck was nowhere in sight. I never even put my foot on the brake as I passed the house. I went straight to the doctor's office. I pulled into the parking lot. I was a little unsure that I was in the right location. I looked around for an address and saw Kennie's truck sitting in the last parking spot. My heart fell to the floor and what was left of my breath went too. I knew right away this was not good. I parked and ran into the office. The waiting room was packed with patients and not one of them was Kennie. I pushed my way to the desk even though it was not in my nature to do so. The clerk had several people waiting to talk to her and all were staring me down for taking cuts. I was a nervous wreck but a determined nervous wreck.

"I'm looking for my husband!" I rudely said.

She looked up at me, her eyes widened, she stood up and yelled into the back, "Mrs. Johnson is here!"

That was the first time I was ever referred to as "Mrs. Johnson". I had not introduced myself and no one knew that I was on my way down there – no one could have known. She never asked what my husband's name was and yet, she knew exactly who he was. This made the bad worse.

Within seconds a nurse appeared at the door leading into the examining rooms.

"Mrs. Johnson?" She said.

My breathing was shallow as I walked over to her. She held the door for me to enter, which slammed shut when she let go of it. A bit startling considering I didn't know what to expect and no one had clued me in on why Kennie had been there for over six hours. She led me down a long hall and in the very last room on the left she pointed to the open door. I cautiously looked in and there was Kennie. He looked up at me with a blank look on his face. He was sitting on the examining table white as a ghost, with both of his work boots off and the doctor was pounding on his knees with an instrument to check his reflexes. Nothing from his knees down was moving, no matter where or how hard they hit his knees. The same with his arms - there was no movement. The doctors saw me enter the room quietly. Nothing was said to me and then they left the room. I walked over to Kennie and gave him a hug.

"How are you doing?" I asked.

"The doctors have been running tests and continuing to check my reflexes on my knees… nothing. When I first came into the office, I was able to still move my hands and feet. Now my hands, arms, feet, and legs are going numb."

Kennie's limb movement was deteriorating. In fact, Kennie was deteriorating. His demeanor, understandably was confused. He was clear about his physical condition but puzzled, as were the doctors, about what caused it. The doctor came into the room, introduced himself and three others to me. The first was the family practice doctor, next the two interns and then the nurse who had walked me to the examination room. They all seemed friendly enough. The doctors and nurses had been devoting all their time only to Kennie and still had no answers. This explained the packed waiting room. The doctors at this facility had never seen anything like this before.

They kept asking strange questions like, "Have you eaten any raw fish in the past forty-eight hours?"

Our answer was, "No". Needless to say, if raw fish can do this to you, we surely wouldn't be eating any raw fish in the future.

The family practice doctor was unable to diagnose Kennie's condition when one of the interns, just out of medical school, spoke up. He was still "wet behind the ears" but I'm very thankful that he put his two cents in. He said that he read of a case in medical school about a person whose nerves quit, he pondered a minute, tapping his chin and said, "Guillain-Barré". The doctors and interns left the room. The nurse went back to her regular duties. We both just sat there. There was nothing to say. I guess just the comfort of being together was enough for the moment.

After a bit the doctors returned to the room to update us on what they were pursuing. They had been gone for over thirty minutes, it felt like a lot longer. The family practice doctor told us that they had been looking up Guillain-Barré in the medical books. He also told us that he called two out-of-town neurological doctors and then a local neurologist. He still had no diagnosis, but Guillain-Barré was the only thing they had to go on. Once again, the doctors left the room without giving us a chance to ask any questions. My mind was wandering as I sat there. I was planning the weekend, trying to modify it so Kennie wouldn't be over worked. At 8:00 p.m. the doctors finally returned.

The doctors explained, "If it is Guillain-Barré, your nerves will shut down. Your white blood cells, which help fight off infection and illness, like the common cold, have been working overtime. Your body is probably producing too much of these white blood cells and they are now attacking your nerves, which is why you are starting to lose control of your hands and feet. It will continue to spread through your body until it reaches your lungs, you'll stop breathing and you can die. In years past they put people with Guillain-Barré into an Iron Lung."

The doctors last words I remember were, "Well, you have a choice. You can go to the hospital tonight and pay your $500 co-pay or you can dial 911 when your lungs stop working."

To us of course there was no choice. What kind of a

choice was waking up to a dead husband? We were going to the hospital.

    The doctor called the hospital and arranged for Kennie's hospital stay. The plan was just an overnight observation and go home no later than Sunday. I called Roger and Ruth (Kennie's parents) and told them what was going on. I needed help driving Kennie's truck home since Kennie couldn't drive and I had my own car to drive home. They lived close and were there in just a matter of minutes. Then I called my dad and mom and told them what was going on. They also lived just a few minutes down the road. They agreed to meet me at my house. It was after 8:30 p.m. before we left the doctor's office. Kennie had been in the doctor's office for over eight hours. He walked into the packed doctor's office thinking he would get a prescription, a recommendation for bedrest, and just go home. Instead he's wobbling through an empty, dimly lit, closed doctor's office not knowing what was wrong with him.

    We managed to get Kennie out and into my father-in-law's Buick. Ruth drove my car. She was uncomfortable driving Kennie's truck, a stick shift. I can't blame her, the truck did have touchy gears. Roger drove Kennie to our house in his car, with Ruth following. Ruth parked my car and the three of them proceeded to the hospital. I drove Kennie's unruly truck. It gave me time to think a bit. The doctor gave a detailed description of the illness, but never said how he contracted the illness and I didn't think about it until I was alone. I finally pulled up to our house and parked Kennie's truck. I looked up at the house and there stood my mom and dad on the front porch waiting for me. They had all jumped at a moment's notice.

    I ran by them quickly, unlocked the front door

mumbling something like, "Hello, thanks for coming" and into the house with my dad and mom right behind me. My job was to get the comfort items: change of clothes, socks, underwear, toothbrush, etc. and feed our dog, Lady. I started to notice I was in shock.

I was saying things like, "How can this be happening to Kennie? How can this be happening to me? We're young! We're not supposed to get sick! Not like this!"

I was running around the house like a mad woman almost hyperventilating, pulling stuff out of drawers as fast as I could open them, when I looked up and saw my dad and mom standing at my bedroom door just looking at me.

My dad said, "Take a deep breath. It will be okay." How could he know it was going to be okay? But it did the trick. I took a deep breath and I did calm down. I got into their car and we went to the hospital.

The parking wasn't exactly convenient to the lobby. After a couple of elevators and a bit of a walk we were finally at the front desk. I was informed that Kennie was still in admitting. What? I thought. I was at least 40 minutes behind Kennie's arriving at the hospital. Once again, I was shown down a hall where Kennie was sitting. He had lost all control of his hands by this time and was unable to hold a pen well enough to sign himself into the hospital. I had to sign him in. Why they left a man in his condition waiting in the admitting room all this time, just so I could sign him in I'll never understand. Why didn't they just have him make his mark and have a witness sign alongside of him?

Once I signed Kennie in a nurse asked him if he wanted a wheelchair, he refused. That was just the way Kennie was, never trying to put anyone out and always trying to prove he was strong.

When we got to the room Kennie managed to change his clothes and get into bed with no assistance. He had a small room all to himself, not far from the nurse's station and it was quiet. By this time it was around 11:00 p.m. Kennie had been at the doctor's office from lunch on and had nothing to eat since breakfast and was brought a small meal. Kennie's inability to grip a spoon, like the pen, meant he needed help eating. His mom helped Kennie eat while I stepped out of the room to call his boss to tell him what was going on. We all believed Kennie would be back to work on Monday. The floor Kennie was on was an all-male floor so I couldn't stay the night. Kennie's dad stayed with him and I went home. No matter how tired I was I couldn't sleep.

The next morning, I was at the hospital very early. I don't even remember the 45 minute drive. The nurses let me in to find that Kennie couldn't even get out of bed. I could only hope my poker face was working for me. I needed to be there for support, not breaking down in his time of need. Kennie was in bed and smiled. He couldn't move his hand to wave at me, but he waved what he could of his arm. He was so weak his brother had to help him use the port-a-potty that was on wheels next to his bed. I couldn't believe this was my Kennie. Here's a man who loaded a full size, side-by-side refrigerator in and out of his lifted truck all by himself, not three days earlier and now he can't even get out of bed by himself.

The nurses kept having him blow into a handheld machine to check lung capacity. The doctors then started tests: blood work, heart monitors, urine tests, and not one but two spinal taps. There was still no confirmation on the illness and Kennie continued to decline. I felt helpless and I'm sure Kennie did too. All kinds of doctors were called from the East Coast to the West Coast and the question still came up about the raw fish.

I stayed until they made me leave Saturday night and I returned bright and early Sunday morning. When I went into the room the doctor was holding onto Kennie and attempting to get Kennie back into the bed. The doctor explained that he wanted Kennie to walk across the room to see how far he could walk. Kennie stood up, never even took a step, collapsed and the doctor caught him.

After getting Kennie back in bed the doctor announced, "Okay. Done. Time for Intensive Care Unit." (ICU: A step up from a normal hospital room for helping critical patients.) By that afternoon we were informed that Kennie would have to go on a ventilator to support his breathing. The lung capacity test had shown a major decline, which meant Kennie was not going to be able to breathe on his own much longer. He was only able to move his head and very little of anything else.

I was told by the doctor that there are two ways to insert a ventilator. One way is to place an oxygen tube through the mouth down into the lungs, but if the tube remains in his throat for weeks it could affect his vocal cords and he may lose his voice. The second was a tracheotomy surgery option. A tube is placed into the windpipe that goes down to your lungs with a stub sticking out of the neck/throat right below the vocal cords and you can connect an oxygen machine up to it. Surgery is required to cut the hole in his neck/windpipe. In both cases oxygen is then pumped into the body to help Kennie breathe or worst case breathe for Kennie. This was the first time I was made aware of a wife's responsibilities. With Kennie's hands unable to grip a pen, I was told I would have to sign the authorization on Kennie's behalf. This meant I was the one signing to have Kennie's throat cut. So many things happening and so quickly. Decisions to make and no time to think things through. Just a quick explanation and go with it.

I was sitting next to the bed waiting for the orderly to take Kennie to the Operating Room (OR) when a nurse mistakenly gave the OR consent forms to Kennie's mom, Ruth, to sign.

The head nurse noticed and started yelling, "He's married!! The wife must sign the paperwork, not his mother!"

Ruth must have felt awful. Here she raised him and looked after him for 20 years and me, well I was only married to him for a mere three and a half years. The rights were quickly taken out of her hands and put into mine. I could see how the nurse could make that mistake. Kennie was very young. He still looked like a kid and at 140 pounds, he had yet to fill out his body to look like a man. Ruth handed me the consent forms and I signed them.

Reality really hit when the doctor told us Kennie might not live and at best he could expect to spend the rest of his life in a wheelchair. I'm 23 and faced with the fact that I'm going to be a widow. No! I married him for better or worse, in sickness and in health and we were going to get through this!

Our brothers and sisters and their families started to show up to check on Kennie. They had learned about the surgery and wanted to be there for us. It seemed to take forever for the OR to be ready for Kennie. While we were waiting, the doctor came into Kennie's room to talk to us privately. The doctor informed us that Kennie had a rare illness called Guillain-Barré. This was the first time the doctor gave the illness an official name. The spinal tap finally paid off. He continued by telling us that it's a condition where the body has had some kind of trigger or illness that caused the immune system to react. The body's defense is to produce white blood cells which fight an infection or a cold. Kennie's body has been working overtime in producing too many white blood cells. The original trigger is gone but Kennie's body is still producing white blood cells which are now attacking his own nerves and causing them to shut down. Guillain-Barré first attacks the furthest part of the body - the hands and feet. It then makes its way to the torso, heart, and lungs which will leave the victim paralyzed and unable to breathe. This is the stage where Kennie is. The doctor asked us if we would consider plasmapheresis treatments, explaining that this was an experimental treatment but it had helped other patients with Guillain-Barré. The plasmapheresis treatments involved putting a tube the size of a standard straw into his main artery in his upper right leg and then from time to time hooking a mobile machine up to the tube and removing about a pint of blood from his body at a time. The machine would separate the red blood cells from the old plasma, which holds the white blood cells and then mix the red blood cells with the new plasma and return it back to Kennie's body. The hope was that with less white blood cells in the plasma, the body would stop making more white blood cells. It seemed to be the only thing we could try. The answer was, "Yes". The procedure of inserting the tube into Kennie's artery started immediately. The entire family and I were asked to leave Kennie's little room while they inserted the tube into his leg. The team of doctors and nurses congregated around his bed, a tray with the instruments needed was brought in and placed next to the doctor, then the curtain was pulled shut.

  I heard the doctor say to Kennie, "This might be a little uncomfortable, but it won't take long." Within seconds I heard a painful sound coming from Kennie. The curtain was then opened. The tube was in. As the doctors were calling us back into the room, the orderly came with the bed to take Kennie to the OR. I watched as they moved Kennie's almost lifeless body from one bed to the other. The family gave him kisses, said their goodbyes, wished him well, and then it was my turn.

    I looked into his eyes and told him, "I love you and I will be waiting for you when you come out. We will get through this." I leaned into him and gave him a loving, reassuring kiss. The bed started to move and the orderly pushed him away. Standing there as Kennie disappeared around the corner, I noticed the room full of tears including my own. I realized the strong family support. Most of the family was there - crying but there. The doctor told us that the tracheotomy would prevent him from eating and talking. A nasogastric (NG) tube would be placed through his nose, down into his stomach and green colored baby food would be pumped through it so Kennie could eat. Yummy! I was informed that the doctors tried to place the NG tube before they inserted the leg tube but were unsuccessful because Kennie had a sensitive gag-reflex. Instead Kennie and the doctors agreed to place the NG tube when he was knocked out during surgery.

    Kennie came out of recovery and went into the ICU. The nurse came to tell us that he was out and that we could see him. I asked if the NG tube was placed, successfully. Her answer was, "Yes". She informed us that only two at a time could go into the ICU so Ruth and I went in first. The nurse, trying to prepare us for what we were about to see as we walked into the room, explained that Kennie would be groggy from the anesthetics, would only be able to move his head from side to side, was no longer breathing on his own, and the tube might be a bit frightening. As I entered the room, the first thing I noticed was the smell. A combination, of plastics, oxygen and some other smell that I couldn't quite put my finger on. It smelled like an old musty house, a smell that will stay with me forever. I'll never forget it. My eyes hit Kennie - tubes everywhere and machines making all kinds of sounds. Nurses were running in and out of the room, checking on the machine's bells, whistles, and writing on charts. It all was so busy and yet somewhere in there was my husband, a man that had barely begun to experience life. I walked up to the bedside and took hold of his non-responsive hand.

I leaned in, kissed him, look into his eyes, and said, "I love you. I'm here and will always be here. No matter what."

The doctor had advised us prior to surgery to keep Kennie's mind on the here and now, as we needed a distraction when Kennie returned from surgery. The only thing I could think of was starting a family. Kennie couldn't talk because the tube in his throat was blocking the airway to his vocal cords. I had to do all the talking. No problem. I had been given the gift of gab. I started by asking him to close his eyes and imagine what our future children would look like. Boy or girl? Color of hair and eyes? Whose eyes, nose, all the way down to the toes? He would blink when he agreed. It seemed to do the trick. It kept his spirits up.

Ruth left half way through my talk with Kennie so that other family members who were waiting could come in. It was hard for me to endure the sight of Kennie like this. I'm sure it was just as hard on Ruth to see her son in the bed unable to move or even breathe on his own. I felt for everyone else, but I wouldn't allow myself the negative. I had to stay strong and focused. No self-pity for me. One by one family members came and went. I just couldn't leave his side. That night Kennie and I decided that when (positive thinking) he came home we would start trying to have children. It was something to keep us focused.

Family members and friends continued to come and go

until visitor hours were over. I kept Kennie's boss informed. Needless to say, Kennie did not go back to work on Monday. It was amazing how many people were concerned for Kennie and started to research this illness. I received all kinds of calls and literature on Guillain-Barré. Some from people I didn't even know. One of Kennie's coworkers looked up the illness and explained it to the rest of the coworkers.

My own employer was very understanding and I was able to come and go as needed. I would go into work around 2:00 a.m. The night guard got to know me pretty well. I would stay at work until visiting hours started and then go to the hospital until the nurses kicked me out around 1:00 p.m. or 2:00 p.m. for a shift change. I would do some work and check messages at my desk for about an hour and then return to the hospital where I stayed by Kennie's bedside for as long as the nurses would let me. I would also spend one night at home to make sure the dog was fed and then spend the next night in Ruth and Roger's motor home, which they had parked in the hospital's parking lot so they didn't have to leave. I would spend every minute I could with Kennie, talking about whatever came to mind.

Ruth and I would stand at his bedside and move Kennie's legs and arms for him, to keep them from becoming stiff. The nurses, for the most part, were nice. They not only helped Kennie, but they also helped me by offering me food and drinks. They understood that I only cared about being with Kennie.

At night it was clear that Kennie didn't sleep well and for some reason he didn't want us to leave him. The doctors and nurses assured us that it was just anxiety and they would give him a shot of morphine or valium or both to help him calm down. Kennie fought it, the drugs didn't affect him at all. He couldn't wait for us to show up in the morning, because this meant he could sleep, knowing we were there to watch over him.

I arrived at the hospital one morning and noticed that Kennie was trying to tell us something. Kennie was unable to speak due to the trachea tube in his throat so I wrote the alphabet on a sheet of paper and stuck a pen in his mouth. The only part of his body Kennie could still move was his head. We then held the paper up so he could point to the letters with the pen. Slowly he was able to spell out what he wanted to say. Communication finally. What he told us scared me.

The bed he was on rotated from side to side by deflating and inflating. This was to keep the fluids from settling in his lungs. The ventilator that was connected to his throat was off to the right of his bed. (Remember this is the only thing keeping Kennie breathing.) He had a button also to the right of his head, which was propped up on his pillow so he could hit it with his head to call the nurse. The problem was when the bed deflated to the left, the ventilator would randomly disconnect from Kennie's throat and he couldn't hit the call button to call the nurse until the bed re-inflated itself. This deflation and inflation process took two or three minutes. It took another two or three minutes for the nurse to respond after Kennie managed to hit the call button. The whole time Kennie was without air and understandably panicking. No wonder they had to inject him with so many drugs to calm him down, he couldn't breathe! By using the alphabet chart Kennie was able to explain what was wrong and something as simple as a rubber band around the air tube connected to his throat fixed the problem. He still didn't sleep well at night, but after that who could blame him?

In addition to the whole tube disconnection thing,

Kennie also had a nurse that was inattentive and just mean to him. With our new-found communication pen-in-mouth and alphabet chart, Kennie was able to tell us how rough she was with him. In some cases, she hurt him when she didn't have to. She must have figured because he couldn't speak, she could do a half-assed job and who is he going to tell? Well now that he can communicate, he let us know that he didn't want her as his nurse. I went to the Charge Nurse and informed her of the situation and how the night nurse treated Kennie. Kennie believed the night nurse must have known that the oxygen was coming apart from the tube when she eventually responded to the call button. Her solution to the situation was more morphine and valium, not to attempt fix the problem. His main complaint was that there was no one there at night to make sure she did her job the way she was supposed to. The Charge Nurse took the report from the nurse, but never investigated the excessive use of morphine and valium on Kennie. If she had she would have seen for herself that the tube was popping off and leaving Kennie in a panic with no oxygen. Even though the rubber band solved the problem, Kennie didn't trust the night nurse anymore and didn't want her as his nurse any longer. The Charge Nurse understood and assured me the night nurse wouldn't be his nurse in the future.

    The night nurse was no longer taking care of Kennie but she was still working in the ICU. This nurse had to be almost six feet tall, with blond hair, brown eyes, and was about 30 years old. Her size was intimidating, especially when I noticed her coming directly toward me one evening when I was alone in the room with Kennie, who was asleep. She asked if I would step out into the hall for a minute and talk with her. I did. She backed me up literally against the wall and began to tell me how I got her into trouble by complaining about her. She said she had a talk with Kennie, he was okay with her being his nurse and that I had no business making a formal complaint to her boss.

When she paused, I took the opportunity to speak.

"First. I wasn't the one who complained about you. It was Kennie, but I was more than happy to do it for him. You left him without oxygen! You never caught or corrected the tube disconnecting problem. You didn't respond quickly when he finally was able to hit the call button. He felt like he was dying under your watch. He doesn't want you as his nurse, especially after this. You just proved to me that you are incapable of being compassionate. You'll be lucky if you don't lose your job. I'm sure that yelling at a patient's wife is not protocol."

Looking around the hall I realized that she timed it so that most of her coworkers would be at dinner. After that I didn't see her again. Good riddance! It was one of the most powerful things I had ever done. I not only stood up for Kennie but for myself.

Kennie also had to endure the suctioning of fluid out of his lungs. This involved disconnecting his ventilator from his throat and shoving a small snake-like tube through the opening and down to his lungs, which would suck out any phlegm that he couldn't cough up. Yuck! In between suctioning they would give him breaths of air by squeezing a bottle that looked like a two-liter bottle of seven-up that was held up to the opening of his throat. The first few times they did this I had to leave the room. I couldn't take watching Kennie struggling for air, but little by little I became numb to all the procedures. So much so that one time I found myself helping the line from his urine catheter empty into the bag hanging on his bedside. I stopped myself saying, "Gross, what I am doing?"

Ruth and I counted the equipment connected to Kennie: eight. Eight tubes sticking out of him: a heart monitor, the ventilator, NG tube, intravenous (IV) line, urine catheter, the plasmapheresis tube, oxygen monitor, and the "moon boots" (as Ruth and I named them). "Moon boots" were inflatable boots wrapped around his legs and feet which would periodically inflate to keep his blood circulating.

The plasmapheresis treatments started within a day or two. A big machine was wheeled into his room with a bag of plasma about the size of a bag of ice you buy from the store. I still don't fully understand how this machine did what it did. I watched as the technician connected the machine to the straw-like tube sticking out of Kennie's leg. The machine was programmed to Kennie's specific needs and it did its magic one pint at a time. The first time they forgot to warm the plasma and Kennie got cold. Lots and lots of warm blankets were placed on Kennie to warm him. The next time the plasma bag was brought up to body temperature before they started and Kennie was fine. The treatments were done about every six to eight hours.

I continued my running from motor home, to work, to the hospital and home for almost ten days. I was tired and determined never to give up. My life had changed and so did I. I became more outspoken. If we needed something I didn't sit quietly and wait for it like before. I got up and got it one way or another. The hospital seemed to have become my home and so I helped myself to whatever I needed.

I had been calling Kennie's boss every few days to let him know how Kennie was doing. His boss never came to the hospital to visit Kennie. Halfway through a phone call his boss told me that he had Kennie's final checks and wanted me to come pick them up. I was dumbfounded. How was I going to tell Kennie? He's in the ICU fighting for his life and one of the things that he could return to that was normal for him was gone.

I asked his boss, "If Kennie got better could he return to work?" He told me yes. Kennie has always been a good, loyal employee. I asked about the insurance. Would it continue to cover him? He said he would work it out so I could pay the premiums and we would still have insurance. My work offered insurance but it was more expensive and not as good. I had the only income and quite frankly I'm not sure how much longer I could keep this up. But once again I had no choice. Later that day Kennie's boss called. He found out that one of Kennie's coworkers was coming by to visit Kennie and had him bring Kennie's final checks. I thanked him for his time and told him I would call him when Kennie was better. Hanging up the phone I couldn't help but think his boss believes Kennie's going to die or at the very least never walk again.

"No." I said to myself. "He's wrong." I couldn't tell Kennie what I suspected his boss was thinking. It seemed pointless.

I could tell Kennie was starting to feel restless and thought maybe a bath would help. The nurse ordered some bathing supplies and a rinseless shampoo for his head since he couldn't get out of bed for a shower. I gave him a sponge bath. The nurse helped me with the shampooing. He seemed to enjoy the head massage. Brushing the teeth was something that we would tackle another day. This did seem to make him feel better.

After several of the plasmapheresis treatments Ruth and I were at Kennie's bedside. Ruth was on one side and I was on the other and I could see in Kennie's eyes that he was frustrated about something. We got the chart and pen out to find out that he was cold. When we covered him up, we could tell he was upset. Two seconds later with his own hands and arms which were crossed over his chest, he shoved the covers off. Ruth and I looked at each other. Kennie was clearly upset and we were smiling from ear to ear. I started to cry with tears of joy. This was the first time in over a week Kennie had moved on his own. This was also the first sign that he was getting better and proof that the plasmapheresis treatments were working.

Excited about what Kennie had just done I called for the nurse. She called the doctor.

    I couldn't wait for the doctor because I had to return to work and we didn't know when he would arrive. I was sitting at my desk working and returning phone calls when the phone rang.

    I answered it, "Hello."

    The voice on the other end said, "Hello. I love you."

    It was Kennie!

    I could hardly speak and started to cry with relief. I was listening to Kennie talk again. He told me that after I had left the doctor came in and removed the tube from his throat. Better yet, he was out of the ICU and in a regular room. I hung up the phone and continued to cry. The girls in the office thought the worst had happened. I explained it was good news. I dropped everything and went straight to the hospital.

    I walked into a packed room of people smiling, talking, and laughing. Right in the middle of the room was Kennie sitting up in bed, breathing on his own, talking, smiling, and laughing. Kennie told me that they were talking about releasing him soon. When I got closer to the bed, I took a closer look at him. He had no tubes, only an IV. I could handle the IV. He had a bandage over his throat where the tube was. He didn't have to eat anymore green baby food through his nose. He was chewing and swallowing. Something most of us take for granted. He also got to brush his teeth, after a week.

Kennie also had to start walking again. This came back easily for him. The nurses said it was because Ruth and I never stopped working Kennie's legs for him when he couldn't. Watching him walk was like watching someone get back on a bike after not riding one for some time. He was a bit wobbly but little by little he was moving.

The day finally came for the doctors to release him. Kennie had been in the ICU for a week and the hospital for two weeks. We were ready to go home. Packing was easy. I threw everything in a bag to deal with it when we got home.

I looked at Kennie and asked, "Are you ready to go home?"

He was already sitting on the side of the bed, fully dressed and even managed to put his shoes on. I had gone by See's Candy shop on my way to the hospital and bought a few boxes of candy. Kennie, now able to walk and talk, took the boxes of candy to the nurses, ICU nurses and doctors to personally thank them. Some of them were shocked to see him walking and others didn't realize how tall he was since he was always in a bed, but all of them were happy that he had recovered. Out the door we walked with no wheelchair. The next stop: home. Kennie weighed only 120 pounds, had a hole in his throat, and was alive!

Home. Kennie got out of the car and walked on his own into our house. I almost cried, considering the doctors said that at best he would be in a wheelchair for the rest of his life. Lady, our dog, was happy to see Kennie again. I believe that she knew he was sick. She was very gentle with him, not jumping all over him like usual. I made both of them dinner. I thought it was strange for Kennie to swallow food with a hole in his throat. You would think food would come out. I know the cut was far below where the esophagus meets the trachea, but it still makes you think. I was told that before he goes to bed, I had to change the bandage on his throat where the trachea had been. I prepped the new bandage as directed and pulled the old bandage off. I was surprised by the hole I saw. The doctors told me that the hole would close by itself but I wasn't expecting a hole. I was expecting some kind of stitches or butterfly bandage. It was strange to feel his breath coming out of his throat and his mouth closed. This took a bit to get used to. After a day or two the doctor called. The hole in his throat should have closed within a few days, but it didn't. The doctor thought it was due to the loss of weight. The lack of fat tissue on his neck didn't allow the wound from the trachea tube to close naturally. Back to the doctor we went to stitch it closed.

    We walked into the doctor's office and they sat Kennie down in a chair that reminded me of a dental chair. In fact, they even put a paper bib on him like the dentist does. The doctor asked me if I wanted to have a seat in his office while he stitched Kennie up.

    I said, "No."

    After everything I had been through with Kennie I thought "I can handle this". Seeing the doctor cutting away at the scar tissue started to make me lightheaded. I sat down on the chair next to Kennie, assuring myself that another ten minutes and we'd be out of there. I thought I was coping well when the doctor held up a piece of scar tissue that he had just cut off around the hole on Kennie's throat. Shaking the piece of skin towards me, he began to tell me that you have to cut off the scar tissue so the fresh meat will have a chance to close the opening on his throat.

    I promptly said, "I'll take you up on that 'waiting in

your office' offer." I went into the doctor's office to catch my breath and found there was nothing in his office to take my mind off the cutting and stitching of Kennie's throat. There were pictures of trachea surgeries all over the walls. As expected, another ten minutes Kennie was all sown up and we went home. Kennie returned days later to have the stitches removed. The next appointment was with his doctor from the hospital. Kennie had made a full recovery. He was cleared to return to work and resume his normal activities. The next call was to his boss. He was true to his word. Kennie got his job back.

    The amazing part, considering what we were told at the beginning, was two weeks to the day Kennie was home and one month to the day he was back at work. He had beaten the odds and Thank God he had the will to live. We both realized how precious life is and remembered the promise we made in the hospital. It was time to start working on the "Family Portrait". It was time to start having children.

CHAPTER TWO: STARTING A FAMILY

Almost losing Kennie made me realize how precious life is and how little time we may have to live. I also realized that even though my employer was nice to me during Kennie's illness, I needed to try something else. I quit my job and started my own business assisting small car dealerships with registration. This gave me more free time and time for Kennie and I to be together. I also spent time with my dog Lady, the light brown cocker spaniel that we adopted when she was a year old. Lady was already named and the name fit so we kept it.

My sister-in-law also had a cocker spaniel who had just had a litter of puppies. There was one puppy that didn't have a home and because I was at home most of the day and had the time, she asked me if I wanted "Tramp" to go with "Lady". My niece had named him Tramp, to try to convince Kennie that this was our dog. I was already sold on him. Tramp had a black coat with white paws and a black and white face. If you laid him on his back, he had a white path on his tummy that went down each leg that looked like a skeleton. He was beautiful. The bonus was he would give Lady a playmate. Kennie gave in and Tramp came home with us.

Now it was time to start our human family. After several months of trying it finally hit us, we had already been trying. By all accounts we should have been pregnant at least once since we had used condoms as our only protection for the last four years. Four years and no baby! We decided it was time to start looking for an infertility doctor. We had to use the list of doctors provided by the insurance company. The doctor we chose (doctor #1) turned out to be one of the better doctors. I was naive back then and as they say, "ignorance is bliss". I was shy and very reserved, so being put through all kinds of painful, degrading and just down right horrible tests was something I was not prepared for.

The doctor started with a consultation. He asked, "Do you drink?"

I replied, "No."

"Do you smoke?"

Again, "No."

The doctor handed me a temperature graph chart and explained that I was to record my temperature every morning and that a spike in body temperature meant I was ovulating, which was the ideal time to get pregnant.

The doctor decided to begin tests, starting with checking my uterus to determine if it was healthy enough to carry a baby. The procedure involved inserting a small instrument into my cervix to scrape the uterus lining and collect a sample. That sample was then be sent to the lab to check for anything abnormal. The procedure was supposed to take about five to ten minutes. Nope. My cervix was too tight for the instrument to fit. Plan B: a seaweed wrap, as the doctor called it. An instrument a little bigger than a toothpick was to remain inserted in my cervix for two to three hours to widen my cervix. The seaweed wrap was intended to swell and open up my uterus and then the instrument removed so the doctor could insert the instrument and collect the sample from my uterus.

It was 5:00 p.m. The seaweed wrap was placed. After getting dressed I went to make an appointment to come back in two to three hours. I was informed that the office would be closing soon. Now what? I made an appointment to come back in the morning at 11:00 a.m. I was having some discomfort but no real pain. Plus, I was assured by the doctor that there wouldn't be a problem. I went home. The pain hit me. It kept getting worse and worse. I took ibuprofen every four hours, all night long, and it didn't help. Morning came and I left early for the doctor's office. They made me wait, in pain, with tears rolling down my face and every expecting mother in the room staring at me. Finally, I was called back. It had been 18 hours for what was supposed to be a two- to three-hour procedure. I felt instant relief when the seaweed wrap was removed. After an uncomfortable collection of the uterus lining, I was done. All this pain to have the lab results show that my uterus lining was fine and had nothing to with infertility.

  Another week the doctors shot dye into my uterus to check for blockage. The appointment was at the hospital in the x-ray lab, a large cold room, and I was wearing only a hospital gown. I climbed up on a flat table with a large x-ray machine hanging over me. I was told to scoot down on the flat, cold table in the OB position so my bottom was hanging off the table. There was nothing to put my sockless feet into but I somehow managed to keep them on the table next to the rest of my body. Looking around I noticed people coming in and out of the room. I counted eight new faces before I recognized the doctor, who sat down and told me to scoot down again. How much further can I go without falling off? There were more techs coming in and out before I realized that the room also was the main supply room. No privacy. Lucky me. The doctor explained the different equipment and pointed the monitor towards me so I could watch as the dye made its way through my tubes and into my ovaries.

In the OB position, I was nervous and sweating. The doctor then explained that there would be three tubes placed into my uterus. One to put the dye into me, one to remove the dye, and one just in case I have a reaction to the dye. As if I don't already have enough to worry about.

I was in the OB position, on the x-ray table, with three tubes sticking out of me, when the doctor says "Okay, you need to scoot back on the table."

Yea right. I thought, you've got to be kidding me!

He also told me to watch my head around the x-ray machine hanging over the table and be careful not to let the tubes fall out.

What kind of an insane person does this? I thought to myself, "One who wants a family." I somehow managed. That's when I started actually counting the number of people in the room. Fourteen! Why? I don't know. I just wanted it over. The doctor started the procedure. The dye went in and no blockage. Everything was fine. I had endured a humiliating test for nothing.

No. To rule out what might have been the problem.

The next test seemed a little less stressful but still strange. This time Kennie was in the office with me. Kennie and I were told to go home, have intercourse and return to the office within 12 hours so the doctor could take the sample of Kennie's semen out of my cervix. Timed sex. This provided us no real answers either, other than everything is fine.

The next step was also a timed intercourse procedure. The only thing Kennie had to do was produce a semen sample. He started to complain to the doctor and then shut up when the doctor handed him a special condom for the test. The doctor instructed us to go home, have intercourse, and bring the condom back to him within a certain amount of time. The doctor neglected to tell us that after the specimen is collected it must be kept at body temperature – we had to read this in the instructions that came with the condom – and this could be done by putting the specimen filled condom in your underpants or in your bra.

OH, No, No, No. You're handling this one Kennie.

After collecting the specimen and placing it in Kennie's underpants, we went straight back to the doctor's office. We were cracking jokes and laughing all the way. A great stress release. As the ultimate joke, Kennie walked up to the reception desk where a lady sat answering the phone. She was a larger lady with big fluffy hair that stood four inches high above her head. This made her face very easy to see.

In a squeaky voice, that didn't match her appearance, she said, "May I help you?"

Kennie said, "Yes" and then reached into his pants and pulled out the specimen filled condom. The women's eyes almost popped out of her head. I lost it. I could hardly breathe I was laughing so hard. Tears were coming down my face and then I noticed everyone in the room was looking at us and for a change, I didn't care. Kennie never gets embarrassed and wasn't bothered a bit.

The semen test was useless because all sperm, except one, died before the lab could look at them under a microscope. In fact, all of the tests proved to be useless, including the temperature graph that the doctor took one look at and tossed into the trash. For months I had faithfully taken my temperature every day and charted it. My temperature never spiked and the doctor never told me what I did wrong.

Finally, in September, the plan of action was Clomid, an infertility drug that may produce multiple births. My instructions were to wait for my cycle, take the pill for five days and then let nature take its course. Clomid caused your ovaries to either release more than one egg at a time or release eggs more frequently. Twins! Great! I can have two and not worry if I can't get pregnant again. Let's go.

I thought Clomid would be foolproof - like a guarantee - but I started my cycle after my first time taking it and several times after that. I became depressed every time I got my period. I felt I had failed. This had to be my fault. The tests proved there was nothing wrong. Can you have intercourse wrong? Our friends and family joked that we didn't know how to correctly have sex. We got all kinds of advice, from standing on your head after intercourse drinking orange juice, to some kind of a clinical wash. We know they were just trying to help. I did read that you can decrease the amount of sperm count if you have numerous back to back intercourse, sit in a hot tub, or wear tight underwear.

Caught up in my own life of trying to have babies, I didn't even think to separate the dogs. Tramp was only three - maybe four - months old. To my surprise Lady was going to be a mommy. Her pregnancy would only last two months. This would make Tramp a father at six months old. Somehow this all seemed unfair. Lady and Tramp would be a "Mom and Dad" before Kennie and me. I thought of my dogs as my kids and that would mean that we would be grandparents before we were parents. This was funny to me.

In true Carol fashion, I wanted to make sure that this was a successful pregnancy for Lady, so I researched and found out high protein was good for a pregnant dog. Every morning Lady and I each had one egg with cheese. Of course, Tramp would get one too. We would also boil or barbecue boneless chicken for them. Lady was so happy and playful and seemed to enjoy being pregnant. I hoped that I would feel the same way one day.

    I knew it was getting close to Lady's due date and didn't want to leave her, but I knew I had to from time to time. We had a nice porch out back. I set up a box with lots of blankets in it, just in case she had her puppies when we weren't home. If nothing else, it gave her something nice and soft to lie on - she was getting pretty big. On the mornings I had to leave, I would get up, let the dogs out into the back yard, bring them in, have breakfast, put them out in the back yard for the day, and then go to work. Kennie was usually home around 2:30 p.m. and let the dogs in. Following the normal routine one day, I went to work. The dealers kept me longer than I had anticipated and I arrived home at dusk. Kennie drove up right behind me. I went to let the dogs in. I opened the sliding door, Lady was in her box and Tramp just sat there barking at me. I went over to the box, looked inside and there were two puppies. Kennie moved the bed inside and then put clean towels in the dryer to warm them for the new puppies. It was clear to see there were more puppies on the way. Lady was a pro at this whole thing. She would push one out, open the sack, clean up the mess and her new born. She had six puppies in four hours. Tramp just stood around, panting. Silly puppy. It all seemed to wear him out. We finally went to bed. We had six healthy puppies. When we woke up, we had seven healthy puppies. They were so much fun. The puppies took the stress off of us for a while. We had something to focus on besides getting pregnant. When the puppies were old enough, we found good homes for all of them. It wasn't hard. They were so cute.

    It was December. I was sick with a head cold that turned into an infection. I went to my primary doctor for antibiotics. The stress of the infertility, Christmas as a reminder that we didn't have a family yet, the cold and flu season, I'm sure all played a part in my getting sick. In that I was of childbearing age, the nurse needed to do a pregnancy test before giving me an antibiotic. I then realized that after several months of taking Clomid, I may have missed my period. Taking the pills and then getting a period had become so routine, I didn't even give it a second thought. Until now. I was trying not to stress about the results. I convinced myself it would be negative like all the others. The doctor on call did an exam and went to treat me for my cold. The nurse stuck her head in just as the doctor was finishing and handed the doctor a piece of paper. I guess because of my age and looking very young the doctor used extreme caution in telling me that I was pregnant. She thought the baby might have been unwanted.

I started to cry tears of joy. I explained that I almost lost my husband, plus how long we had been trying to conceive and that this was most definitely a wanted baby.

Pregnant! I was going to be a mom. I finally knew what it felt like to be walking on clouds. I held two prescriptions in my hand - an antibiotics prescription for my cold and a prenatal prescription for my baby. I was smiling all the way to my car thinking "This is it. I'm going to be a mom." I'll have a baby to take care of. We would no longer be just Kennie and Carol, but Daddy and Mommy. We were going to be a family by the end of next year. I could hardly contain myself.

I went to the pharmacy to fill my prescriptions, telling everyone in my path that I just found out I was pregnant. I bought Kennie a card and balloons. I wrote "To Daddy. I'll see you in August". I left it on the kitchen table, right where he drops his keys and wallet, knowing he wouldn't miss it. When Kennie got home he opened the card and read it. He didn't get it. I had to explain it to him. HELLO! You're going to be a father. He was so excited. He started calling everyone in the family. Our families told friends and extended family. The news spread like wildfire.

Kennie loved baseball and was coaching our nephews in little league. He had dreamed about what it would be like to coach his own child one day. What a great day. We even started planning for a nursery. We had a little room in the front of the house that got the morning light. Perfect. How exciting! We were going to be parents.

I made a follow-up appointment with the doctor to discuss what comes next. When I arrived for my appointment, I was informed that the doctor who had helped me achieve the pregnancy had left the practice and that another doctor had taken over (doctor #2). I was instructed to drink plenty of orange juice for folic acid, milk for calcium, and eat full meals with the recommended fruits and vegetables. After what we went through, I was going to leave nothing to chance. I followed every instruction. I didn't even like milk. I forced myself to drink at least one glass a day.

The new doctor was concerned because I had conceived the baby on Clomid. She had me come into her office every other day to have my blood drawn to check my human chorionic gonadotropin (HCG) levels. She explained that if the baby was growing at a normal rate, the HCG levels would double every other day. She was thorough and I knew I was in good hands. One day I was in the office having my blood drawn when the doctor informed me that my HCG levels were more than doubling and that usually meant twins. Wow! Twins! We hit the jackpot. All the tests finally seemed worth it.

My doctor called the next Friday late in the day. At first, I was upbeat; she called me with HCG levels all the time. She told me my HCG levels had stopped doubling.

"You're either miscarrying or you are having a tubular pregnancy." She explained that a tubular pregnancy is when the baby plants itself inside the fallopian tube and can't grow anymore. When this happens, the doctors usually have to remove the baby and the tube surgically. She then pointed out that the lesser of two evils was a miscarriage, trying to give me hope for future babies.

"What can I do to stop this from happening?" I asked.

"Nothing, there is nothing you can do."

"My babies are dying and there is nothing I can do?" I said, pleading with her to help me somehow.

She said, "Lie down and put your feet up."

I went numb. I hung up the phone contemplating the difference between a miscarriage and a tubular pregnancy. I actually hoped it was a miscarriage. A few minutes later Kennie walked through the door. That's when it hit me. I had to tell Kennie. I started to cry. I managed to tell him what the doctor said. She said I would start bleeding if it was a miscarriage, but there was no blood. I had hope - she must be wrong. I found blood the next morning. Her prediction was right.

All alone in the house with my thoughts was not good. I called my sister. Since she'd had a miscarriage, surely she would know what to do. She told me to call my mom. Both came over to sit with me. Their voices were comforting but not much help. What seemed like the inevitable was coming. I continued to lie on the couch with my feet up all day and into the night. Waiting, crying, and hoping there was something that could be done to save my babies. The conversations had quieted when Kennie had arrived home. Four people sitting there with nothing to say, the silence was more than I could take. I said goodbye to my mom and sister. Kennie and I went to the hospital. The emergency room was empty and I was taken right back. I changed into a hospital gown and was then shown to a private room where I was greeted by a very young doctor who ordered a clean stream urine sample. I found out soon enough that this meant pain. The doctor performed a vaginal exam and found everything still intact. He then ordered an ultrasound.

The sonographer was in a trailer behind the hospital. It was dark and scary. I was glad Kennie was with me. I couldn't help but think why the nurses would send a pregnant, bleeding woman, in a hospital gown down a dark path to a trailer. I should have been in a wheelchair being pushed by someone who knew where they were going. The sonographer made apologies for the walk and told me that there were plans to move ultrasounds into the hospital in the next year. Already in a gown, I followed her back to the examination room and climbed up on the examination table. The sonographer asked if this was my first baby.

I replied, "Yes."

She asked my age.

I responded, "25." I told her that we had been going through infertility and were very happy that we were going to have twins, but still getting used to the idea. She pulled up my gown to expose my belly and squirted cold, wet gel just below my bellybutton. She began moving a wand around in the gel which produced a picture on a monitor. Nothing made sense to me. It looked like when a television goes to snow. She then told me that the babies were too small to see without a vaginal wand. This was yet another procedure I was not prepared for. When the vaginal wand was inserted the image came up on the screen. You could see our beautiful little babies and that their hearts were beating. They were in the uterus, where they should be, not in the fallopian tubes.

She smiled and said, "It looks good." She also said that she had heard of women going the whole pregnancy with spot bleeding and then giving birth to healthy babies. This gave me hope. I went to the waiting room where Kennie was sitting, told him the good news and that I actually got to see the twins. Knowing our babies were alive gave me hope that the doctor was wrong about the HCG levels.

When I got home the plan was to once again lie down, put my feet up and hope that the bleeding would stop, but every time I went to the bathroom I found blood. A reminder that this was not just a bad dream, but reality. A few days came and went. I had some pain, but it was manageable, until early one Saturday morning around 2:00 a.m. I had major cramping that wouldn't stop. We went back to the emergency room where I told another set of doctors I had been bleeding for six days. They looked surprised. Back to the trailer behind the hospital for another ultrasound. This time the girl didn't smile. In fact, she didn't say anything. At first, I thought this was bad news, then figured she was having a bad day. It was early in the morning and she was almost done with her shift. This was one of the few things she told me.

I was back in the emergency room, ready to be examined when the doctor on call (doctor #3) walked into the room talking to his staff, telling them to prepare the OR for Mrs. Johnson. I was thinking that the staff was going to do a procedure to help me and save my babies.

I finally got the chance to ask, "What is going on?"

The doctor looked surprised and said, "The sonographer didn't tell you? Your babies are dead. They have no heartbeat."

I thought, How heartless! You're a doctor in the medical field. I just did everything I was told to do and I'm still losing my twins.

When I started to tear up, he changed his tone and informed me that I had an "incomplete spontaneous abortion". All I could hear was "Abortion". I didn't want an abortion. He explained this was just a term that meant "miscarriage".

I was barely far enough along to show, but at nine weeks I was attached to my babies. I was crying. Kennie was crying. I was told that a dilation and curettage (D&C) was going to be done. The purpose was to clean out the uterus after the miscarriage. I started thinking. I really hadn't been in a hospital since I was born. There was a foot emergency and of course the infertility work ups. Now the unthinkable: they were going to extract my babies, or what was left of my babies, from my body.

I was directed to a makeshift bed where the nurse was to prepare me for surgery. The first thing she did was poke an IV into my left arm. I almost passed out. I had never had an IV before. Kennie was standing next to me and holding my hand. The nurse gathered up my things, placed them into a plastic bag, and handed them to Kennie. We walked out the door and slowly down a hall. I was dragging an IV pole, wearing nothing but a hospital gown, my underwear, and socks. The nurse opened two big doors and told Kennie that he was not permitted to follow me. I said goodbye and continued down the hall into a very cold room with a bed and two huge circle lamps that hung out of the ceiling facing the bed. Nobody really explained to me anything about the procedure. I then realized I was in the operating room and being asked to climb up onto the operating table. This stunned me. Everything was happening so quickly. My thoughts were racing. My heart was racing and I was numb. No Kennie to hold my hand. Our hopes of having a family were leaving me. I couldn't wait to be knocked out so I could stop thinking.

When I woke up in recovery, I was unaware of my surroundings. I didn't have a clue what to expect. I opened my eyes to find something smothering me. In reality it was an oxygen mask. I heard a nurse tell another nurse, "Someone is waking up". My throat was dry, scratchy and it was painful to swallow. I later found out it was because they used a tube that went down my throat to prevent my airway from closing during the D&C surgery. After an hour I was told that I could get dressed. The nurse closed the curtain and left me on my own. I could hardly stand but somehow I managed to get dressed. I was then wheeled out to a room where Kennie, mom, dad, Ruth, and Roger were waiting. I had no idea that anyone other than Kennie was waiting. It's nice to know how much our parents care about us.

I walked through the front door at home. I felt as if something was missing or empty. I felt incomplete. Now the "incomplete" in "incomplete spontaneous abortion" meant something to me. Everything we had planned and worked for was gone. The family we had hoped for was gone.

After a few days I went back to work. This was another hard part. We were so excited about being pregnant we told everyone. Now I had to deal with friends and customers asking, "How are the babies?" and "How's mommy?" Kennie also had to go a whole season of Little League wondering if he would ever coach a child of his own. I wanted to put up a sign in the front yard that said, "We lost our babies. Please, don't ask."

A week later I was at my doctor's office for my checkup. She encouraged us to try again and told us this was probably a fluke and wouldn't happen again. She carefully asked if we wanted to know the sex of the babies. Yes. She told us that they were boys. Boys, a feeling of excitement followed by a sadness knowing Kennie would have had boys to play catch with. The doctor pointed out the positive things, like the fact that we did get pregnant and that we would more than likely get pregnant on our own next time. We thanked her and told her we would give her a call when we were pregnant again. She then informed us that she was leaving the practice and going back to school to become a high risk OBGYN and that the doctor who helped us in the operating room with the D&C surgery would be our new doctor (doctor #3). Confused and feeling abandoned, we left the office.

    Questions running through my mind:
    Should we try again?
    Could we try again?
    Would we try again?

CHAPER THREE: BACK TO THE DRAWING BOARD

We had a game plan to be a family by the end of the year. Now we had to erase and start over. The thought of what happened to our twins was on my mind constantly. I was replaying it like a bad movie I couldn't turn off. Kennie hadn't missed a day of work since his Guillain-Barré illness and was able to keep his mind busy at work. I had a lot of free time and spent it with our dogs Lady and Tramp. Lady quickly became my best listener. I seemed to vent most of my sadness to her. I was still working through each day one at a time, trying to get on with my life and the fact that my twins were gone. I felt my body had failed. I felt that I had failed. I questioned myself. What did I do wrong? I tried to keep a stiff upper lip by remembering that the doctor said losing the twins was a fluke and that my next pregnancy would be successful. Kennie was great at staying positive. He would make me laugh by clapping his hands together, then quickly rubbing them back and forth, with a smile on his face saying, "Back to the drawing board". Knowing, of course, this meant more sex.

Kennie and I still figured that we would need a doctor's help getting pregnant. We believed the Clomid helped us achieve our first pregnancy. We had spent every day for the past six plus months trying to conceive and decided to wait awhile and give ourselves a little bit of time to heal. I had never lost a family member before. Shoot, even my Great grandmother on my father's side was still alive. The only family members that had died in my life time were my uncle, who I didn't know very well (we saw him occasionally at Christmas) and my grandfather on my mom's side. He died when I was three. The only thing I remember about him was crawling up on his lap and watching Jackie Gleason in the "Honeymooners" with him. The only family member that I had ever grieved for was my dog Snowzee, who we got when I was three and died when I was seventeen. That was my only education in death I had until now. The loss of a dog doesn't compare to the loss of our twins or the loss of our future family that should have been. How was I ever going to get through this? From the moment you find out you are pregnant you start to plan for life. Your dreams start to take off. You start to envision yourself as a mom or a dad. When I was pregnant, I could see myself rocking my babies to sleep, one in each arm. I could also see them playing with each other in the yard and being best friends for life. These dreams were quickly shattered overnight.

    Knowing that we needed the doctor's help to achieve the pregnancy of our twins we never gave birth control a second thought. After all of these years and never getting pregnant on our own there was a fat chance we could do things the normal way now. As luck would have it, five months later in May, I missed a period. I went down that aisle that most women dread every month, the "feminine pad" aisle. But this time I wasn't there for feminine products, I was there for the pregnancy tests in the same aisle. Standing there looking at all of the different choices, I was lost. I had never bought a pregnancy test before. Nor had I ever talked to anyone about buying one. I started with the first test on the left and worked my way right. Picking up the box I read, "Plus sign shows you're pregnant." Another box read, "One line you are not pregnant and two lines you are pregnant." They were pricey too. They ranged from $7, not so bad, to $25 and up. As I was considering the tests my grandpa's words were ringing through my ears: "You get what you pay for". Of course, he was talking about car parts not pregnancy tests. After figuring out my budget, I bought the seven-dollar test and went home.

    I walked through the door to find Kennie home. I was questioning myself -should I or shouldn't I tell Kennie that I missed my period? I had stressed myself out and missed a period when I was going through infertility. This could be the case and besides, we weren't trying to conceive. Why get Kennie wondering too? If the test is negative, we would both be depressed. I decided to spare Kennie the anxiety and not tell him. I made my way down the hall, clutching my little brown bag behind my back without Kennie noticing, and through the master bedroom and into our small master bathroom. I went in and promptly closed the door behind me. I opened the bag, opened the pregnancy test box and read the directions. The words "first morning urine is best" burst my bubble. I would have to wait another day. I packed up the test, put it back in the brown bag and hid it under the bathroom sink. I then flushed the toilet and washed my hands in an attempt for Kennie not to notice, which he didn't. I had mixed emotions. Part of me was excited and the other part of me was talking myself down. "It's only going to be negative. Why are you getting yourself all worked up?" Bed time, at last! Goodnight.

    1:30 a.m. The alarm clock goes off. Kennie gets up to go to work. The truck driving job requires him to go from San Diego to Los Angeles daily, pick up a load and have it back in San Diego by 8:00 a.m. This meant an early wakeup call. The good thing was that he was normally home between noon and 2:00 p.m.

On a normal morning I could sleep right through the alarm going off, but not today. I needed him gone. I was trying to act as if I was sleeping while Kennie went through his morning routine. Thinking to myself, "Does he always take this long to brush his teeth?" Finally, the kiss on my cheek, the light goes off, a little movement in the kitchen, the front door closes, his pickup truck starts and drives away. Two in the morning you can hear everything, even the crickets who are still on the clock. I was feeling sneaky. I had never kept anything from Kennie. This was harder to do than I thought. It's two in the morning, what the hell am I doing? Then thinking this was probably just a waste of time, money, and sleep. I got out of bed and opened the bedroom door. I was greeted by a wonderful coffee smell that engulfed the entire house. I headed out to the family room to look out the front window just to make sure Kennie was gone. I returned to the master bathroom where I pulled the bag from under the sink and once again read the directions. My frugal mind was having second thoughts. Maybe I should have bought a second test or the better one that cost more. I finally stopped questioning myself and started the test.

Step one: collect urine specimen in cup. What cup? I dumped the box upside down into the sink and this cup, smaller than any cup I have ever seen, including the tea party set I had as a small child, falls out.

Holding up the tiny cup I said, "You've got to be kidding me!"

I know I have a full bladder. I have held it all night and this cup is going to over flow. Tired and trying to get this over with, I sat down and collected my "first morning urine" in the teeny, tiny, itty, bitty cup.

Step two: remove test stick from wrapper and dip the

"test strip end" into the cup of urine for five seconds. Trying to figure out which end was the "test strip end" I continued to read. Make sure you don't touch the "test stick end". That is when I realized that I was holding the wrong end of the test stick. OOPS! Shit! Oh well, looks like I'm going to get my $7.00 worth. Remembering what my Grandpa said. Placing the test stick into the urine cup, I counted to five. I then removed it and put the test stick on the tissue next to the cup.

Step three: Wait three minutes; if there are two lines you are pregnant. If there is one line you are not pregnant.

I could not believe how long three minutes would take. It seemed like hours. Sitting there I could smell the fresh brewed coffee Kennie left behind. To calm myself and give myself something to do I went to the kitchen and poured myself a cup of coffee although I didn't drink it. I returned to the bathroom to read the results and saw two lines. That crazy fear kicked in. The fear that makes you question everything you read. Does this mean I'm pregnant or not? Apparently three minutes was a long time and I forgot what I read. It's too early in the morning to be doing this. I grabbed the instructions and quickly reread them. Two lines equals pregnant. I thought how could this be? We didn't have the doctor's help. A normal person wouldn't be thinking like this, I thought. A normal person wouldn't be up at two in the morning either. I started to question what I could have done wrong. I must have done something wrong. I know. It was when I touched the wrong end of the test stick. I must have ruined it. Or I woke up too early and maybe the urine needed more time to be more potent to work? Maybe I left the test stick in too long before looking? Then the guilt. Why didn't I get up when Kennie did and tell him what I was doing? Then he would have been here to double check that I did it right. What to do? I can't call

Kennie now. He is on the road. It's also 2:30 in the morning and all the stores are closed. I can't buy another test kit to double check if I did anything wrong. That means I will have to wait another day anyway. Then I remembered the pharmacy where I bought the test kit is open all night. Duh! I dumped my coffee out. I didn't need the caffeine anyway, considering the possibility of a pregnancy. I got dressed and off I went back to the store.

    I pulled into the parking lot excited and felling like a nut. I dashed through the door like teenager who missed her curfew and headed straight to the uncomfortable aisle again. This time I grabbed the $25 test. I'm going to get my money's worth. The cashier behind the counter must have been thinking "There is a crazy lady at my counter at 2:30 in the morning buying a pregnancy test?" Trying not to concern myself with this for too long, I made it home. Back to the bathroom, reading directions. Funny this one didn't require first morning urine and much easier. No little cup. Just hold the stick in the urine stream. Within two minutes it was confirmed twice. I was pregnant. I was so glad I dumped out the cup of coffee. I would have felt so guilty if I had swallowed even one gulp of caffeine.

    I closed the lid on the toilet seat, sat down and looked at myself in the mirror. A tear was starting to form and make its way down my face. I couldn't believe it. This baby was not conceived on Clomid. I was probably only carrying one baby. I wanted to tell someone. Kennie should be the first and I had deprived him of knowing when I found out. The time was 3:15 a.m. and the earliest I could get a hold of him was 8:00 a.m. I stretched out on the bed. By taking deep breaths I somehow fell asleep. When I woke up it was 9:00 a.m. I rescheduled my appointments for the day and called Kennie at the trucking office. He should be there by now.

"Hello." Kennie answered.

"Hello. How are you? Are you sitting down?" I inquired.

"No, should I be?" He answered with a chuckle.

"Yes. I have something to tell you." I gave him a few seconds to find a seat and then continued. "After you left for work this morning, I took a pregnancy test and it came out positive. We are pregnant."

There was a moment of silence. Then he asked, "Are you sure?" Two peas in a pod – we think alike.

"Yes. I took two tests and they were both positive." I then confessed to hiding the test, messing up the test, going to the pharmacy at 2:30 in the morning, the cashier with the look on his face, then redoing the test. Kennie thought it was amusing and announced to his office that we were pregnant again. I could hear happy congrats in the background. Saying goodbye and hanging up the phone I felt an almost reassuring that everything would be okay this time.

I called the doctor and was informed that I did not need an appointment for a pregnancy test and just to come in at any time. I was excited. Within minutes I was in the doctor's office. They gave me a slip of paper to take to the blood lab and have my blood drawn to confirm the pregnancy. I wondered why I needed blood work when I had already done the home pregnancy tests. The nurse assured me that the blood test was more accurate. I left thinking I may not be pregnant. Driving to the lab, looking down at the lab slip sitting on the seat next to me, I remembered a conversation I had with the OBGYN doctor when I was pregnant the first time. She had handed me a slip of paper to take to the lab. She quickly took it back and wrote on it *stat* and explained that *stat* means urgent or top priority and that we would get the results back within 24 hours. I remembered my sister-in-law telling me it took her several days to find out if she was pregnant. I couldn't wait several days to confirm the pregnancy so I pulled the car over to the side of the road and wrote *stat* on the paperwork. I felt like I was cheating the system, but I figured heck, the system cheated me the first time around. I arrived at the lab and went to check in. I was nervous. I thought that they would somehow know that I was the one who wrote *stat* on the paperwork. I went up to the counter, the woman sitting at the counter asked me for the paperwork and I handed it to her. She looked at the paperwork and then looked at me. Busted I thought. I was just about to confess when she stood up and said follow me. I thought I was in trouble and then realized all she was doing was walking me down the hall to draw my blood. Relief ran through my body. I sat down in the chair, turned my head away, felt a small poke in my arm and it was over. I received a bandage to remind me of my cheating the system and I went home.

    Feeling a bit guilty and yet vindicated about writing on the lab paperwork, I poured myself a glass of water and waited for Kennie to get home. Happy and excited I told him about the doctor's visit. I then confessed to him about how I wrote *stat* on the lab paperwork and explained to him what that meant. Kennie laughed. Basically, I lied twice. I was getting good at this "sneaky" thing. It was around 5:00 p.m. when the doctor's office called and confirmed I was pregnant. She also commented on the lab having the quickest test results that she had ever seen. I was trying not to laugh as I thanked her for calling and said goodbye.

    Kennie and I started telling everyone we thought should know about our being pregnant again. Mostly just family and close friends. It was so difficult telling people that we had lost our babies, telling people now that we are pregnant again seemed to make up for all those uncomfortable conversations. We achieved this baby on our own it seemed natural and gave us hope that a miscarriage wouldn't happen again. We forced ourselves to get pregnant the last time, so this time is different. This baby will make it. I found myself starting to bargain, pleading with God that this baby must live. That he or she will make up for all of the physical and emotional pain from losing our twins. That this time there will be no problems. We paid our dues.

     The OBGYN appointment I had made finally came. It seemed to be a normal appointment: Allergies? None. My health? No problems. Family history? High blood pressure, cholesterol, type two diabetes. Normal aging problems for family members. Then came the conversation about infertility and the loss of my twins. This OBGYN was the doctor who told me my babies were dead and he didn't even remember me. Nor did he pre-read any of my records. It was obvious. I decided to educate the doctor on my history. I ran through a play by play of the infertility, Clomid pregnancy, loss of our twins, and our amazement of the new pregnancy. I asked if I needed to come in for blood work daily considering it was the last doctor's way of watching the development of the babies. He said that since we didn't achieve this pregnancy with Clomid "why would you?" I wasn't comfortable with this answer and I wasn't very fond of this doctor. I didn't know or even think that I had a choice in doctors. I thought that the doctor the insurance company assigned you was the doctor you had to keep so I was determined to make the best of it. I was given prenatal pills, pregnancy literature, and made an appointment on the way out to see the doctor in eight weeks. I filled the prescription and went home. Reading the literature, the doctor gave me reminded me about drinking milk and orange juice, and eating full meals.

I felt normal and even started to get a belly. It was small, and only Kennie and I could see it, but it was there. I found cute maternity shirts on sale and bought them for the future. I was starting to not worry about the problems I had before. I had passed the time frame that I lost the twins and felt more relaxed. I was in the clear. I started singing to my baby and connecting with him or her. I was back to being blissful. What a great feeling.

One Saturday Kennie and I went over to my sister's house for dinner. I brought the prenatal books I received from the doctor. My sister had two children, a six-year-old son and a three-year-old daughter. My niece had flyaway blond hair, big green eyes and was very inquisitive. She was the first to meet us at the door. Kennie bent over and picked her up and held her a shoulder height. It was summer and Kennie was wearing a tank top.

She pointed to the scar on Kennie's neck and asked with a concerned look, "What is that?" She was pointing to Kennie's tracheotomy scar that he got from the oxygen tube when he had Guillain-Barré.

Knowing that she wouldn't understand he said, "It's a boo-boo."

With a more concerned look. She asked, "Did you fall down?"

Kennie laughed and then admitted, "Yes. I fell down." That was good enough for her. She kissed his boo-boo and wanted down.

We said hello to the family and sat down on the couch. My niece then crawled up next to me and asked, "Do you have a baby in your tummy?"

I thought for a moment then realized someone had been talking to her and answered, "Yes."

With a disgusted look on her face she then asked, "You ate your baby?"

I smiled, chuckled a bit and thought this was a question for her mom and dad. I just answered "No. I didn't eat my baby." We began looking through a booklet that I had brought to sidestep the awkward question. It showed the progression of the baby's development in stages. The first page I stopped at showed a picture of a 12 week embryo baby that almost took up the entire page. An "actual size" picture of the embryo was in a smaller box off to the bottom side of the page.

She asked, "What is that?" and pointed to the big picture.

I told her, "That is a picture of a baby in its mommy's tummy."

She pointed to the small picture, wrinkling up her nose and asked, "What is that?"

I told her, "It is the real size of the baby in its mommy's tummy."

She pulled the book from my hands and looked at it really closely. Everyone in the room was watching as she took her time analyzing the picture. Then she handed the book back, crossed her arm, stared up at me and informed me, "No it isn't! That's a bug!" In just a matter of minutes she had managed to make us all burst out with laughter. She seemed to be annoyed at first with our laughing then she cracked a smile. On the drive home, I was thinking about my niece and was hoping that one day we would have a little one who will answer the door and make everyone laugh.

My eight-week appointment had arrived. I was just a

day shy of my first trimester. We had made it. Kennie went with me to my appointment. After what happened last time, Kennie was not going to let me go see the doctor alone. He wanted to be part of the whole thing. We sat down in a packed waiting room which was oddly quiet. A woman, also waiting, informed us that the doctor was at least an hour behind. She made it seem like it was a normal occurrence. We began talking about our pregnancies. It was her first pregnancy. I didn't dare tell her about my twins. I didn't want to scare her. It was nice to talk to someone who was excited about their baby and had no clue what can go wrong.

    Finally, my name was called. The doctor examined me for a total of 15 minutes and informed us that everything was going great. He measured my belly and told me to keep up the good work. Not knowing exactly what should happen at a trimester exam I didn't know if this was normal. I did wait eight weeks for this appointment, you'd think it should have lasted more than 15 minutes. I didn't really understand the measuring thing but figured I could look it up later, since the doctor didn't seem to have the time to explain it to me. In the car on the way home it crossed my mind that we must be having a normal pregnancy if the doctor doesn't want to see me for eight more weeks. I smiled, took a deep breath and exhaled.

    We got home and I called my mom to let her know how the appointment went. There was a pause when I told her that he was an hour behind and the appointment was only fifteen minutes long. She seemed to think that I was cheated out of my appointment and that the doctor was trying to make up his lost time. I said that I didn't have any questions for him anyway, but next time I would make sure that I had a list.

    A few days later I woke up singing, the dogs were playing, I ate my breakfast of eggs, milk, orange juice and went to take a shower. I turned on the water, got undressed and went potty. My world stood still. There was blood on the toilet paper. Oh my God, I thought, not again. This can't happen again. I know I did everything right. No, no, no! I must have scratched myself. I tossed the bloody tissue in the toilet and grabbed more. I checked again to find even more blood. NO! I yelled. The dogs ran and hid. I started to cry. I turned off the shower and got dressed. I attached a feminine pad to my underwear, something I was happy to not use over the past months, and called Kennie. The whole time I was saying to myself "This can't be happening! We paid our dues!" While waiting for Kennie to come home I laid down, put my feet up, and tried to relax. After about 30 minutes Kennie walked through the door and off we went to the hospital. We pulled into the first parking spot, right up front. It was as if they knew we were coming. I didn't like the familiarity. Same exam and uncomfortable urine procedure then off to the sonographer behind the hospital. This time I was pushed in a wheelchair, up the ramp, and into the trailer. The sonographer was very nice. She invited Kennie into the room after learning about the last trip back to the trailer. She also talked to Kennie and me the whole time. She told me everything she was going to do before she did it. Jelly on the belly, wand on the jelly, and then the look. She knew I could tell what was coming when I saw the look on her face. So she said the words.

"I don't see a heartbeat."

This was very hard news to take, but it was better than last time when I found out that my babies had died on the way to the OR for surgery.

She said, "I'm sorry."

We all began to shed a few tears and she called the doctor. The doctor was at another hospital and we were instructed to meet him there. Lying there I clinched my fists then pulled them to my face shaking them, in a kind of rage. Why, why is this happening to me? The car ride to the other hospital seemed to take a long time. I realized that this was the last time I would be carrying this baby, my baby. Sadness really started to kick in. I was crying and talking to my baby, telling my baby how much I loved him or her and that one day I will see him or her in heaven. Nonstop tears were just gushing down my face. We arrived in the Emergency entrance as instructed. A nurse was waiting for me with a wheelchair and a caring smile. Kennie parked the car as I was taken into the hospital and prepped for a D&C surgery. The routine was becoming far too familiar. Kennie arrived just in time to kiss me goodbye. I tried to be strong as I was wheeled on a gurney down the hall into the operating room for another D&C surgery. A song came to my mind that was popular at the time and I started to sing "I Love Your Smile" by Shanice. I had been singing songs throughout my pregnancy and I needed to let my baby know that I was still with him or her. I got a funny look from the technician pushing my gurney but I didn't care. I kept singing. This was my moment and I knew I wasn't going to get it back.

    When I got to the operating room the anesthesiologist told me to start counting backwards, ten, nine, eight and I was out. When I woke up, I was once again smothered by the oxygen mask, but this time I quickly realized what it was. The same scratchy, sore throat. I began to look around and unlike the other hospital the nurses were already starting to attend me. After a while I was permitted to leave. The nurse assisted me in getting dressed, helped me into a wheelchair and wheeled me out to the waiting room.

    When I was leaving, the nurse who greeted me at the car

with a wheelchair when I first arrived caught up with me and handed me a white teddy bear and said, "I know this is a sad time and I'm sorry for your loss." She hugged me and continued "The teddy bear will give you something to hold onto."

I knew exactly what she meant. Kennie had informed the family of what happened. Once again the family I love was in the waiting room. It started to bother me that the doctor didn't come to me. I started to wonder: Why did I, a patient who was in pain and bleeding, have to get dressed and drive all the way to another hospital to have a D&C surgery done? Why couldn't they just assign the D&C surgery to another doctor at the previous hospital? These questions were never answered.

Home. We were finally home. We pulled into the driveway and the next door neighbor, who had four little ones of her own, ran up to the car and said, "You lost another one." In a quiet voice she continued, "I knew it. I just knew it."

She gave me a hug and went back into her house. I know she meant well, but what a welcome home.

CHAPTER FOUR: NOT GIVING UP

What do you do when your body fails you twice? I started thinking about stories I'd heard of girls who became moms by getting into the backseat of a car and how easy and uneventful their pregnancies were. Why is it so difficult for me? Being pregnant and giving birth are the most natural things a woman can do and I couldn't do it. No. I'm not the type of person who feels sorry for myself and I'm not going to start now. The old "pull yourself up by your bootstraps" attitude kicked in and I made every attempt to move on. Months went by. Of course, everyone who knew we were pregnant now knew about the second miscarriage. We decided to focus our attention elsewhere. We put our house on the market. We traded a three bedroom, two bathroom, one car garage house for a four bedroom, two bathroom, a two car garage house across town and doubled our square footage. Not long after we moved, my self-employment came to an end. The economy was changing and I had to too. I got a job as the manager of a video store and life seemed to have some normalcy to it except the house just had Kennie, the dogs, and me rattling around in it. It was obvious that something was definitely missing. It was the middle of spring when we started talking about trying to have a baby again. I started an aerobics class to prepare my body for another pregnancy. I figured it couldn't hurt. My body had changed a bit for the better. By summer I once again missed my period. This time I didn't hesitate telling Kennie. I bought a test and the following weekend when Kennie and I were home I took the test. Positive. At first, I was excited and then my emotions went from flat out scared to almost a numb feeling. Could I really do this again? I had no choice. I was pregnant for the third time, with my fourth baby.

Monday morning I went down to the family practice doctor by myself. Kennie couldn't go because it was too early and he was still at work. Besides it was just a blood test to confirm the pregnancy. Blood was drawn right there in the office – a huge change from the last time. Wow, I didn't have to be sneaky. I was given a referral back to the same OBGYN. Our insurance had once again changed but I still had the same doctor. Lucky me.

Kennie drove me to my first appointment with the OBGYN doctor. It seemed to be the same thing as before. I had to re-educate the doctor with my prior pregnancies, health, and family history because clearly once again he didn't read my chart. This will be technically the third pregnancy with him. I felt he should have at least remembered my face or a part of my story. Finally, the doctor asked if I had any questions.

Hell yes! I thought. "Why do you think I've lost so many babies?"

"Who knows?" Was his response.

Wasn't that his job?

He said, "Lots of women have numerous miscarriages and no one ever finds out why."

What a confidence booster. This seemed like a lame answer to me. I asked about my family history of diabetes would have any barrier on this pregnancy? A funky frown appeared on his face. He asked me if I ate this morning.

I said, "No". It was still early. Kennie and I were planning to eat on the way home. He asked the nurse to bring in a glucose test monitor to test my blood levels. She returned with a white handheld machine about the size of a paperback book. She prepared a little stick with a tiny needle and a trigger on it and then sterilized a spot on my finger. She picked up the needle stick and used it. A little needle shot out and poked my finger. A quick pain from the needle and a drop of blood started to pool at the tip of my finger. Apparently, it wasn't enough. She began to squeeze my finger and the drop got bigger. She took a little strip out of the bottle about the size of a matchstick and placed it in the machine. My finger's drop of blood was about to drip when she touched the matchstick strip to the blood. Somehow the blood was absorbed into the strip and within seconds a number appeared on the machines face. I was clueless. After the nurse tested my blood, the doctor looked at the results and announced I didn't have diabetes. The doctor never explained the results, only that he ruled out any possibility of the disease.

I had read about scar tissue caused by D&C surgeries and how they could cause miscarriages. I asked if scar tissue could be an issue and the doctor said no. Everything I asked or challenged was ruled out with borderline answers at best. It seemed I was not going to get help in a diagnosis of my losses. Toward the end of the appointment the doctor appeared anxious to leave the room. Maybe I asked too many questions.

The doctor concluded the appointment. "Don't forget to make an eight-week appointment before you leave."

I asked him while he was still standing in the hallway trying to make his escape, "Can we make it earlier, in light of my problems I have had in the past?"

He said, "No need, you should be just fine with this pregnancy." He immediately disappeared. I made my eight-week appointment and left. I had lots of questions and terribly sad thoughts that this was not going to work out. I clearly didn't connect with this doctor. He seemed to not really want to talk to me. I felt like my concerns and questions did not have merit.

I guess after repeated losses you start to put up walls to protect yourself. I believe that is what I was doing. I tried to be positive but not one person could answer my question; "WHY AM I LOSING MY BABIES?

Kennie and I decided that other than our parents, brothers and sisters, we would tell no one about the pregnancy unless they asked. I was back to eating healthy - eggs, fruit, milk and orange juice. I also started to notice that other than an occasional stomach stir, I didn't have any morning sickness. I had no idea when the morning sickness was supposed to start.

Routines were starting to set and days went on as normal. I started to show. It seemed my body started showing the baby bump a little earlier than last time. After a while people started to ask if I was expecting. When I would tell them why I wasn't announcing that I was pregnant they totally understood. Kennie tried to keep my spirits up by talking to the baby. He always talked into my bellybutton as if it was an old telephone receiver.

"Hello," He would say. "It is daddy. I love you."

This would make me smile, but inside I was so scared. I had a little soul inside me and I was trying not to get attached for fear that this baby would end up like the last babies. I'm pretty sure the detachment was not good. I had pleaded before with God and I didn't get the answer I wanted. I thought reverse psychology would be an option. Like I knew anything about reverse psychology.

I was just about eleven weeks when I went to the bathroom and saw a very faint blood mark on the toilet paper. I sat there in my sadness once again with my head hung low. I felt as if everything was draining out of me, almost emotionless. It wasn't like before. The blood was faint. Having no sense of urgency, I waited around the house for Kennie to get home. When he arrived home the doctor's office was closed so our only option was to go to the hospital. Same routine, little room, trailer, and then we were discharged. Only this time I was sent home with a yellow toilet/commode hat to catch anything that fell out. I figured out that the nurse meant to catch my baby when it fell out. I was told to follow up with my doctor. Wonderful. The man who doesn't know me or want to know me. It seemed as if he was just in it for the paycheck.

The next morning Kennie and I saw the doctor. During the physical exam the doctor informed me that everything was still intact and looked fine. He then asked to do a rectal exam. I said no. He explained it could have something to do with the bleeding and told us how many women he has saved diagnosing rectal cancer. I just couldn't see how a rectal exam would benefit the situation I was in. I felt it would do more harm than good. It could wait until after I had the baby. After saying no the second time, I found myself in the middle of a rectal exam against my will! I was uncomfortable. I told the doctor to stop and was told by the doctor in a stern voice that his finger was smaller than a bowel movement. As if that was supposed to change things. I also noticed that there was no nurse in the examination room and asked where the nurse was. He stopped his procedure instantly and responded as if Kennie was the respected third person in the room. Kennie was sitting in the guest chair behind me and clueless. I guess Kennie never noticed the missing nurse or what the doctor had just done to me. The exam was finally over. I was uncomfortable and upset. I couldn't get dressed fast enough and get out of there. We didn't get any diagnosis to the bleeding. In fact, the exam caused me more stress. I was a wreck. I felt violated. Like I had been raped, clinically.

The next day the bleeding was worse but tolerable. No wonder after the horrible doctor visit yesterday. I was told by many people that you can bleed throughout your pregnancy and still have a healthy baby. It gave me some hope. Then the pain got worse. There was a lot of pain all at once. I ran for the toilet with the commode hat already on the toilet seat and sat down. I grabbed the towel hanging on the towel rack and rolled it up and bent over it in pain. I felt a clot, or something like it, fall out. The pain lessoned. Kennie had just come home and found me in the bathroom, crying. He asked if I was okay. Looking up at Kennie, I told him something just fell into the commode hat.

"Was it the baby?" Kennie asked.

I said, "I don't know I didn't look." However, the pain was considerably less and subsiding. I stood up, took a breath and looked. It didn't look good. There was a mass about the size of my fist in the commode hat with a lot of blood. Kennie went to look for something to put the mass/clot/baby in and all he could find was a used, washed out empty butter tub. If this was my baby, I really didn't want to put it in a butter tub, but I had no choice. I called the doctor's office and the doctor on call (doctor #4) invited me down to his office. He told me to bring the butter tub and what was in it.

The doctor's office was close to my home but it felt like one of the longest rides I have ever taken. Tears were falling out of my eyes as I looked down at the container with what I thought was my baby in it. I started talking to the butter tub telling it all our hopes for a long life that we should have had together. I talked life experiences we were going to have: Disneyland, local parks, walks with the dogs, daddy and me, etc. I stopped and realized that it wasn't ever going to come true and started to cry again. I couldn't believe this was happening again. What happened to already paying our dues? We pulled into the parking lot and made our way to the doctor's main door. When we walked into the office, I was unprepared for the packed waiting room. We walked up to the counter and started to sign in. The woman asked my named then pointed to one of the seven clipboards to sign in. I was told to have a seat and that I would be called back soon. I looked around the room at all of the pregnant women and took a deep breath. By now I had gotten good at taking a deep breath to relax. How was I going to handle this? I have my baby (or what was left of my baby) in a plastic butter tub. I needed to take a seat among all of these pregnant women. God help me please! I thought. The next name was called. A woman got up from a corner seat. Kennie and I sat down. Protected by Kennie on my left and a table with magazines on it on my right I felt a little more secure. I was trying to conceal my butter tub to make sure no one would ask what was in it. I tried not to make eye contact with anyone and then the unthinkable happened.

    A very young pregnant woman sitting on the other side of the table asked, "Are you going to breastfeed your baby?"

    She had no idea the emotions she stirred. Fortunately, Kennie heard this and made a beeline for the front desk, while my eyes filled up with tears. Kennie told the clerk that I needed out of the waiting room at once and explained the problem. The door to the back rooms opened and we went in. I never even spoke to the young woman. It was more for her than me. I guess I was still trying to protect the ignorant bliss that some mothers-to-be still had. The nurse at the door explained there was no open room. Then showed us down the hall to a storage room with a broken exam table in it and supplies. She apologized for the room and went to get Kennie a chair. When she returned with the chair, she handed me a gown to change into then left again. I told Kennie at least it was better sitting in a storage room than out in the waiting room trying and having people looking at us wondering what was up. I changed into the gown and began to assess the exam table before climbing up on it. it seemed to be still functional, mostly just ripped and a leg holder gone. I cautiously climbed up on it and it held me. After about a half hour the doctor stuck his head in the room. I'm guessing that he didn't believe we were in there but then he put on his game face and introduced himself to us. He was a very young doctor. Young doctors are okay in my book because I credit a very young, right out of college doctor for saving Kennie. I explained to him why we were there and then showed him the butter tub. He took the container out of my hands and sat it down on the counter. He wasn't careless with it but no matter what he did with it, it was not going to be good enough for me. He did a physical exam and told me my cervix was closed so I couldn't have miscarried.

    I said with hope, "Then what fell out of me?"

    He then picked up the butter tub, took a quick look inside and stated that he would be right back. When he returned he was still holding the tub.

I asked "Is that my baby? Did I miscarry another one?" He told me "No."

More puzzled now than before. "Then what is in the tub?"

He told me it was just a blood clot and tissue. I didn't buy it. He had the tub and opened it in front of me. He asked if I wanted to see the clot.

"Yes." I replied.

He brought the tub over to me and pointed out the mass.

I asked, "Couldn't that be the sack?"

He thought about it and grabbed a glove. How convenient we were in a storage room. He put the glove on and tore into the tissue with his finger to reveal my baby. Tiny and no denying my baby. Not a clot as the doctor was saying. The doctor was puzzled because the cervix was closed. Not knowing how to proceed he left the room again. I think he wanted to consult another doctor. He reappeared with two prescriptions and his apologies. With my cervix closed he disregarded the baby as a blood clot. He handed me the prescriptions explaining that one pill was to get my uterus to clamp down and get rid of what was left in my uterus. The other pill was to lessen the pain. I was in disbelief. It happened again. It was like I was in a fog. I got dressed and we left. It didn't even dawn on us that there was no D&C surgery performed. No sonogram. Just that it was over once again and still no baby.

I was lost, figuratively speaking. I just lost a fourth baby. What kind of cruel joke was being played on me? Being told "It's a clot. No, it's a baby". My doctor doing a rectal examination against my wishes. The poor woman who just asked a simple question in the waiting room causing me to burst into tears. The storage room that was my makeshift examination room. The only good thing that came out of this was I got to see my baby. A tangible memory.

I was visiting family later that week when I heard a story that made me smile. It seems that some of our family members and friends who knew about my story were sitting around playing cards. When it came up that I had lost another baby there was young boy in the room who overheard the adults talking. He heard "She lost another baby." The child jumped up ran to the table and started saying "Well why are we not out looking for the baby?" They had to explain to the boy in a delicate way, that the baby had died. I'm told the boy felt very sad for me and my baby. What a great kid - he wanted to start a search party for my baby.

About a week later it still bothered me that I didn't know what happened to my baby's remains. I quickly dismissed the idea because it hurt too much to think about what happened to him. I was also bothered by the fact that I did not have a D&C surgery like in the past. I called the doctor's office that treated me and was told that I needed to call my OBGYN doctor. The doctor on call was only filling in for my doctor. I didn't like my doctor but I called his office anyway. The clerk who answered the phone informed me that there was a new doctor in the practice. I asked what happened to the doctor who saw me just a few weeks ago. I was informed that my previous doctor was let go and not re-signed, because he was too much like a horse doctor and patients were unhappy with his bedside manner. After the rectal exam, I knew exactly what they were talking about. Good riddance! Karma at its finest. I was then informed that the doctor who had replaced him didn't have any openings for new patients. Wait. I'm still a patient. I was then told that I could choose a doctor from a list provided by my insurance company. What? Then it hit me. I didn't have to go with the OBGYN that my family practice doctor sent me to. I just needed a different referral to another doctor. No one ever told me this. It made sense. I thought I didn't have a choice.

Okay. I know I'm not really that stupid. Why wasn't I questioning the doctors? My whole idea about trusting doctors was starting to change. The lack of confidence in all the doctors out there was fading. The drive that I had next to Kennie's bedside when he was sick was starting to return. I was finding my voice again.

CHAPTER FIVE: ONE MORE TRY

It had been over three years since Kennie's Guillain-Barré illness. We had lost four babies and moved to a different house. With my new found education in how health insurance companies work with referrals, it was time to do some research and find a doctor who would listen to us. Looking for a new doctor was also a way of giving myself some time to heal, sort through what happened, and process the reality of things. I also started to focus on a job. I went back to work for a car dealership transferring ownership on vehicle titles.

It was late August when I lost my last baby and it was now the middle of December. I started to look for a new doctor who could handle my undiagnosed condition and one who would be more concerned about what was going on in my body and who would try to provide answers as to why I was losing so many babies. Kennie told me that our health insurance was changing once again the first of the year so we put things on hold until then. Plus, it would be a waste of time to start with a new doctor and the insurance changes in January. I guess this was Gods way of saying enjoy the holidays.

The first of the year, after the paperwork for the insurance was done, I called the insurance company to get a referral for a doctor to diagnose my problem. I explained to the operator at the insurance company my loss history and problems having babies. The operator informed me that my primary doctor would have to give me a referral to the OBGYN doctor. I then asked the operator if she could recommend an OBGYN doctor.

"A high risk, OBGYN?" she asked. Since I had lost so many babies, I was now considered high risk.

I said, "YES." She started rattling off names and locations of doctors who handled high risk pregnancies. She named the location that we went to for my last loss. At least it was close and they should have some of my medical records.

"Are you sure this doctor is a high risk doctor?" I asked one more time just to double check. She assured me that he was.

I made an appointment with my primary doctor and asked for a referral to the high risk OBGYN. I was then informed that unless I was pregnant I didn't need a referral. It was a fee consultation. Mislead again but I insisted on a referral anyway just in case – might as well cover the bases. My doctor gave me the referral and I felt empowered.

When I got home, I called the high risk OBGYN and was told they did offer a free consultation. I made an appointment three weeks out. That got me thinking. I could interview other doctors and then choose the one I wanted. I could do all of this for free. I called another high risk doctor and made an appointment. This doctor was female and I thought this might be the change I needed. She had an opening that day so off I went. When I got there the room was almost empty. At first I thought this was a good thing - no waiting and I could get ahold of her easily when I had a question. While filling out the standard paperwork I came to a page about waving my legal rights and left it blank until someone could explain it to me. I started looking around the room and noticed it was beautifully decorated with a modern flair. There was comforting water trickling from a waterfall table display in the corner of the room. It was soothing right until they called my name. Game on. I was prepared with my story and questions, hoping this was the doctor who was going to make a difference. I was sitting in the littler waiting room (the examination room) when the door opened and the doctor walked in. The doctor was a short woman with dark hair and stared at me as if she was sizing me up for a fight. This immediately made me feel uncomfortable. This is the first time I had "mommy antennas," a term use when you know something is not right and you are not just looking out for you but for your children too – even if they are future children.

She said hello and asked, "What brings you here today?"

I went into my story and started to ask my questions.

"I see." She said. She began going through the paperwork I filled out - the forms they have you fill out and never really read. I noticed she wasn't really reading it either, just flipping through the pages. She found the legal rights page I didn't sign, at the bottom of the stack on the clipboard. This stopped her frantic paper shuffling. The form stated I would waive my rights to sue her for malpractice.

"Well," she said, "We can't go any further until you sign this."

I asked her to explain "this"? I was told that in lieu of a lawsuit, a group of people plus a retired judge would decide if a lawsuit could be filed and on top of that the group would decide the final outcome of any lawsuit.

In light of the last doctor and things that he did and didn't do I said, "Why would I trust someone who can do whatever they want and not have to pay for their mistakes, if they make one?" I then told her, "No." I was not going to sign the paper. She left the room and I started to put it together. She must have been sued before. No one in the waiting room, a nice calming atmosphere and an opening right away, where most appointments are at least two weeks out. She then returned and said she could not continue unless I sign the paper. She explained that she had called her insurance broker and it was mandatory for me to sign in order for her to treat me. This confirmed my suspicions. I was done and I told her so. I thanked her for her time and excused myself.

When I got home, I started calling doctor's offices and asking questions. The first question I asked was if they had such a form. Some did and some didn't. I called an attorney and was told that it may or may not hold up in a court of law depending on the situation. That was good enough for me.

After calling different offices I decided to wait for my consultation/interview with the doctor who was a colleague of doctor #4 who treated me for my last miscarriage.

The appointment was made for the end of the day which allowed Kennie to join me. I was uncomfortable waiting to be called back because the last time I was in this waiting room I was holding my baby in a butter tub. Fortunately, it wasn't like last time. There weren't as many people in the waiting room. It appeared that the doctors had taken care of most of their patients. I went to sign in and was told that the doctor would see me now. I was handed the paperwork to fill out in the examination room. I fanned through the papers looking for the legal document to sign. Surprisingly there wasn't any document to sign waiving my rights to a malpractice. Good sign. The door opened to the back offices. We followed a lady to the end of the hall toward the familiar storage room. She opened the door next to it. A normal room. I felt myself sigh with relief and exhale. We were told the doctor would be right with us. She wasn't kidding. Within minutes the door opened and in walked the doctor. He wasn't very tall, had dark hair, a kind handshake, and a very heavy accent.

He started with a routine question. "Why are you here?"

I answered, "To have a successful pregnancy."

He continued. "Family history?"

I gave the same answers as before, except this time I asked a few more questions regarding diabetes. Like the prior doctor he had his assistant bring in a monitor to check my sugar levels with a finger stick. Again, no diabetes present.

He continued with, "Do you have any known health problems?"

Everything was the same. Back to the reason I was there, "What can you do to help us have a successful pregnancy?" As he went into his plan of action, I realized that it sounded a lot like doctor #1's plan when we went through infertility. This got me to say, "It's not infertility. I have been through that before."

His reply was, "But this time it's to see what is causing the miscarriages. Not to find out why you can't get pregnant. We know you can get pregnant, that's not the problem now." At least one of my problems was solved - I can conceive. A small smile came across my face realizing that I had accomplished something. His approach is much like doctor #2 (one of the doctors I liked) and he is giving me an explanation for why. He asked me when was my last miscarriage and D&C. He was surprised that I didn't have a D&C after the last loss and it was his colleague who treated me. He then said that the D&C was the first thing he was going to do. I could see a question cross his mind.

He said, "I need to get a referral to treat you for your chronic miscarriages."

That's when I proudly reached in my purse and pulled out the referral and said, "Will this do?"

He looked at it and nodded his head agreeing that it was enough. Yes! I looked at Kennie and he smiled back at me. A moment of fate. I'm in the right place (doctor #5). I asked Kennie if he had any questions for the doctor and he said no. The doctor had me set up an appointment with the front desk to have a D&C done. He also wanted me to go to the lab for blood work. The doctor then assured me that we would take one step at a time. A reassuring handshake and we were off to the receptionist at the front desk. That is where I got confused. The appointment for the D&C that I was setting up was at the doctor's office. The other D&Cs were done in the hospital and I was knocked out.

I asked, "Why here at the doctor's office?"

I was told that D&Cs were done in the doctor's office all the time because it was handled a little differently and was not as traumatic to the body. The receptionist told me to take 800 mg of ibuprofen before the appointment to take the edge off. Still puzzled when we got into the car, I asked Kennie what he thought about the D&C being done in the office.

Kennie's reply was, "They couldn't do it in the office if they weren't supposed to." That made logical since.

I continued, "What did you think about the doctor?"

Kennie paused and asked "Do you like him?"

"Yes. He seems to know a lot more than the last doctor and he appears to be much more caring."

Then he said, "Good, because I couldn't understand a word he was saying. His accent was too strong to make out one word." I laughed and started to imagine what it must have been like to set and listen to a one-sided conversation. He could understand me and not the doctor. It must have been like

Charlie Brown when he's talking to an adult in the "Peanuts" shows.

The day came for my D&C. I took my 800 mg of ibuprofen and we went to the doctor's office. I walked into the office, signed in, and took a seat in a packed waiting room. Looking around at all of the people I wondered "Doesn't anyone work anymore?" I had to take the time off of work as usual and Kennie started work at 2:00 a.m. so he was off at his regular time. We had a seat and waited over an hour beyond my scheduled appointment time. The doctor was late. He wasn't even in the building yet. Here we go again. I wondered how many patients were ahead of me. I had taken my ibuprofen and wondered would it still be in my system by the time we did the D&C. When the doctor arrived, I was one of the first to be called back. I climbed up on the table. I didn't want to look around. I was somewhat afraid I would see something to make me change my mind on this procedure, so I focused my eyes on Kennie. The doctor came in and began with the familiar, "Scoot your body down more" as he pulled the foot stirrups out of the table for my feet to go in. Then with another request, "Scoot down more." Your lower back could be hanging off the table and you're still told to scoot down.

He said, "You'll feel a bit uncomfortable but no real pain." He continued, "It will only take a few minutes to complete the procedure. You can hold your husband's hand if you want to." Kennie was right beside me. The nurse was almost repeating every word so Kennie could understand what the doctor said. The nurse picked up on the fact that Kennie couldn't make sense of what the doctor was saying with his heavy accent. The doctor squirted the cold gel for the ultrasound machine on my belly, placed the wand in the gel and brought up an image of my uterus on the screen. He inserted the suctioning device and then turned on the machine. Holy crap! I squeezed Kennie's fingers, closed my eyes and tried to remember to breathe. The machine sounded like an extremely loud vacuum. This was by far the worst pain I had ever felt. I didn't time it, so I don't really know how long it took but at one point the doctor assured me it was almost over saying, "Just a little more." The pain continued. When he noticed I was feeling weak and almost ready to pass out, he finally turned off the machine. I felt my body collapse and exhale. That's when I noticed Kennie's fingers were blue and let go of his hand.

      Still in pain as the doctor finished up by saying, "I think we scraped it all." That's good because we are not doing this again. Different procedure, my butt! Now I know why I was knocked out with all of the other D&Cs. I continued to lie there for a few minutes in pain, very aware of how fast my blood was pumping through my vessels in my head. The doctor left. Kennie helped me slowly sit up. It seemed that everything was in pain and throbbing including Kennie's fingers. I could just imagine what Kennie's face looked like when I had ahold of his purple fingers. The doctor returned and informed us that when we were ready, we could start trying to conceive again. He handed me a prescription for Clomid, the fertility drug I had taken in the past, plus a prescription for progesterone suppositories, a hormone to help enrich the uterus and support a future pregnancy. He explained that the blood work came back normal. The prescriptions were a precautionary procedure just to ensure that everything was covered. He informed us that my body will discharge what it doesn't need from the D&C procedure. He also wanted Kennie to have a sperm count done and handed him a paper with the address on it. I waited for it because last time this was done at home in a condom. You could tell Kennie knew what this meant. This was the first time he understood the doctor.

Kennie's face kind of wrinkled up and he asked the doctor, "Is this really necessary?"

The doctor responded quickly with, "With what your wife just went through this is easy." How could Kennie say no?

We had no problem filling the Clomid prescription, but the progesterone prescription needed to be ordered and then made at a different pharmacy. The progesterone suppositories also had to be refrigerated or they would melt - just the natural heat from my fingers started the melting process.

I went with Kennie to his appointment at the infertility center for his sperm count. He had gone with me every time to my appointments so it only seemed fair. We walked into the waiting room. There was only one man in the waiting room and he looked up at us with a startled look and then looked away. Okay. I get it. No eye contact. I guess it's like being in a men's public restroom at the urinals. I can only imagine how uncomfortable this must be for men in general. Kennie signed in. The other man was called back. It was late and they were going to close soon. It wasn't long before Kennie was called back. I had a seat and within a half hour the man that was in the waiting room came out and left. Still no Kennie. I'm not sure how long this should take but the other guy finished in a short amount of time. Finally, Kennie came out. He was told to have a seat.

In my normal joking manor, I asked, "What took you so long? Did you have a hard time in there?" We both smiled at first and finished with a laugh. The technician came out, locked the main door and the office was closed. He informed us that this procedure was not covered under our insurance plan and we would have to pay for the visit out of our own pockets. He said a lot of plans will reimburse the fee to the patient. We would have to contact them to find out.

He then asked us, "Do you want to see the sample under the microscope?"

Cool. "Yes." Kennie thought differently and declined. I went with the technician into a small laboratory room. He motioned for me to come over and look in the microscope. I focused into the scope. Wow! I had never seen anything like this. There were lots of black and white images of tadpoles (sperm) moving all over a squared off frame. He then informed me that the squares in the background helped measure the amount of sperm and how quick they move. From my own analysis I could tell that there were a lot of sperm, maybe millions and they were active. This was so unlike the first test that Kennie had to do with the condom.

I went to the waiting room where Kennie was and told him this was a once in a lifetime chance to see what your sperm looked like. At first he started to decline again, but then I said, "The office is closed and the technician is willing to educate us with this." Kennie followed me back and reluctantly had a look.

He looked up, smiled and said, "My boys are swimmers!"

I corrected him and said, "Some of them may be girls." The technician explained what we were looking at was just a drop of the semen and there are millions more in just one sample.

I asked, "How many is normal?" I was told over 15 million per milliliter and they can live in a woman's body up to a week. Outside of the body they live only an hour or two. Wow, I thought, women produce only one egg. Men produce this much sperm in their semen. It's a wonder why women don't get pregnant every time they ovulate. We thanked the technician for his time and he let us out.

When we got into the car Kennie was snickering over something.

I said, "What is so funny?"

He started to explain that on his way to the sample providing room the technician handed him a small specimen cup, pointed to the instructions on the wall, and told him to press the call button if he needed anything.

Kennie said, "I went into the room, closed the door and realized that the lock was broken. Great! This didn't help the situation. The instructions were on the wall. The first instruction was to relax. How do you do that when the lock on the door is broken? Knowing what had to be done I looked over at the magazines sitting on the table. They looked disgusting. They were wrinkled and who knows what was on them. Then I saw the tv videos. Okay. I turned on the tv and put one of the videos in and it was already past the good part."

He had me laughing so hard I couldn't breathe and my side started to hurt.

He told me, "I started to rewind it but after looking at the magazines on the table who knows how clean the buttons on the recorder were. I decided to just do what I had to do and collected my sample."

Oh my gosh! Laughing was the release we needed for our stressful situation.

I called the insurance company and yes, they would reimburse us for the clinical costs. One less thing to deal with.

That month as instructed I started the routine of taking the Clomid, followed by the progesterone suppositories. After a few months of this routine I still wasn't pregnant. I read that there was a study done on the extended use of Clomid that proved Clomid can cause ovarian cancer in some patients. I called the doctor and told him about my concerns. He informed me that the Clomid study was done on women that were on it for a long period of time. I won't be at risk because I won't be on the medication for long. He told me the sperm count results came back normal. He wanted me to consider artificial insemination. He explained in detail what it entailed and said Kennie would need to go back to the infertility center for a semen collection for the insemination. I made the appointment and then told Kennie the plan which was to collect his semen, keep it at body temperature, then quickly get the semen to the doctor or the semen would die in just a few short hours. A quick insertion into the uterus and let mother nature do her job. The day came. Kennie took the day off work and we went to the infertility center. I prepaid the bill knowing this time I could send it in like the other bill and get reimbursed. Kennie was almost a professional at this. He went into the little room and 15 minutes later he was out with the specimen in a warm spot up against his body and off we went to the doctor's office. Everything was running like clockwork. We arrived at the doctor's office to find a packed waiting room. We went up to the desk knowing we had a timed appointment, to find out that the doctor wasn't even there. What? How could this be? Who is going to help us? Especially considering what Kennie had just gone though. I asked the receptionist if there was anything she could do. She asked around to the doctors in the office and nobody was available.

  Meanwhile the sperm were starting to die. She finally found a doctor willing to help at the local hospital across the street. Off we went. When we arrived at the hospital, we found out we had beat the on-call doctor to her office. This didn't help our urgent situation. (We'll call her doctor #6, because she could have made a difference after we explained our story to her.)

By the time the doctor arrived to help us she realized how old the semen was and said, "It probably won't take. However, you're here and we might as well go through with it." I'm guessing she did it because she wanted a paycheck for her troubles. Once again to an examination room, change to a gown, climb up on the table, scoot down and scoot down once again after the doctor comes into the room. The doctor inserted the tube, added the sperm and in went the semen. A pillow was placed under my buttocks to keep the pelvis tilted upwards. The room was quiet, just Kennie, the doctor and me with nothing to do but wait.

My sense of humor goes off, "Does anyone want a cigarette?" I don't even smoke but somehow it seemed humorously appropriate.

That month I got my period. What a waste of time, Kennie's day off, and money. The doctor never even apologized for not being available for an appointment that he wanted scheduled. Nor did he reschedule the procedure. I couldn't help but think if he had just been in his office when he said he would be, the sperm wouldn't have died and we would have conceived a baby that day.

I got a call from the infertility center. They had received our reimbursement check and it was several hundreds of dollars. I picked it up to discover it was made out to the infertility center. They signed it over to me to fix the insurance company's mistake. It was Friday and Kennie went to deposit the check while I waited in the truck. Kennie returned to the truck fit to be tied. He told me the teller would not except the check because it was a third-party check. I took the check and went back into the bank. I returned to the truck with successfully depositing the check with a three day hold. I was a teller once and my experience paid off. Kennie was impressed.

I realized that there were a number of people who know my story, family, friends, neighbors, clients, Kennie's co-workers and now even bankers.

Months had come and gone. We added another year to our struggles. We had been through so much: Clomid, progesterone, artificial insemination, doctor appointments, DNCs, scraping of the uterus for samples, Kennie giving samples, dealing with insurance companies. Plus all of the stress we had endured with the miscarriages and infertility procedures was almost more than we could take. We were armed with an extensive hands-on education and yet we still felt like we were losing the battle. There was so much effort put into the tests that I started to wonder if anyone noticed that I was not pregnant yet. I decided to stop taking the Clomid and progesterone and I canceled all of the workups just to give us a break from the constant stress. We would start fresh again in January. Another January. I could hardly believe I was saying it.

Halloween was a reminder about what I was putting on hold when the kids, dressed in their costumes, came to the door trick-or-treating. But I still didn't take the Clomid. I passed again on the second dose the following month. Before we knew it Thanksgiving had come and gone and I noticed that I had missed my period. Well, I thought, I had missed a period before and I wasn't pregnant. It was just late. I thought about it and decided to restart the regimen of progesterone suppositories just in case I really was pregnant. I wanted to help support the baby in the beginning of life. I did not want to leave anything to chance. I called the doctor. I asked him for the paperwork to have blood work done to see if I was pregnant. I figured why spend the money on the test if the doctor's office was going to have to do a pregnancy test for their own confirmation. A urine test confirmed I was pregnant. I contributed it to the lack of stress. Unlike the last convenient blood confirmation, I was sent to the laboratory for blood work to officially confirm the pregnancy. I pulled over on the way and again wrote *stat* on the lab paperwork with no guilt and within less than a day my pregnancy was confirmed. The doctor called to tell me I was five weeks pregnant and due August 11th. I didn't conceive on Clomid. More than likely no twins. Per the doctor, I was to continue to eat and drink healthy. Back to the milk, orange juice, and eggs. I started prenatal pills and continued the progesterone suppositories and made an appointment to see the doctor in three weeks.

    As I hung up the phone, I was thinking sure here comes the hard part, trying not to get too attached to the idea that I was pregnant because I probably won't carry the baby to term. This is not normal. Not connecting was probably a way of self-protecting. Why can't I be normal? This was the first time I really felt like I was walking on eggshells and knew very well what that meant. It all felt so clinical. Not the normal excitement, "I'm pregnant!" In fact, everything had become clinical until one night I was stretched out in bed with Kennie. He turned towards me, leaned over my belly and started talking to my bellybutton again.

    "Hello." He said.

    It made me smile and at that moment I started to connect again.

    By Christmas all of the family knew about the baby. Some even bought the future baby gifts. I just couldn't get into it yet. I smiled and thanked them but no one except Kennie knew that deep down I was a wreck.

January came and our insurance changed again. Luck had it that we got to keep our same doctor. This was a surprise. We went for our first "real" baby appointment and the doctor was running late. Waiting in the little waiting room (examination room) Kennie was bored. First, Kennie was sitting on the little doctor's stool spinning around until it came off and Kennie hit the ground. Oops! Then he put it back together. He then noticed the faucet was leaking. Project. He took the faucet apart and I started freaking out because the doctor could walk in any minute. Kennie fixed the faucet and was back to being bored.

He was like a two-year-old. He started opening drawers and pulling out instruments. Saying, "I wonder what they use this for?" As he was holding up something like a speculum.

I would answer just to get him to put it back. "That's used for an examination. Oh my God. Stop! Just sit down!" I guess I was stressed a little. I just couldn't relax and Kennie was adding to my stress. We were in the room a long time without anyone letting us know how much longer. That's when Kennie decided to start singing to me with hopes of making me feel better. Okay. Kennie can't sing. Then he noticed the light, on a bendable stand, which was turned off. Every woman knows about the focus light that the doctor uses during the examination. Kennie grabs it by the bulb top and uses it like a microphone. He starts singing "Burning Love" by Elvis Presley. He was in the middle of one of the verses, one hand in the air with his knee bent in the Elvis pose, when the doctor knocks and enters the room quickly. He looked at Kennie and smiled.

Kennie replied with "I was just trying to make Carol smile and have a little fun."

The doctor said with a smile, "You've had all your fun since your wife is now pregnant." Then the doctor jokingly said, "Besides that is an expensive light - wait until you get my bill."

Kennie smiled and said, "Wait until you get my bill for fixing your leaky faucet." The doctor looked at the sink and noticed that it was no longer leaking.

The doctor replied, "When is your next appointment? I have other rooms that need repairs." The real funny part is Kennie understood every word the doctor said.

We all laughed.

We finally got to the reason we were there.

The doctor asked, "How are you doing?"

I said, "Everything seems to be going okay." The doctor asked about morning sickness. "You know I hadn't thought about it much, but no." At that moment I realized that I never did get morning sickness even with my prior pregnancies. According to the doctor, if I was going to have morning sickness, this was the time for it, at the beginning of the pregnancy. He assured me that not having morning sickness was not a problem and not to worry about it. Not all women get sick. He wrote me another prescription for the progesterone and told me that the prescription was just enough to get me though my first trimester.

He also said, "After the first trimester the baby will be fully implanted and you will no longer need the help of the progesterone suppositories." This was very scary for me. I had come to rely on the medicine as a sure thing to get me through this pregnancy. I guess I never realized that the progesterone was short term and not used throughout the whole pregnancy.

Plus, I had never made it beyond the first trimester. Time to shift gears again. The day finally came when I ran out of the progesterone. It was nerve-wracking to go without the progesterone but it did mark the time that the first trimester was over. I had some weight gain and I had a baby bump.

Somewhere around that time I was at the doctor's office with Kennie. The doctor was telling me about a blood test for down syndrome and other illnesses that was done around the second trimester. He said I should consider it given my age. The thought hit me I was almost 29. Kennie got sick when I was 23 which meant we had been trying to have a family for almost six years. The doctor handed me reading material about the blood work for the tests. A simple blood test. I then read about making a decision to abort the pregnancy before you're 16 weeks along if the birth defect test came back positive. I had never gotten this far and I'm taking a test to see if I want to abort my baby. A simple decision for me. I'll do the blood work but there is no way I would abort my baby. I don't care how much work it would be. If this baby makes it to term, he's mine to keep. Period.

We had entered another year of Little League. Kennie was back to coaching a team. Only this time I was pregnant and I was starting to show. Most everyone at Little League knew my story and checked in with me when they saw me at the field. I started to feel as if I was normal. The fears of losing this baby were fading. It was around mid-April and I was sitting watching a game when I first felt the baby move. I wouldn't say a hard kick but a definite movement. I was connected. From there forward I called my belly-bump "Bumpkins". What a great feeling. Then the day came for me to take the dreaded six-month blood test for birth defects. Still sticking to my word, I took the blood test but it would not change my decision to keep my baby. I thought of it as giving me a heads up on any problems we may have to be prepared for. The blood work was done and the results showed everything was fine. This marked the end of the second trimester.

Even though Bumpkins was the name I called my baby for the duration of the pregnancy, we did contemplate real names. If it was a girl, we liked the names Megan and Jessica. If it was a boy we were sold on Kevin.

Family and friends were asking to throw me a baby shower. I hadn't even thought about having a baby shower. Not one but two showers were arranged. A lot of people were following my pregnancy this time after learning our story. Our nursery theme was teddy bears because it was neutral. I got lots of teddy bears. One was enormous. We called him "Ted". In addition to teddy bears we got baby clothes, a car seat, and all of the essentials. I was set. Kennie and I started decorating the baby's room. I picked out a number 1, 2, 3 and a teddybear stencil. We painted it on the wall in primary colors. My mother-in-law Ruth, Kennie, and I went out shopping for a crib. Ruth surprised me by buying the crib. Kennie and I bought the matching dresser. The nursery was just perfect. Now we just wait for the big day. My due date was August 11th - it seemed far away. Doing things in preparation for the baby helped calm me and put me back on the normal track. I felt the way I felt when I was pregnant the first time - excited to be pregnant. Excited to have a baby.

Looking over all the stuff we had for the baby – and some for me – it occurred to me that there really wasn't anything for Kennie. I went to the mall, had a custom t-shirt made for Kennie with the words "Daddy in Training" and put it in a gift bag. Kennie opened the bag and immediately put on the t-shirt. In fact, Kennie wore the shirt every chance he could, mostly to the practices at the Little League field.

It was late May when I returned to the doctor's office for a routine visit. The doctor noticed that I had gained weight. The chart showed that I weighed 213 pounds. I'm five foot seven so I justified it in my head. Plus, I'm pregnant. I thought that gaining weight was part of being pregnant. He told me I needed to stop eating so many fast food hamburgers. I don't eat much fast food and I don't eat hamburgers unless there are no other choices on the menu. The nerve of him. The real insult was that I had taken it upon myself to change almost everything I ate to make it healthier for the baby, especially after what I had been through.

I sucked up my hormonal anger and promptly told him, "I don't eat hamburgers." You could tell he didn't believe me. He informed me that this kind of weight gain could lead to gestational diabetes. I reminded him that diabetes runs in my family. He seemed to have a "I wonder" look on his face and ordered a glucose tolerance test to check for diabetes. Wait, didn't he already do a diabetes test in his office when he poked my finger? I then learned that the test he did in the office, poking the finger and drawing blood, was not as accurate as the one they do in the laboratory (lab.). What? All this time I thought there wasn't a chance for me to get diabetes and now this late in the game he tells me it's not completely ruled out. I felt like I just fell down a big hole and hit the bottom. He hands me a blood work request form with (funny it already said *stat* already on it) and wants me to go tomorrow after fasting to the lab. I have to be fasting, no eating twelve hours before the test. The test takes around three hours because blood is drawn every hour to see how my body reacts to sugar after drinking a very sweet soda given to me by the lab technician.

The next morning, I went through the three hours of testing, knowing this was for the good of my baby. After fasting all night, I was hungry, not feeling good and I knew I couldn't eat before the lab work was complete. At the lab I was handed a sugar enriched soda to drink after the first blood draw, a urine specimen cup, and a sterile wipe. I'd done a urine test before but not seven months pregnant. It's not easy. Looking at the cup it again reminded me of the first pregnancy test I took. Why are the cups so small? I had to guess at where to hold the cup because it disappeared around the big pregnant belly. Okay, the collection is done now where do I put the cup while I finish and stand up? One choice was on the back of the toilet. I can't even reach back there so not an option. Metal casing around the toilet paper roll or the handle bar for the disabled. Looks good until I noticed the urine rings from prior patients. Or my last choice on the floor and risk spilling it. I chose the floor; the small cup had a lid. I eventually placed the urine cup in the little cupboard, choosing the farthest back slot and closed the door. Then reopening the little cupboard door quickly to see if anyone took it from the other side. Nope, still there. I returned to the lab for the first blood draw, then I drank the thick, icky sweet, disgusting soda-like beverage on an empty stomach, and continued have my blood drawn every hour for three hours.

Finally home and having something to eat I had a chance to inspect my injection sites. The technician did good. However, the bandage left big red marks on my skin. I've had this kind of reaction since I was little. Kennie came home later and went straight to the kitchen to bake me a birthday cake for the next day. He asked me what flavor I wanted and I told him carrot with cream-cheese frosting sounded good to me. Two things were a bit odd here. One: Kennie didn't bake cakes he usually ordered cakes. Second: Anyone who knows me knows my choice is always chocolate. I sat down at the kitchen counter as Kennie went to work on the cake. The phone rang.

"It's for you, it's the doctor." Kennie handed me the phone.

"Hello?" I was quickly informed that I had gestational diabetes and that I needed to go to an Endocrinologist right away I was told that the Endocrinologist could help me with my gestational diabetes and answer all of my questions. I hung up the phone and wondered what just happened. The conversation went so quickly and then I had gestational diabetes - something he supposedly checked me for early on and told me I didn't have. I made my phone call to doctor #7.

The call was answered, "Hold please." Then silence. I'd learned from experience that this is not a good way to start a relationship with a doctor.

Five maybe ten minutes of silence. "What can I do for you?"

"I'm trying to set up an appointment with the Endocrinologist today." I'm sure I mispronounced that word more than once before I got it right. She explained they were booked. My blood pressure hit the roof. I hate it, and I mean I hate it, when one doctor tells you to do something like it is an absolute emergency and another doctor acts like it is no big deal. I felt a rush of emotions, pregnancy hormones, and the sudden panic that my baby was in danger. I let her have it.

"What do you mean weeks? I need to be seen now! My doctor said...." I explained the urgency. Well guess what? I got an appointment for the next morning. Don't mess with a terrified pregnant woman.

Kennie came home early and went with me to the Endocrinology appointment. The Endocrinologist was in the same building as the OBGYN's office. How convenient. I really had no idea what to expect. Into yet another waiting room. By this time, I may have visited every waiting room in town. At least it seemed that way. Looking around the packed waiting room I noticed all sorts of different people. I was used to sitting with pregnant women and some dads-to-be but there were no pregnant women. No one fit a stereotype. Women, men, different nationalities, skinny, overweight, and then me. I started to wonder if I was in the right place and then my name was called. When we were led back into a room, I started to read the wall information and noticed a box of needles sitting on the doctor's desk. It was starting to sink in. The OBGYN doctor didn't want to tell me because he knew I was going to be put on an injection regimen. Happy birthday to me. The room was somewhat dark with wooden accents and had a normal office desk sitting in the center of the room. This was not a normal exam room. The doctor entered the room and informed me that I would have to have insulin injections. Insulin injections! I can't do that? Sheer panic was racing through me. Oh, and that's not all.

"You'll need to poke your finger four times a day and record the blood results."

I was dumbfounded. I needed time to absorb all of this. I wish the OBGYN doctor had at least clued me in on all of this, at least then I would have had time to let it sink in. Now I have to make an immediate decision. Of course, in reality there was no decision to be made. I was going on insulin. I was panicked and totally scared. The real question, was my baby safe? What if I over or under injected the insulin? The doctor pulled a syringe out of the box on his desk and a bottle of insulin from a small refrigerator. He sat them both on his desk in front of Kennie and me. He tried to explain that the insulin was a 70/30 bottle and that it was easier to pull from one bottle than from two. I was clueless. The doctor tried explaining to me how to get the insulin into the needle and how the lines on the needle worked. I really didn't understand this yet but I trusted him. I had no choice. As he was opening up a new glucose meter, he explained how to use it. The doctor unzipped a little black zipper bag and revealed a meter about four inches by three inches. It looked the same as the one the doctors used on me at their offices to check my blood sugar. At least this looked familiar to me. There was a bottle of test strips to place in the machine one at a time and a little stick like gun that he loaded a needle (lancet) into. It had a trigger button to propel the lancet into your finger, poke a small hole so a drop of blood can be retrieved and placed on the end of the test strip. I was quickly learning a whole new vocabulary, test strips, lancets, etc. After five seconds the results (a number) would appear on the meter. The doctor quickly prepped it with a lancet, then rubbed alcohol on the end of my finger and pushed the trigger at the end of the stick like gun. OUCH! SHIT! He wasn't as gentle as the nurses were. He asked me what I had to eat today and wrote it down in a book. He took out an alcohol pad and wiped my arm with it. He then picked up the syringe stuck it in the bottle and pulled out some of the insulin, talking the whole time but it didn't make any sense to me. He then put the cap back on the needle and placed it on desk. A moment to relax. He then told me I would have to record everything I eat, my blood results from the meter, how much insulin I injected in the morning and at night, call it into the doctor's office and the doctor would make the necessary adjustments with the insulin. The doctor tried to explain it all to me and I was in a fog. Fortunately, Kennie was there to ask all of the questions I couldn't think to ask. I was lost and wanted in the worst way to get out of this. I was to become a human pincushion. I sucked it up and put on my game face. This was temporary. Some people have to do this all of their life. Who am I to complain? The doctor gave me the insulin injection in my arm. Double OUCH! He put the used syringe in a canister and then asked me if I wanted to go on disability. I thought again about all of the people who take insulin and lead a fairly normal life. Besides, my boss would have a hard time replacing me. My answer was "No."

What no bandage at the injection site? Good. I'm allergic anyway but what if the insulin comes out? It didn't. Kennie got all of the information from the doctor and the supplies from the pharmacy downstairs and we went home.

Kennie gave me a pep talk in the car. "You can do this. I'll be there to help. It's not that bad. It's not for the rest of your life. You're doing this for our baby." That's the one that stuck. The big brown paper bag with the diabetic supplies took up the entire space on the bench seat between Kennie and me. In the silence during the ride home, I started to put things together. I originally told the OBGYN doctor the first time I met him that diabetes ran in my family and all he did was poke my finger. In reality, at that time he should have ordered a glucose tolerance test to diagnose my gestational diabetes. Of course, the main reason for the insulin was to make sure my baby was safe and healthy. For that reason alone, I didn't mind being a human pincushion.

The first thing I noticed as we walked through the door at home was the wonderful smell of my birthday cake Kennie baked the night before. My bubble burst. I knew my sweets were cut off. That was one of the only things I heard at the doctor's office after insulin injections. There was no birthday cake for me on my birthday. Oh well. I sucked it up again. I was hungry and I was afraid to eat. I knew a little about diabetes because it ran in my family but even my family didn't really know how to keep their sugar-levels under control. They just winged it. My grandfather was the only one on insulin. The others were on oral medications. Plus, I'm pregnant and on insulin. I'm told there is a difference. I sat down and started to read the materials that the doctor gave me. First, I read about food intake. I was hungry and hadn't eaten much after the OBGYN called and informed me that I had gestational diabetes. I was afraid to eat anything. Oh my god: according to what I was reading, the juice and milk, which I had been forcing myself to drink every morning for the baby's health, was one of the worst thing to drink if you want to lower your blood sugars. In fact, this is what they recommend if you over inject insulin or hit a sugar low for some reason. Why didn't someone tell me? Why didn't the doctor test me earlier? Fruit intake was to be limited too. It's summer and I have been eating fruit because it's healthy. Apparently, it is the wrong choice too. It seemed everything that you know about healthy eating is not necessarily healthy eating for a diabetic. It did suggest to increase protein and lower carbohydrates. More meats and less bread. Twelve hundred calories a day from three meals, limit sugars, starches, fat and juices. I can do that. I got up and fixed an egg and cheese sandwich on an English muffin. Well at least the egg a day that I was eating was good for the protein. I continued by reading the lab report. Fasting blood levels should be less than 100, mine were 140. After I drank the funny looking soda one, two- and three-hour results showed 260, 256 and 231. It should have gone down to below 140 after one to two hours per the book I was reading. I also read that my blood pressure was 128/80. The 128, according to the normal scale, was high, too.

I called in sick to work for the second day in a row. This was not like me but I needed time to adjust. I went into the kitchen. There was the brown bag from the pharmacy. It was still sitting on the counter as a bad reminder that it wasn't just a bad dream. The biggest box and the one I feared the most were the one with the syringes. The word was "syringe" not needles. My language was starting to change every day. I still wanted out of this whole human pincushion thing but knew I had to go through with it.

I stood there telling myself, "You can do this."

I continued reading where I left off the night before. Two insulin injections a day from the 70/30 bottle. I was to take 24 units in the morning and 17 units at night. It hit me I was at home alone and I needed a shot. After the initial panic ran through me, I needed to know how and where to inject. According to the book, the areas to best inject are your arm, thigh or stomach. No, not happening in the stomach. That's where the baby is. I didn't want to poke him. Looking at the syringe I saw that the needle was too short to poke the baby but I wasn't taking any chances. The arm was a "no" also. How do you reach the spot on the arm, pinch up the skin and inject with one hand? I'm sure there is a trick to it but I don't know it. That left the thighs. I continued reading. I opened up the bag then the box and pulled a syringe out. On the side of the syringe were five lines then numbers. Each line represented two units. Following the directions, I got the insulin out of the refrigerator, removed the cap, alcohol swabbed the top and sat the bottle down on the counter. I then took a syringe out and removed the cap. I picked up the insulin bottle turned it upside down. It had a spongy white top which I inserted the syringe upwards into the bottle and pulled back on the end of the syringe to create suction. The insulin started to fill the syringe.

Twenty-four was the lucky number of units. I pulled the syringe out and returned the bottle to the refrigerator. Still telling myself, "I can do this!" I felt like everything was moving in slow motion. I sat down on the couch still in my nightgown and pulled it up to expose my thigh. I used the alcohol pad from the box we got the night before, opened it and wiped the spot to inject. I pinched up a spot of skin on my thigh, picked up my syringe and "SHIT!" I can't do this. What the hell? Sheer panic. I needed to take the shot so I could eat and not eating was not an option. I got up and turned on music. I turned it up and started singing with it to take my mind off of the syringe, as if the music would make the pain less. The reality was it was a little needle less than an inch long and when the doctor did it there was virtually no pain. I sat down and started again. Telling myself this time, "I won't stop." I wiped the spot again with the alcohol pad, picked up the syringe, pinched up the skin and stuck the syringe in. Crap! It hurt and I made the mistake of pulling the syringe out. Instantly I knew I was going to have to re-inject. "Stupid! How can I be so stupid?" A small amount of blood was coming out of the tiny little pinhole. I wiped it up with the alcohol pad. Now I know I could inject a syringe into someone else with no problem but it is a whole different story when it is you injecting yourself. I realized that while my left hand was pinching up my skin, my right hand was holding the syringe. How was I going to push the end of the syringe to inject the insulin? I don't have a third hand. There was nothing or no one to tell me what to do. It was now almost 10:00 a.m. Kennie was due home in a few hours, so I decided to wait for him. My logic was I had gone this long without insulin in the pregnancy, I could go a few more hours. I recapped the insulin, put it in the refrigerator and fixed myself another egg sandwich. Kennie came home I explained what happened. I asked him to give me the shot. I could tell he didn't want to but he said yes. He took the syringe out of the refrigerator and removed the cap. I rolled up my sleeve, wiped alcohol on the spot and he gave me the injection. Some of the insulin started to come out of the hole when he pulled the syringe out. I wiped it, put pressure on it and it stopped. It was a little painful but I was grateful Kennie was willing to give me the insulin injection. Kennie taped an empty coffee can closed and cut a hole in the top and dropped the used syringe into it. Apparently, this is how to properly dispose of the used syringes. According to the doctor when the canister is full you take it to a medical disposal company.

    Night came and I was due for another injection. I decided that I would give it another try with Kennie there. I needed to learn how to inject it myself because the reality was Kennie was not always going to be home. I prepared the syringe and my other thigh. Holding my breath, I pinched up the spot and poked my thigh. I let go with my pinching hand and pushed the end of the syringe to inject the insulin. I continued by pulling the syringe out, wiped the spot with an alcohol pad and held pressure on it for a minute. I exhaled while calming down. Little to no pain, no bruise and I did it myself. Okay, Kennie is off the hook.

    Alternating left and right, high and low on the thigh for the injection site helped. I learned that hitting a small vein caused bruises on occasion. I also learned the hard way you never set the syringe down on the table because it will get bent. Bent syringes hurt because they go into the skin crooked. You have to be careful with pulling the insulin out of the bottle. The syringe also must go straight into and straight out of the insulin bottle to prevent it from getting bent.

I was instructed to call in my eating, blood and insulin records almost daily. About a day or two into it and the Endocrinologist had added a third shot at lunch. It wasn't easy incorporating insulin, blood checks, and recording it all in the book, into my daily routine. I made it back to work and had to deal with the new routine of insulin injections. Something as ordinary as working late became a challenge because I had to plan an injection and a meal. My coworkers were always interested in what I was doing. They were aware of my pregnancy and the gestational diabetes. I would disappear into the bathroom with my bag of supplies and come out wiping tears away from my eyes. I'm pregnant for the fourth time, made it through the miscarriage time frame and figured I was in the clear. Now I'm dealing with being insulin dependent, gestational diabetes, high blood pressure on the rise, possible toxemia (a product of high blood pressure when you're pregnant) and one of the most stressful jobs in the company. I was starting to break. I can't take much more of this considering the hormones too. Cravings weren't even an option.

One day my boss called me into her office and said I was causing a distraction with this whole diabetes thing. I couldn't believe my ears. How cruel and heartless can someone be? I just looked at her. She had no idea what I was going through and the sacrifice I had made for her. One of the reasons I chose to work instead of going on disability was there was only one other person in the office who knew how to do my job and she had the second most demanding job in the office. I didn't want to put them in a bind at a moment's notice but looking at her with a dead silence around us I finally said "I have just decided to go on disability." She argued that I couldn't do that. I left her office, went back to my desk and called the Endocrinologist. I told him I changed my mind and requested that he send the disability notice to me at work. The disability paperwork arrived by fax within a few minutes. I picked it up, went to my desk, packed up my personal belongings, went into my boss's office and handed her the doctor's disability note and said, "Good bye." I felt vindicated.

At my next OBGYN appointment I was told that my sugar scores were going down. That was a good thing but my blood pressure was still a concern.

Kennie took me to a Padre Baseball game to get my mind off of the stressful situation. I was in the stadium watching a Padre game and I needed to eat but knew I needed to take my insulin shot first. I went to the bathroom. There was no private or clean place to sit down and inject my insulin. I went back out to where Kennie was and asked him to walk with me to the truck. It was pretty far for how pregnant I was. I got into our little Ford Ranger and closed the door. I had a little blanket to cover my lower body. I prepped the syringe, pulled my pants down to expose the injection site, wiped the alcohol and started to inject. Suddenly someone started pounding on my window! It was a woman.

I heard her through the glass yelling "Don't do that you'll hurt the baby! No! No!" She was trying to plead with me. I already have enough trouble getting the shot in me and now this? I ignored her and finished. I thought I didn't owe her an explanation but I rolled down the window and told her the doctor prescribed this. She meant well but what nerve. She didn't know me or my situation. She should have minded her own business or waited until I got out of the truck and then approached me with caution and concern. Kennie walked up as she walked away. He was trying to find out who scored in the game. So much for stress relief with the baseball outing.

We found out that there weren't very many diabetic friendly places. We went to Knott's Berry Farm for dinner once and they were the best at providing a place for diabetics. They not only provided a bench to sit on but a collection canister for the used syringe. Even when we planned to go out to eat there were complications. You need to eat within 30 minutes of the injection or you might hit a sugar low. I would usually inject at home so I wouldn't create a scene at the restaurant. If there was a line at the restaurant or we had to wait, I would hit a sugar low and it would be hard to focus. That's when we learned that you let the host know that you are a diabetic and you need to be seated right away. At the very least they would bring you something from the kitchen to nibble on.

Late June I learned an important lesson about insulin. My friend invited me to a party where you can purchase kitchen products. She said that she would be serving dinner too. I had never been to one of these parties and decided I didn't want to give myself an insulin shot in front of everyone and I injected myself before I left. I knew I had a 30 minute window to eat something and that should be enough time. I got to her house and the demonstration of the products started, something went wrong and they had to start over. Apparently, what they were fixing was the dinner. The delay dropped my sugars and I didn't have my meter to check them, but I could feel them go. Trying not to make a scene I excused myself from the party and went out to my car. I felt bad about leaving. I was so sick that I threw up in her front yard. That was a first for me. I got into my car and drove home but I could hardly see because my vision had become so blurry. I got home, grabbed my meter and my levels were 25. That was the lowest I have ever seen it. No wonder I was sick. My normal levels were between 90 and

110. I went to the fridge and downed an ice cream sandwich. It brought it up to 79 and I could focus. I made a sandwich and called my friend and once again apologized for leaving with a short explanation. She had no idea that I had taken the insulin prior to coming to her house. In all honesty I shouldn't have driven myself home, but that was an afterthought.

CHAPTER SIX: MOMENT BY MOMENT

It was somewhere around the middle of June when my OBGYN doctor became concerned about my increasingly high blood pressure. He put me on bed rest saying I had "borderline toxemia". Now, what is "borderline toxemia"? The only thing he told me was no getting up out of bed with the exception of a bathroom need or a quick cool shower. This gave me time to research the illness. I found out that toxemia is a condition in pregnancy where the mother-to-be has both high blood pressure and protein in her urine. I read it can be fatal to both the baby and the mother. This didn't help my blood pressure. The only cure is to deliver the baby. It seemed simple: just get me and my baby to the deliverable stage of this pregnancy. I had been on complete bed rest for a couple of weeks when the doctor ordered a non-stress test (NST). This was a non-invasive test done in the third trimester to measure contractions, the baby's movement, and the baby's heart rate over a 30 minute time span. The test was performed at the hospital.

Wait. I thought I wasn't allowed to get out of bed? Don't they make house calls? The nurse who called me to make the appointment assured me that it was okay to get out of bed for this test. Off I went to the hospital for an NST. I had become a little more secure about going to appointments without Kennie considering that I passed all the timeframes of when I had lost my other babies. I walked into the hospital by myself. This was a little disconcerting considering my experiences there. I was personally walked to the testing area. I was feeling a little nervous about the uncertainties of the procedure until I saw a comfortable chair waiting for me and the nurse pointing to it telling me to have a seat. Draped horizontally across the chair were two pink and blue stretchy bands with small holes down the middle of them. I started to move them out of the way so I could sit down and was told that those were there to wrap around my baby belly.

I said "my Bumpkins?" The nurse responded with a strange look on her face. I explained "Bumpkins" and she said, "Yes, around your Bumpkins."

The holes in the center of the bands were for the nurse to connect a small monitor to by putting the holes over the monitor's metal connector. Instantly you could hear my baby's heartbeat.

Wow.

I was amazed. It turned out that there were two heartbeats: mine and my baby's. The nurse could tell the difference between my heartbeat and the baby's but I couldn't make sense of it. She explained that the baby's heart rate was a lot faster than mine. Right next to the chair was the machine recording the activity. A ticket came out of the machine (it seemed to never stop) recording graph like images onto a paper. It reminded me of a small version of the Richter scale that monitors earthquakes.

I started telling the nurse how Kennie and I were married nine years, lived through Kennie's Guillain-Barré, and how excited we are to be having a baby. I told her that this was the first time I had made it to full term with one of my pregnancies. She then asked about the delivery and choosing a hospital. I guess I never allowed myself to think of the end of the pregnancy. Maybe I thought it would jinx it. She gave me some flyers on birthing classes and a hospital tour. I hadn't thought about it, I assumed I would deliver at that hospital because the doctor only had privileges there and the insurance company listed only that hospital to deliver. Before I knew it the 30 minutes of monitoring were up. I asked if the monitor images showed that everything was in the normal range. I was then informed that the doctor had scheduled a few of the NSTs to keep an eye on me and the baby until I delivered. I thanked them for the information on the classes and tours and said goodbye. Before I left the hospital, I signed up for the hospital tour for later that week. Good timing, I almost missed it.

Driving home it occurred to me that my question about the images from the monitor didn't get answered. The nurse seemed distracted or maybe she didn't hear my question. This bothered me all the way home. It's funny how the simplest of things can play on you.

When I got home the OBGYN called.

Too soon.

What's wrong?

The doctor told me the results of the NST showed potential problems. My question was answered – not normal. Before I could start asking what the potential problems were, he addressed my increasing high blood pressure, the toxemia risk factor, and my diabetic blood sugar levels increasing which he blamed on the lack of movement from being bedridden. Higher amounts of insulin were added to the doses I was currently taking to keep my blood sugar levels as close to normal as possible. I think the doctor was guessing. He suggested doing a Cesarean section (C-section). The doctor said that a C-section is performed when natural birth is compromised. In my case waiting for Mother Nature was not an option. We went back and forth over the pros and cons. My due date was in about six weeks - August 11th. Diabetics typically have large babies and C-sections are easier with bigger babies. We could deliver my baby before anything can go wrong. This has always been a major concern of mine considering my history of trying to have a healthy baby. The doctor assured me that he had performed many C-sections and that it was routine for him. The lung maturity of my baby would have to be checked to make sure my baby can breathe on his or her own. The OBGYN doctor suggested the end of July. There it was. I was looking at my belly and knowing that I would be holding my baby in my arms by the end of July. Oh my God, my dream of having a family are about to come true. I'm really hearing this and I'm still pregnant. The reality of it all was almost putting me in a trance.

"Mrs. Johnson?" I guess there was a long pause on the phone before I said, "Yes." I had tears welling up into my eyes and then spilling onto my shirt and they weren't going to be alone. Before we hung up, I asked about bed rest and the rest of the NST appointments. I was told to stay off my feet as much as possible but I could go to the hospital for the NST procedures, attend the hospital tour, and the birthing classes. The doctor thought these would be more beneficial for me than the risk factors of me being out of bed. Even though I was having a planned C-section, taking Lamaze classes would help if labor starts before the C-section is performed. In theory it would be something to help me get though painful contractions. I hung up the phone and smiled at my belly.

I was a bit stir crazy from the bedrest - the only outings were the NST and doctor appointments. The doctor gave me permission to take small trips to the store but for a half an hour at a time. He also told me to listen to my body for signs to quit and go home. To get a change of scenery and some fresh air I decided to go with Kennie to Price Club one evening to get one or two items. At the store Kennie went to get the items and I waited sitting up front. I noticed a woman staring at me. She was dressed in workout clothes - hair, nails, not a thing out of place. Her stare gave me an uncomfortable feeling. I smiled and she frowned back. The moment I saw Kennie I got up and walked over to him in line. I turned around to see that she followed me. I was shocked and offended when she asked, "Are you always this fat?" I thought what an alarming question. She paused and said, "Or are you pregnant?" My quick response was, "Pregnant." She quickly turned and walked away. No apology. Rude. How could she say something like that? Even if I had wondered that about someone, I wouldn't have said anything. I was pretty big due to toxemia, the diabetes, close to delivering, and every pregnancy I had put on a little more weight. Still, that was just down right rude!

  On the day of our hospital tour Kennie had a Little League game and there would be no time to go home before the tour. Considering that the doctor said I could go to the class because it's mostly sitting, I applied the same logic to Kennie's Little League game. It was my first real outing in a while. I sat quietly in the stands by myself. It didn't take long and I was surrounded by lots of moms asking how I was doing. I was excited for a chance to announce my due date. Before I knew it, the game was over. We went from the game to the hospital in our Z28 candied apple red Camaro which was getting harder and harder for me to get in and out of. A Chevy Camaro is not known for its roomy interior and to boot they are very low to the ground. Because of my body size I was finding it harder to manage even simple daily tasks. Kennie dropped me off in front of the hospital and parked the car. Watching Kennie walking toward me I thought, he's going to be a daddy holding our baby soon. I could envision the whole thing. An excited chill ran through my body. We went in through the hospital's sliding doors and found our way to the starting point where other expecting parents were waiting. We were shown into a room with a big table and had a seat. Our tour guide passed out flyers and requested us all to sign in on a clipboard. Kennie signed in "Mr. and Mrs. Johnson" and I passed the clipboard to a nine or ten-year-old boy sitting next to me. He was there with his mom, dad and a soon to be little sister. His dad gave him permission to sign in for his family. He had his dad double check his work and then passed the clipboard on. He kept smiling at Kennie as if he wanted to talk to him. He was just about to say something to Kennie when the tour of the hospital began. We were greeted by a nurse who was in charge of the tour. She introduced herself, clapped her hands together in excitement, and asked if we were ready to see the hospital. Beautiful birthing suites. Every room had a theme, hardwood floors, lots of space, was nicely painted in brilliant colors, and had a couch for dad and visitors. The bonus was that the couch folded out to a twin bed for the father/Kennie to stay the night. The nursery had many incubators, nice and tidy, with a baby powder smell. The nurse in the nursery smiled and waved at us through the window. She was holding one of the newborns. I squeezed Kennie's hand with excitement. That could be our baby soon. We continued the walk around the labor and delivery floor. The concern crossed my mind about the toxemia but I thought, I'm in a hospital and if something goes wrong, this is where I want to be. The guide told us of other amenities, including a romantic dinner for two before you leave the hospital. Another squeeze of Kennie's hand. What a nice way to celebrate a new family's meal together. This warmed my heart. I never really allowed myself to imagine what the future would be like because I didn't want my baby to die like the rest. How sad that I had resorted to this. Something inside of me was still trying to self-protect. I'm almost nine months pregnant. The delivery will be at the end of July, just weeks away. Why not try to enjoy the rest of it?

Excited, I started talking more freely to the other parents. At first, I was afraid to say too much because of my miscarriages and I didn't want the parents to become concerned about their babies but that was early on in my pregnancies and it shouldn't scare them at this point in the game. There were a few short question and answers and then we were done.

When we headed out to the car it was raining pretty hard. Crazy for June but not totally uncommon. Kennie got the car and helped me in. This was normal. After making sure I was in, he got into the car and put his seatbelt on. A startling rap on the window came out of nowhere. Kennie reluctantly rolled down the window in the rain to see the little boy who was sitting next to me when we signed in for the hospital tour.

"Can I help you?" Kennie asked, with a confused and concerned look on his face.

The boy replied "Can I have your autograph?" Kennie looked at me with eyebrows tweaked. Suddenly it occurred to Kennie why the boy was asking for his autograph. I was clueless.

With a chuckle and a smile he answered, "I'm not Randy Johnson."

The boy with a surprised look said "Oh. I'm sorry." and returned to his car and they drove away. Kennie rolled up the window and laughed. Kennie had figured it out. We were in a nice car, Kennie signed us in as Mr. and Mrs. Johnson and he was wearing a Seattle Mariners cap because we had just come from the little league baseball game where Kennie was managing. I told him he should have just signed it for him. It would have made the kids day and one less that Randy Johnson, the real Seattle Mariners pitcher, would have to sign. We laughed. Kennie is not as tall as Randy Johnson but to a nine-year-old 6'1" might look that tall.

The NSTs were quite a few per week. If something was starting to go wrong, we would know right away. They seemed to keep me calm and made me feel everything was normal. That helped my blood pressure.

The following Monday we started birthing classes. Pillow and towel as required in arms, Kennie by my side, we went in. It wasn't long before we made friends and everyone knew us and our story. The classes were once a week and went beyond the end of July. I was having a C-section at the end of July. Going into this I knew I would not be able to finish and wanted to get whatever I could out of the class. The instructor showed a video on natural and C-section deliveries. The education on a C-section I was not expecting but it made it all worth going to the classes. Kennie got to see what he would be experiencing when Bumpkins was delivered. It was also time to decide on formula or breast feeding. I had thought about it but felt making a decision would jinx the outcome of the pregnancy. Breastfeed. I would breastfeed. We exchanged phone numbers and addresses with the friends we made in class. I was verbally invited to baby showers which were to be after my C-section. I had the first due date in the class which would make my Bumpkins the oldest. I had a vision that I would be holding my baby at their baby showers. How exciting. We also planned baby play dates for the future. Life was exciting and blissful. I had become part of life again.

The birthing class instructor recommended selecting a pediatrician - the first real physical thing I could do as a mommy. Next door to the hospital were pediatric offices. Our friends, family, and my primary doctor recommended one of them. We made an appointment and went in to talk with him. Felt kind of funny in that Bumpkins wasn't born yet and we were visiting his pediatrician. We arrived at the doctor's office after regular business hours and there was a note on the locked door saying to use "sick patient" door. What? I don't want to risk getting sick. I already have enough things to worry about. Kennie opened the door and went in. I followed with an uncomfortable feeling. Totally kid friendly, toys everywhere for every age. I wondered how clean the toys were considering the "sick patient" door sign. I know people think this is a first-time mom syndrome but after what I've been through who could blame me? I signed in using my own pen. Another couple came in to have a consultation with the doctor too. Funny I expected a one on one until the doctor came in and addressed us as a whole. The door opened again and a third couple joined us. The doctor answered all my questions. It was a little uncomfortable asking sensitive questions in front of strangers but I needed answers, so I asked. After what I'm sure was a longer than usual consultation, he was now Bumpkin's doctor (doctor #8).

  Before we knew it the end of July arrived. The OBGYN office called to set up an appointment to check the lung maturity of my baby. Apparently, babies born to diabetic mothers can have problems with lung development. Another problem I was not prepared for. During the appointment the doctor explained that he was going to extract fluid from the amniotic sac. I sat down on the exam table, Kennie helped me lie down and stretch out. I seemed to just barely fit. The tables are usually bigger. Maybe it was me. I pulled up my shirt, belly exposed, Kennie holding my hand, and the OBGYN doctor swabbed my big belly with jelly to make the wand from the monitor move more easily. I was advised to look away towards the monitor. That's when I saw him. Bumpkins. Squishy little face with big eyes. He seemed to be saying "Hi!" The doctor moved the wand down my belly for a better look. Bumpkins had not turned for the birth yet but he was going to be delivered by C-section so no problem. The doctor then informed me that he was looking for a space where Bumpkins wasn't so he could insert a long needle to extract amniotic fluid to test the lung maturity.

He said, pointing his finger on my belly, "That's where we'll go in." The doctor marked it with a blue marker. Looking at the monitor I saw Bumpkin's little foot. So small. It appeared to be turning in. I have had more than my share of sonograms and was starting to understand what I was looking at; at least I thought I was.

I asked, "Is that his foot? It looks turned in or something."

His reply was "Those little guys turn so much in the womb. It's probably his hand."

Ready to question this, I saw the syringe and my attention went elsewhere. The syringe was huge. I wasn't exactly used to syringes but was no longer afraid of them. Until that moment.

"How far is that going in? Will it poke the baby? Is it going to hurt? How much fluid are you taking out? Will there be enough left for my baby?" "Simple test in my office." Ya, right! Here we go again just like the D&C in his office.

The doctor's reply, "No, I won't touch the baby. That's why we have a monitor to aid me in sticking the needle in. A topical ointment will numb the injection site and yes there will be plenty of fluid left for the baby." He rubbed the topical, then the antiseptic, then… the huge stab with the syringe into my belly.

SHIT! (My favorite word when no other words come). The force that the doctor had to use to get the huge syringe into my abdomen was like in horror films when the creepy guy is killing his victim. I could almost hear the sound effects that the movies make and I almost started to respond like the victim. Kennie spoke, "Keep breathing and focus." Kennie got my attention with this. Gee, birthing classes came in handy for Kennie.

"SHIT! When is it going to be over?"

Meanwhile Kennie's fingers are once again turning purple by me squeezing them. My eyes are closed and I'm about to hyperventilate. Breathing, keep breathing. Yes, but I'm breathing too fast. Lightheaded is not good. Finally, the syringe is removed. I could feel the doctor pulling it out of my abdomen. The topical didn't help at all. The pain was still there but my breathing was returning to normal and so were Kennie's purple fingers. The doctor held up the syringe. It looked like about a cup of fluid. Bumpkins on the monitor appeared to be fine. I had a bruise about two inches in diameter at the sight of the syringe's insertion and a bandage that I know will leave a bigger mark later. I was told by the doctor that the results will be in tomorrow and to call the office.

He also added, "If the lungs are not ready there is a shot I could give you to mature the baby's lungs for delivery."

Couldn't he just have given me the shot instead of putting Bumpkins and me through this? Kennie helped me sit up. I could feel a knot at the injection site. Weird and painful but this did get me one step closer to having a healthy baby.

The next day the OBGYN's office called me before I could make a call to them. The test showed the lungs were ready and compatible with life outside the womb. Bumpkins was 37 weeks along and ready to be born. I was asked what day I wanted to deliver. I suggested Friday, July 28th and was told that the doctor would be out of town starting Monday, July 31st and needed to be able to oversee my recovery for three days after the C-section.

Thinking out loud I said, "July 24th is my sister's birthday and the 26th is my father-in-law's birthday. Let's make it on Tuesday July 25th. We can have three days of celebrating birthdays or one big bash altogether for future years to come." Appointment made. The typical rules for surgery were given: no eating, drinking, etc. the night before after 6:00 p.m. My C-section was first thing in the morning.

The weekend before the planned birth was exciting. There were last minute preparations for bringing home my baby. I remembered that the minute you give birth not only did the threat of toxemia go away but the gestational diabetes would go away too. I could go back to eating what I wanted without insulin injections. Of course, I needed to lose weight. I was HUGE. I was so focused on keeping my sugars under control that my weight didn't seem to be that important to me or the doctors. I really didn't know what I weighed but I didn't care. The only thing that mattered was a living, breathing, healthy baby. I didn't even care if it was a boy or girl. I was going to be holding my little Bumpkins soon. Yep. My baby will be in my arms tomorrow. I could hardly contain myself. My thoughts were racing. Tuesday July 25th, Bumpkin's Birthday! Family and friends were making statements like: This is the last night for it to be just the two of you. This is the last night you'll get to sleep for a while. Your lives are about to change. My own thoughts were that Bumpkins has already changed my life.

We spent the evening with my sister for her birthday. I went to bed on the 24th rubbing my belly the way expecting mothers do, singing and talking to the baby, telling him about the big day we had coming tomorrow. As directed by the OBGYN doctor I didn't have anything to eat or drink after 6:00 p.m. I was also told not to inject insulin. I guess since there was no food, there was no need for insulin. I had taken my last shot. FINALLY!

Kennie went to work early and was getting off early to take me to the hospital for the birth. I was hungry and excited when the OBGYN office called.

"Hello. Mrs. Johnson? This is the doctor's office and we are going to have to reschedule your C-section."

My reply, "What the ....?"

"Well it seems the doctor has been delayed with an emergency."

Don't they have on-call doctors for this kind of thing! Panic.... Fear.... I can't have my baby today? Then I let her have it. She thought I was just another patient. Boy was she wrong.

"I'm a high risk, diabetic mom who hasn't eaten or taken my insulin. Toxemia has set in and the only way to avoid a fatality for me and/or my baby is to deliver. Today!" Spoken like a true mom.

There was a pause and I think I heard her exhale a deep breath.

"Well Mrs. Johnson I will see what I can do about rearranging the OR for delivery today but it won't happen this morning the way it was planned. I'll call you back with the time once I know."

The call ended. What just happened? Considering the toxemia, I needed to keep my blood pressure down and my doctor's office is the one who's spiking it through the roof. I called Kennie in a panic and in tears. Fortunately, he was in the office. It helped to vent to him. Hours went by with no phone call from the doctor's office. All packed and trying to keep calm, I was bored, hungry, scared, and nauseous. I called the doctor's office.

"Hello. This is Mrs. Johnson. Have you got a time for the OR yet?" It was like they got busy and forgot about me sitting at home scared and waiting.

The woman said, "I'll see where we are with that and call you back."

No. I fell for that once, not again. "What can I eat? I'm shaky and about to throw up."

A pause on the phone, "A small amount of sugar free Jell-O."

Yummy, I thought, at least it was something. "When can I expect a call or what time should I call you back?" She finally got the hint. Don't mess with me anymore.

"I'll call you in 30 minutes one way or another."

The call ended. I ate my jello and a half hour later the phone rings at the same time Kennie walks through the door.

"Hello. Mrs. Johnson. The time is set for 5:30 p.m. Check in at 3:30 p.m. at the hospital. I'm sorry for the inconvenience."

Inconvenience? I already lost four babies and they are putting two lives at risk, my baby's and mine. I was relieved. I was supposed to have Bumpkins this morning early and now, after five? It's okay. I'm having my baby, I kept reminding myself. I have borderline toxemia and stress is not my friend. We were told in the birthing class that after a C-section delivery the mom's abdomen takes time to heal and just sitting up is difficult at best. Heeding the warning Kennie insisted on staying home with me.

Three o'clock came and it was time to leave. Kennie and I walked in together. It was symbolic walking in as two and later walking out as three. Kennie arrived and there were my in-laws waiting on the other side of the sliding doors of the hospital entrance. I guess they were more excited than we were. No way. In through the doors Kennie and I walked. A picture was taken as we were checking in. All smiles. You couldn't wipe them off of our faces if you tried. I walked in with no pain and a plan to walk out with a beautiful distraction for the pain afterwards.

After the paperwork was done, we were led into a room with gurneys waiting for patients and yellow dividing curtains drawn back to welcome the patients. An ID band was placed on my left wrist. The nurse asked my name, age and date of birth.

I replied, "Carol Johnson, 29" and gave her my birthdate. I changed into a hospital gown, filled out paper work, climbed into the bed and in walk my mom, dad, and niece Traci. Traci was nine and, bless her heart, wanted to see me. A nurse attempted to insert an IV, it took her four tries before she finally got it. My mom tried to tell Traci everything carefully. The question Traci had was more like "Why is she having the baby this way instead of the normal vaginal birth?" Mom's response was "Well some babies have to be delivered by surgery." She just watched from there on and smiled every now and again.

I was given a small amount of fluid/medicine to drink for nausea while in surgery. Another yuck to put on my list of unpleasantries. After the nurse's check list was complete, she went to check on the OR and returned promptly.

"Time to go."

Everyone except Kennie said their goodbyes. The curtain was pulled back and the gurney was moving me out and down a hall to the OR with Kennie right beside me holding my hand. Just before entering the OR Kennie gave me a kiss on my lips.

He told me, "I love you. I'll meet you in there" pointing to the OR. He had to change for the OR. He kissed my forehead, the doors opened, and the bed was pushed into the OR. Kennie's hand slowly left mine. I could hear the doors close behind me. I started feeling like I was all alone but reminding myself it was only for a few minutes and Kennie would be joining me. The room was well lit, cold, with big metal cabinets on the walls, and lots of people walking around. The nurse had me move to the operating table and sit on the side of the table with my legs hanging over facing her. One of the men was the anesthesiologist. He was not friendly at all. Absolutely no bedside manner. He never said hello, didn't introduce himself. Nothing. The nurse told me to lean towards her and curl into a ball as much as possible to open my spine for the epidural needle to go in. I had seen and held a needle like this in the birthing classes. It was about four inches long, thick and to be taped to my back once it was in, to hold the tube in place. The medicine would be injected into my spine to numb me from the upper chest all the way down my body. Good thing I couldn't see him working behind me.

The anesthesiologist said the first thing since he walked into the room, "Here we go."

Crap that hurt and they want me to push toward this long needle, curled into a BIG ball and everything in me is saying

NO. Not just no but Hell No! Talking to myself saying, "Just do it and get it over."

"Didn't work." He announced to the room of the failure. Then he tried again. "No. Still not in." Over and over. It was getting painful and so sore. After 35 minutes of trying and dozens of pokes, I started to sweat in a room that was ice cold. That's when I saw that the anesthesiologist was upset.

My first thought was, what did I do wrong?

The anesthesiologist threw the needle on the tray with disgust and hastily cleaned my back. A doctor shouldn't lose his temper like this especially in front of his patient.

He announced to the room, "Doctor, this one is going to have to be knocked out. Someone tell the dad he can't come in and that he can take his paper OR scrubs."

No one was talking to me. I felt really alone now. They had me lie down on the table. Still not a word to me from any of the many people in the room, just motions and gestures. A steady stream of tears fell down my face to my ears and no one in the OR even noticed.

Did they forget I'm still here and awake? My thoughts were racing. No one in the now very busy room was telling me anything. I had to make out what they were saying to each other and figure it out on my own what was going to happen to me next. I was still thinking it was all my fault and because it was my fault, Kennie couldn't come into the room to watch Bumpkins enter the world. I kept saying "I'm sorry Kennie" and no one even acknowledged me. "Knocked out" was what I heard. At least when I wake up this will be all gone and I'll have my baby. Soon this will be gone and I'll be asleep. I felt straps being placed on my body. They strapped my legs and arms down. Still no one has said a word to me. This in itself was scary. Still crying, tears running faster than a faucet down the side of my face into my ears and not a peep coming out of me. Shallow breathing was all I could do. Thoughts racing through my head. Everything was going so well for this pregnancy. I had made it through miscarriages, toxemia, diabetes. This wasn't supposed to happen. Focus. Bumpkins will be here soon. My Bumpkins will be in my arms.

I begged the nurse "When will I be knocked out?"

Her reply, "Soon, very soon."

Tears were at a steady stream and someone finally said, "Count backwards from 10" and put an oxygen mask over my mouth.

I started… ten… nine… and I was out.

In the recovery room I started waking up. I saw light through my eyelids and a slight pain like a period cramp started. As my eyes opened the pain got more intense quickly. At first, I was not connecting to where I was.

"PAIN! OH MY GOD! PAIN! Horrible PAIN! PAIN, PAIN, PAIN, KENNIE!" I screamed! The nurse came over and tried to tell me there was no pain medication given to me in surgery because I was knocked out and I would get it when I woke up. I imagine the pain was equal to a shot through the stomach with a 12-gage shot gun. Why is she talking to me? Get rid of the PAIN!

The nurse wasn't ready with the medication and she seemed to just mosey around. PAIN! Someone stop the PAIN! Finally, the nurse put the medication into my IV. It seemed to take forever to work. When the pain medicine finally started to kick in and I could focus on something other than the pain, I noticed Kennie in the room standing over me. He was crying and the tears were falling down his face. He was choking on his breath with gasps of air trying to talk.

"What? Where is Bumpkins? Oh My God Bumpkins is dead!"

Kennie said, "No, but there is a problem." Pausing at every word and wiping away tears he managed to tell me, Bumpkins is a boy. Kevin is three pounds ten ounces, 15 inches long, with a cleft lip, cleft palate, club feet and his hands are not moving. The hospital is moving him by ambulance to another hospital with a level three nursery with a Neonatal Intensive Care Unit (NICU).

I just gave birth to the only baby I was able to carry to full term and I'm not able to hold him. Then I remembered learning in Lamaze class: "One of the most important things in life is to hold your baby the minute he's born".

The pediatrician came into the room, introduced himself, and reminded Kennie and me that we had met in his office during the consultation.

He told us with confidence but looking directly at me, "Kevin is a trisomy 18 or 13 baby, which is not compatible with life and will probably not make it through the night."

My body went limp. I looked at Kennie. Words could not be said. The tears filling our eyes said it all.

The doctor said something like, "It was so hard to intubate him. His airway was so small. He is going to another hospital, more than likely not make it and will die".

Then my words came with an intense panic. "I want to see him. I want to see Kevin."

The Doctor said, "I don't think that's possible."

"I don't want my first time seeing him and holding him to be when he's not breathing. Please." I pleaded.

The doctor quickly left to talk to the ambulance driver and then returned. "The ambulance driver will bring Kevin by for a brief minute and only a brief minute. He's in an incubator so you can't hold him." He began to say something else and was interrupted by the incubator rolling into the room.

There he was. My baby Kevin. He was the most beautiful baby I had ever seen. I didn't see the imperfections, I saw my baby. He was on his back with his throat extended to help with the airway, an IV in his arm and a teeny tiny diaper. The ambulance driver pushed the incubator up to my bed for a closer look. There was a top cover on the incubator that didn't permit me to reach into it, but there was a hole big enough to put my hand through on the side. I reached through the hole, touched my son's little arm and held his tiny hand. His hand was no bigger than the tip of my thumb, soft and fragile.

I told Kevin with as much voice as I could muster, "I'm your mommy. Mommy and daddy love you so much."

The ambulance driver told me that they had to get going. I knew it was for the best, but I wanted more time. I wanted to hold my baby. A natural thing for a mother to do and I wasn't allowed. As the incubator rolled away, my hand came apart from Kevin's tiny fingers. Then the incubator left the room with Kevin in it.

I said again, "I love you Kevin." I watched the driver disappear through the door. Kennie was trying to decide whether to stay with me or go with Kevin. I told him, "I'm as strong as a horse. Go with Kevin."

Kennie kissed me, said goodbye and out the door he went. I was alone. A new mother with no baby.

I just kept praying and pleading, "Please take me not Kevin. Please. I've lived a life. Don't take him. He's just a baby. I would gladly go in his place."

At that moment I remembered the movie "Dumbo". The part where Mrs. Dumbo was locked up and the mouse brings her baby Dumbo to visit her trough the bars on her cage. I knew exactly how Mrs. Dumbo felt when she had that tender moment with her baby and then Dumbo was taken away. That was me.

My doctor never told our families or friends in the waiting room what happened. That would have been the appropriate thing to do. The family told me that they saw my doctor purposely looking away from the waiting room towards the wall, walking as fast as he could out the front door making him look very cowardly. Knowing the doctor for some time, I would have thought he would have had more integrity than that. Instead Kennie had to tell the family what happened. I'm sure it was much like he told me. Gasping for air in-between his words. I was told that shockwaves rippled through the waiting room of great grandparents, grandparents, aunts, uncles, cousins and friends. We were all expecting a normal birth. Telling the group was, I'm sure, one of the most difficult times in Kennie's life. He was supposed to be a proud new daddy showing off his new baby boy. Instead he was telling the family that his baby son Kevin will probably die according to the doctors.

If it wasn't for some family members trying to peek through the mini blinds with excitement into the nursery, they wouldn't have known there was a problem until Kennie started speaking.

Later I found out that not only was the medical staff not talking to me in the OR but no one told Kennie that there was a problem and he wouldn't be able to come in. He was just left outside the OR door in the hallway all by himself waiting the whole length of the surgery.

He thought he was still going into the OR for the birth until the nurse finally came out and said in a stern voice, "The doctor will be out to talk to you." Afterwards she just walked away.

Why would a medical professional say something like that, so vague and then leave? I can only imagine what sheer terror was shooting through Kennie. He must have been thinking Kevin, me or both of us were dead. Heartbreaking. She could have at least sat with him but she didn't want to take on any more than she had to. No compassion.

After everything finally quieted down, I started to notice I was still in pain and that my throat hurt too. The nurse put pain medication into my IV. Funny, she wasn't prepared with it when I was waking up and needed it the most. I had a thought and suddenly became concerned.

I asked, "Could the medicine you're giving to me through my IV get into my breast milk? Then Kevin couldn't eat anything I produced?"

The nurse just looked at me like I had two heads or something. It then occurred to me that she believed that Kevin would be dead and wouldn't need breast milk anyway. I was hopeful that the doctors were wrong. Nothing more was said.

My mom and dad were the only ones left at the hospital and entered the room. Kennie's parents went with him to Kevin's hospital and everyone else went home. There was nothing anyone could do. With the adrenaline rush over I was giving into the medication that was making me drowsy. An orderly moved me to my own room down a long hall, the very last room on the left, far away from the other moms and their babies. It might have been with best intentions but I figured it was because my baby wasn't with me and was expected to die. I was sad and crying. The orderly pushed my gurney parallel to the bed in the room.

I said, "You don't expect me to move over to that bed, do you?" Knowing very well that I was just cut wide open and then stapled shut.

The orderly said "No. You just relax and let us handle it." This was the first kind thing that was said to me since I got to the hospital and it came from an orderly, not a trained medical professional.

I looked up to smile at his kind words and realized there was a second orderly standing over me. They each grabbed a side of the sheet I was on and lifted me enough to scoot me onto the stationary bed in the room. Painful. I let out a controlled scream followed by a deep breath. The first orderly made sure I was comfortable and advised 20 minutes before the pain medication is due, I should start calling for the medication. "You don't want them to be late with a dose. It's harder to get rid of the pain after it happens than to keep it from happening in the first place." He cautioned me to not let them miss a dose. He gave me a smile, a wink and left the room. At a time when my life was falling apart and a moment when I need someone to be sensitive, he was kind to me.

Looking around I noticed the earth tones in the large room and the hardwood floors. To my left was my IV pole, an empty tray table for food, a window which was covered by the heavy curtains to block all light from the room and a chair big enough for two. In front of me was a closet, a TV hanging on the wall, and the door heading to the bathroom. To my right was an ugly green couch with my mom and dad sitting on it and then the door leading to the hallway. I was told the couch folded out to the size of a twin bed when needed. Dad told me to just sleep and they would stay until Kennie returned. That was reassuring.

I went in and out of sleep. Each time I opened my eyes I didn't know where I was. I would then see mom and dad and fall back asleep. I had no idea what time it was when Kennie returned. He told us that Kevin was in a high level NICU. I recognized the ICU part. He said that the staff there was running all kinds of tests. Most of the tests would take over 24 hours to complete and another would take close to a week.

Wiping tears away, Kennie pulled a Polaroid picture out of his pocket of Kevin. Kevin was on his back with the oxygen tubing taped to his tiny little face and the connecting attachment suspended above his head. His color was pink with a slight blue tone (could have been the Polaroid). The diaper that was on him was meant for a normal size baby not a 3 lbs. 10 oz baby. It was too big. He had cords stuck all over him to monitor his vital signs, a tag on his ankle saying his name and that he belonged to Kennie and me. The ankle tag made me smile. The nurse at Kevin's hospital took the time to put a teddy bear and heart stickers on the picture with Kevin's information reading: "Johnson, baby boy. July 25, 1995. Born at 5:41 p.m. Kevin Paul. 3 lbs. 13 oz." His weight seemed to vary. What a way to start life. All I could think of was that I was supposed to be holding Kevin in my arms and singing softly to him, not having him miles away in another hospital hooked up to equipment making noises in a NICU bed. Mom and dad listened to what Kennie had to say and decided there was nothing more they could do. With Kennie there now they decided to go home and get some rest. Their experience with hospitals told them and us this was going to be a long journey. Kennie made the couch into the little bed and stretched out. Well, the best he could for a six-foot man. I could hear sniffles coming from Kennie throughout the night.

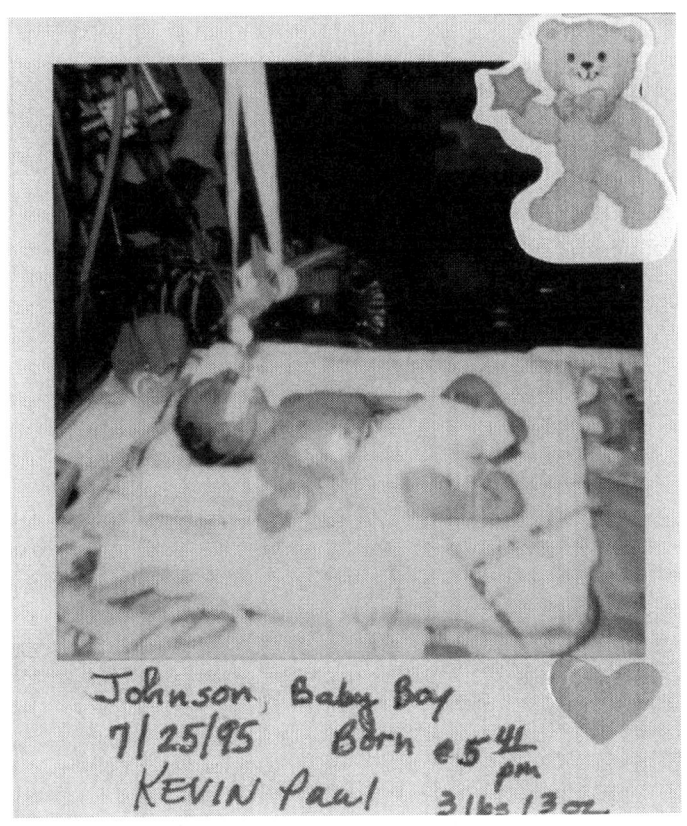

Johnson, Baby Boy
7/25/95   Born @ 5:41 pm
KEVIN Paul   3 lbs 13 oz

My thoughts took off. What did I do wrong? Nothing. I did everything that I was told to do and did nothing to endanger Kevin. So, what happened? Breastfeeding! I was supposed to be breastfeeding. What are they feeding him? Is he hungry? I cried all night. I turned away from Kennie towards the window with an attempt to muffle my crying from him, so he could sleep. Will Kevin be alive in the morning? Will I get to hold him while he's alive? I've got to get over to the other hospital to see him. "Oh God please don't take him. Take me instead." I began pleading with God again. "Take me instead. Let Kevin live. We've come so far. We've come so far. It can't end like this."

At around 5:00 a.m. I called the nurse for pain medication.
The minute she walked in the room I asked her "Did Kevin make it through the night? Is he still alive?"

She didn't know.

I told her I wanted to go see Kevin.

She told me that wasn't a good idea because I just had major surgery.

I said that didn't matter to me. That was my last concern.

She informed me the doctor would be making his rounds and I could talk to him about it. She left. Meanwhile Kennie called the hospital to check on Kevin. It didn't take him long to get ahold of Kevin's nurse. Everyone he talked to was eager to help. My prayers were answered. Kevin had made it through the night. I became antsy. The doctor couldn't come through the door quick enough. I was in pain but I didn't feel it. It didn't matter anyway. My son was alive and I needed to get to him. Seeing him alive and not being completely out of it from the pain medication - that was the prayer I was hanging onto.

Finally, the doctor appeared somewhere around 8:30 in the morning. He asked how I was doing.

I ignored his question and went straight to my need. "I need to go to the NICU where my son is. When can I leave to go see Kevin?"

He started by trying to talk me out of it but then realized that wasn't going to happen. He asked about my pain level. Another thing that was the least of my worries but he prescribed a pain killer to be taken now. My pain was hardly noticeable with everything going on. He tried to start a conversation that began with Kevin's trisomy condition and removing Kevin from life support.

What? I just had Kevin, prayed all night that he wouldn't die and you want me to consider taking him off the ventilator so he can die? NO! Not an option. I just ignored him once again.

The look on my face was enough and the doctor finished with, "I'll write you a day pass to leave this hospital and go to the other hospital for a limited time. The nurse will help you with the prepping for going. Do you have any more questions?"

Thinking only of Kevin and not even a thought for myself. I said "No."

He picked up his paperwork with a disappointing wave and left. I didn't even think twice about it. I'm going to see my son and a smile appeared on my face.

The nurse came into the room within seconds. I think she wanted to get rid of me. I was about to start getting ready but I couldn't even sit up by myself because the C-section had severed all of my nerves and I was still healing. The nurse gave me a painkiller, removed my IV, and warned me that I needed to continue to drink lots of water because the IV wasn't there to hydrate me. She then went over to the closet took a towel out, I was thinking that I was going to take a shower. She came over to me and placed it on the floor next to the bed I was on. She lowered the bedrail, helped me sit up on the bed then had me swing my legs over the side of the bed. It took a moment for my lightheadedness to go away. That's when I remembered the catheter I still had. No shower. It took some effort on my part but with help I was now standing on the towel. She then grabbed the urine fluid line, gave it a tug and it fell to the floor. It came out easily. The towel soaked up the body fluids that came out with it. I was then told I could go use the bathroom. I noticed how far away the bathroom was from the bed. The big plush suite was not so nice at the moment. Kennie came over and took my arm on the left side, the nurse on the right side of me and I slowly made my way to the bathroom. Every step was so painful that the next step felt impossible until I finally reached the toilet. I pulled the gown to my side out of the way, it was only covering my front. I noticed the gauze taped to my stomach covering the incision. It was pretty massive and well taped. I wondered if this tape was any different than the tape I'm allergic to. Sitting down on the toilet was yet another painful movement. Thank God I had strong legs. I was trying to relax myself to allow the stream to flow. Just as it got started it instantly stopped. SHIT! PAIN! More pain I was not expecting. Pain or no pain I knew I had to go. I grabbed the towel sitting next to the shower, rolled it up placed it on my lap and leaned over it. I continued by talking myself through the pain a little at a time, going and stopping until I was done. The nurse came in to check on me. I told the nurse about the painful urinating. She said that was normal. It will go away as the muscles and cuts heal inside and out. That made sense.

    Still wearing my hospital gown with the opening in the back I was handed a second gown to wear like a robe to cover the opening. As I was putting on the robe-gown the wheelchair arrived. I was ready. Fifteen hours after major abdominal surgery and I'm leaving my hospital to go see Kevin in his hospital miles away.

    The nurse handed me a pillow as I sat down and positioned my feet onto the wheelchair. I started to realize how fragile I was. I had very little control of my muscles that I normally take for granted. No. Pain is not an option. I blocked out any concern for myself. The nurse told me to bear down on the pillow to hold the staples in place so they don't pull apart or cause pain. What... Staples? I hadn't even allowed myself the time to think about me. I have staples holding me together? I was thinking that's "crazy" as I was being pushed out of the room. There was intense pain whenever the wheelchair rolled over the slightest seal or crack in the floor. I stopped thinking "crazy" and replaced it with "mind over matter". I quickly pushed the pillow into my abdomen in order to comfort the shocking pain. The hall seemed to go on forever. Even the seams in the carpet brought pain but it would all be worth it. I get to see my baby. My thoughts kept focusing on last night when I got to see Kevin before the ambulance driver took him away. The picture Kennie brought me with all those tubes and machines. Kevin needed his mommy. My voice was what he listened to the past nine months. Kevin needed to know I was still here and I didn't leave him. Passing the nurses station not one of the nurses looked at me. They were avoiding making eye contact. I didn't have a healthy baby in my arms. No compassion at all from the very people who are supposed to help me through this devastating time. In fact, they were getting "paid" to help me. I reached the doors we walked through just the day before with smiles. A totally different story now. The double sliding doors opened to a blue Buick with my dad, mom, and Kennie waiting for me. The nurse handed me a second pillow and we drove off. I was feeling a bit guilty that I was in the front seat and my mom was in the back with Kennie. The carpet seams were tough to take but the dips in the road were more challenging by far. I was thankful for the pillows I was given to travel with. On the drive over to Kevin's hospital we passed an ambulance.

Kennie said, "That looks just like the ambulance Kevin rode in."

"How can you tell?" I asked.

"Look at the side of the door? See the picture of the baby crawling? That was what was on Kevin's ambulance."

It was gone in seconds. The distances between the two hospitals was over 16 miles and took over 30 minutes. It felt much longer.

We finally arrived at Kevin's hospital. It had a grand entrance with glass walls as high as my neck could bend upward to see. Glass doors that opened so quietly I didn't even hear them. I was wheeled over the rubber mat. Oh my GOD! I didn't remember the mat at the hospital I left causing this kind of pain. Then relief: a tile floor. The entry was bright from the cathedral window walls. The naturally well-lit room had plush, cushioned seats close to the windows. The cool air-conditioning was welcomed after being in the July sun. Kennie watched person in a wheelchair being backed into the elevator and did the same with me. The car ride over was painful with the bumps in the road but nothing compared to the gap between the floor and the elevator. Funny how observant I became with the floor. Knowing I had to endure it again leaving the elevator I took a deep breath and braced myself for the exit. Going down the hall it occurred to me I would have to do that again later that night.

I noticed as we went down the halls the walls were covered with pictures of critically ill babies, their stories of how they survived and pictures of the babies all grown up. That gave me hope for Kevin's future. I looked up. A sign read "Neonatal Intensive Care Unit". We were here. I could feel an adrenaline rush. I was wheeled into a room where we washed our hands and put on a yellow isolation gown to protect the babies. My heart began to race more as we entered the room. Close. We were close. Nothing but lights, monitors and bells. A familiar oxygen smell sent me back to the time Kennie was in the hospital with Guillain-Barré. The only difference was a baby powder smell that filled the air. Babies, lots of little babies in high equipped incubators. As my wheelchair passed them, I looked inside. There were small babies, normal looking babies, but I'm sure they were there for a reason. Some were shaking which made me sad. Most were crying. The room had maybe 30 beds and most were full. We passed the main nurse's station. The nurses standing at the desk smiled at me and I smiled back. Then the wheelchair stopped. There he was. My son Kevin. The child I had waited for all my life. From the time I held my first "Betsy-Wetsy" doll I knew I wanted to be a mom and now I am one. I'm a mother. A rush of excitement, tears, gasping for breaths, and a loving chill ran down my body. I wanted to pick him up and never put him down again. I knew that couldn't happen. There was too much equipment keeping him alive that prevented me from holding him. Everything inside of me was just jumping like a line of race cars engines before the light turns green. A calming came over me as my wheelchair was pushed closer to Kevin's bedside. I instinctively reached into the incubator and touched his tiny arm. It was smaller than the length of my little finger. His hand was barely big enough to cover the tip of my index finger as I molded his tiny fingers around my little finger.

    I told him "Mommy is here and everything will be fine now." I began to sing to him a song I sang when I was carrying him. He seemed to react with his eyes and a deep breath. Tears fell from my face onto his blanket. Looking at him, he was so small. Yet one of the reasons the doctor delivered him early was because they feared he was going to be over ten pounds. I then noticed he had green eyes peering out of his tiny face, curly black hair that curled around his ears, beefy legs, and a pretty large chest considering his small size. His feet were curled in from his clubfeet with little blue hand knitted booties on them. It occurred to me that his feet were what I saw on the monitor during the sonogram in the doctor's office when he was drawing out the amniotic fluid. Unfortunately, I was right and the doctor was wrong. It was Kevin's feet I saw. The unusual clubfeet fooled the doctor into thinking they were his hands.

      The nurse told me that the powder blue booties and the pink and powder blue blanket she was holding were knitted by some talented grandmas. They donate them from time to time to the babies to use and the parents to keep. I smiled and thanked her. Kevin appeared to take deeper and calmer breaths as he listened to me sing. In fact, I continued seeing comforting exhales and a slight smile on his face. Looking beyond Kevin, I could see the bed he was in was made of a clear plastic mold with a heat lamp raised above it. The cushion he was on was covered by a receiving blanket. The height of the bed was equal with my wheelchair which made it easy for me to sit next to him and hold his hand. The nurse explained to me that Kevin was so small that it was very difficult to intubate him and they were afraid to move him because the oxygen tube could fall out. The tubes were taped to his face to prevent that from happening but made it difficult to really see his facial features. He was on his back with receiving blankets rolled up on both sides of him keeping him in place to support the oxygen tube. The ventilator was keeping him alive. He couldn't breathe on his own. The machine was almost at full capacity. There was a pink heart sticker on his chest to monitor his pulse.

Kennie was standing next to me the whole time I sang to Kevin. Singing not only soothed Kevin and comforted me but it seemed to bring back something of our normal life.

The doctors started making their rounds. You couldn't miss them. They were like a sea of white coats consisting of eight men and one woman with a ponytail. They were mostly interns with one or two doctors. The doctors made their way towards us one incubator bed at a time. I realized that Kennie and I were the only parents in the room of about 25 babies. How sad. Maybe the moms are like me and just had surgery. I just couldn't imagine babies in the NICU with mommies or daddies even though there were nurses to take care of them.

The faces of the doctors and interns turned toward us. We were next. The sea of white coats moved towards us and the head doctor spoke.

He didn't say hello or introduce himself, instead he addressed the group. "Team this is Kevin Johnson."

I almost burst into tears. Someone spoke Kevin's name.

He addressed Kennie and me, "I'm doctor (doctor #9), I'm a neurologist and I will be heading up Kevin's care."

I said, "Hello I'm Carol and this is Kennie, my husband. We are Kevin's mom and dad." Wow, another first. I actually acknowledged that we are parents.

The doctor then turned to the group and said "Kevin is a trisomy 13 or 18 baby, with anomalies: cleft lip, cleft palate, clubfeet, inability to move his hands, a hole in his heart…"

What? I stopped listening after that. Couldn't hear any words coming out of his mouth even though his lips were moving. I knew about everything until then.

"Excuse me. I hate to interrupt, but a hole in his heart?"

"Yes. It's normal and it will close in a few days."

Kennie continued to ask questions until the doctor redirected his speaking towards the group. I was a bit out of sorts and had a hard time concentrating. As they walked away, I noticed that none of them were wearing isolation gowns as required for us. It didn't seem right.

The head doctor returned without the big group and had a heart-to-heart with Kennie and me. The nurse was there too. He told us that the likelihood of Kevin making it (living) and the quality of life Kevin would have based on his trisomy prognosis was not good. The doctor finally explained that a trisomy diagnosis is a chromosomal defect where the body is unable to continue growing correctly in utero.

The doctor then began to say things like, "You need to consider taking him off life support."

I looked at Kennie and said, "I just gave birth and you're asking me to help him die? Not only that but to make the decision for Kevin to die? No. I can't make that decision right now. We haven't got the test back yet to determine that he has a life-threatening problem." I suspected that the doctor knew that if Kevin was taken off of the ventilator now, he would surely die, but why does he want him to die? I didn't get it and I couldn't bring myself to ask the question of why. Plus, if the trisomy illness was not compatible with life why not let Kevin's body determine the time of death? We all agreed that we would wait to make a decision when the results of the trisomy test came back.

After the doctor left the nurse reassured us that the choice was ours and we should do things in our own time not the doctor's. We would know what to do step by step as things came up and we were responding like a mom and dad should. I so appreciated her words. They were spoken at the right time.

It was also another milestone; she was the first person in the hospital to address us as "mom and dad".

Family members started showing up to visit and were allowed to come in one at a time. Because there were no other parents in the room the nurse allowed more visitors and didn't enforce the time limit. My niece Traci, who was in the room when the nurse was preparing me for Kevin's birth, walked up to Kevin's incubator and looked inside where he was stretched out. I had no idea what might be going on in her little mind, but knowing her it was compassionate. She handed me a picture she drew for Kevin to help him feel better and a red teddy bear. It made me smile. The nurse then asked if she wanted to take her picture with her brother. I looked up at mom who had walked in behind Traci. She was making a "shhh" sign and holding her finger to her lips. Apparently, my mom told the nurse Traci was my daughter because only immediate family members were allowed in to see Kevin.

Traci stood next to the incubator, smiled and the picture was taken. Family continued to come and go. The support of the family was comforting and a great way to share the time with Kevin.

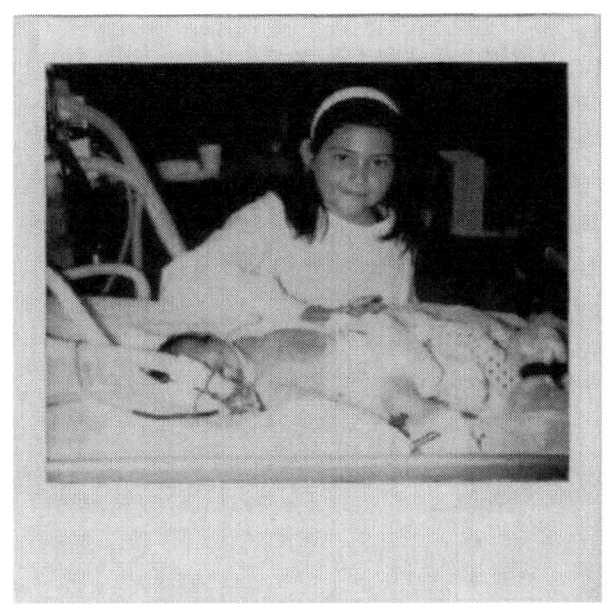

Nurses reported to us as the test results came in. Other than the obvious conditions the tests came back negative. Which meant Kevin didn't have "it" whatever "it" was. The trisomy test was the only one that seemed to take the longest. I was told it wouldn't be in for a while, maybe days. I asked couldn't they just put a rush on it or write *stat* on it to hurry things along? I was told it had something to do with the cells having to be watched as they grew and it couldn't be rushed. Not too clear of an explanation. I was approached by a social worker about religious needs. I told her that I was raised Presbyterian and if she could get a pastor to come pray for Kevin I would be grateful.

Kennie and the nurses brought me snacks. No more diabetes. I could eat whatever I wanted without needles. Bathroom trips were still very painful and required assistance, but it started to get easier. There was a scale outside the bathroom I managed to get up on and when it went past my normal weight I wanted off. The doctor who was treating Kevin was walking by and saw my disgust on my face while I was stepping off the scale. He smiled at me and with words of encouragement he said, "Don't worry it will come off eventually. You just had a baby. Give yourself time."

Kleenex was a big deal in my life. I must have gone through several boxes. I was crying for Kevin, for Kennie, and myself. I'm sure the excessive hormones didn't help. I didn't want to leave Kevin's side. I was making every second count. He had made it through the first night, but I still wondered how much time do we really have together?

I was approached by another social worker from the hospital. She introduced herself and handed me a stack of literature.

Before she removed her hand from the stack of papers she said, "Read through these and use them when the time is right." She then ended with a smile on her face.

The first thing I read from the packet said, "Babies Death packet".

Nope not for me right now.

She saw my face and said "Take it home put it in a drawer and if you need the information it will be there."

I didn't want to talk about death. We were supposed to be celebrating life.

She continued trying to do her job. I just sat and listened to her softly suggest looking into what to do if Kevin does die. She pointed out the local mortuaries and cemeteries that were on some of the literature she had handed me. Kennie recognized one. His grandpa was buried there. I told her we would look into it. Kevin is alive and starting to thrive. This information is not needed right now. I thanked her for her kindness, concern, and the information.

The next visit was from yet another doctor (doctor #10). He introduced himself as a genetics doctor and told us he too was waiting for the trisomy results. I liked this doctor. He was calm and made a lot of sense. He took the time to answer our questions without any concern of how long it took. We discussed the Do Not Resuscitate (DNR) order. He said that when a person is dying you do all you can to save them, but when a person is terminally ill a DNR is put into place so the person doesn't suffer and can die in peace. Of course, we didn't know if Kevin was terminally ill, the diagnosis of trisomy wasn't back yet. After much debate we signed the DNR as a limited DNR. Only to be used in the event Kevin dies naturally, not like a choking incident. I did not like this discussion or the decision we made. It was so difficult because Kevin was alive and starting to breathe on his own, but I also didn't want him to suffer. I loved him.

I watched the nurses as they cared for Kevin, not realizing that I was in training. His temperature needed to be taken frequently. A premature size baby's temperature fluctuated and checking it often was the only way to find out if he was cold or warm. Kennie noticed that I was so involved in spending time with Kevin I hadn't ordered my medication. I was in pain and trying not to show it. Kennie asked Kevin's nurse about getting medication for my pain. Within 30 minutes I had my medication and a makeshift dinner to boot. I was singing softly and enjoying every minute getting to know Kevin.

The nurse noticed that my pass from the other hospital had expired hours ago and brought it to my attention. I had been gone for over 14 hours and I didn't want to leave Kevin. What if he doesn't have that much time left? What if this is all the time Kennie and I get with Kevin? Especially after all of the DNR talk today with the last doctor and the social worker. Kevin was in good, caring hands. The nurse assured me that if anything changed with Kevin, she would call us immediately. The medication was kicking in and making me sleepy. It was getting late so reluctantly I agreed to go back to my hospital. Kennie helped me stand. I attempted to lean in to give Kevin a kiss goodnight and couldn't reach him with the warming lights hanging over his bed and my limitations with my incision. I kissed my fingertips and placed them on his little cheek and said "I love you". Kennie push me to the door and out we went, praying the whole time that Kevin would still be alive in the morning.

The wheelchair ride back to the car was just as painful as the initial ride from the car. It was just a little less intense because we weren't in as much of a rush. Consumed by the day's events

I had forgotten that it was my father-in-law's birthday. I'm sure he understood.

All of our family and friends were gone. Being alone gave Kennie and me time to think and talk. The one thing that was bugging me was I never got to hold Kevin. That hurt. I understood I couldn't hold him - he was fragile, on a breathing machine, had so many tubes and monitors hooked up to him. My arms began to ache. It sounds strange but it felt like there real pain coming from my arms. I told Kennie about my aching arms.

So many questions were randomly crossing our thoughts. Could the trisomy problem have something to do with my diabetes? How were we going to handle this? If he comes home how will we take care of him? If he dies what do we do with his little body? I don't know the first thing about burying someone. I reluctantly picked up the literature that the social worker handed me. My entire gut ached and not from the incision.

I said to Kennie, "I don't want to be scrambling for a place last minute to bury Kevin and he ends up in someplace awful. Maybe we should go over to the cemetery and check it out before we see Kevin tomorrow?"

He agreed providing I was up to it. I didn't want to waste valuable time with Kevin, but we needed to look into it.

I know I shouldn't have concerned myself, but I asked myself, what do we tell people who don't know what happened? I will have to repeat myself over and over, considering the experience with my miscarriages. What do I do about the baby's room? Do I return the gifts? Again... No. He's alive right now and not an option for me to consider. I'm not going to concern myself about that. Besides what if the doctors are wrong about Kevin's condition. A tear started to form in the corner of my eye and I realized that I left my Kleenex box at the hospital. Kennie's sleeve came in handy.

Other thoughts filled my head. The OBGYN doctor was wrong about lots of things: the turned up foot in the sonogram (which was clearly his clubbed feet); the estimation of larger birth weight when Kevin was actually less than four pounds; my diabetes being undiagnosed during the majority of my pregnancy; trying to eat right and then finding out everything I was eating the whole pregnancy was wrong; and not knowing the outcome problems existed before birth because of lack of efficient knowledgeable medical attention. Finally, a good thought crossed my mind; maybe the doctors are wrong about the trisomy thing. God, I hope so. This started my assessment of all of the doctors that let me down. I put my trust in every one of them. So many doctors could have diagnosed my diabetes long before Kevin and maybe saved my other babies/pregnancies from ending in miscarriage. I told every one of the doctors about my family's diabetic history. I thought about filling out all of those questionnaires, writing about my family's diabetes prior to my appointments. Did any of the doctors even read them? Or was it just to sit me down, keep me quiet, and hope that I lost track of the time they left me waiting? They should be held accountable somehow.

Back at my hospital Kennie went to get me a wheelchair and a nurse so he could park the car. It took forever but he finally came out with both. It was a long painful push back to my room at the end of the hall. We passed plenty of other nurses and it was obvious they were avoiding eye contact. I was in pain and still holding onto my pillows, but I made it into bed. Enduring the pain and focusing on Kevin was making me stronger. It was after midnight. Kevin was officially three days old. A small victory. He was born on the 25th and today was the 27th. This gave me something to smile about.

    Kennie returned to the room about the time the nurse was finishing taking my vitals. We both were in tears, understandably, when the nurse asked about Kevin. We told her about the ventilator, that the tests that came back negative, and that we were waiting for the trisomy results. She began to counsel us about taking him off life support. The nerve of her! She's not Kevin's nurse or even at his hospital. We had just spent the day dealing with things new moms and dads shouldn't have to deal with and discussing this particular topic with Kevin's doctor. I had no intention of talking about Kevin with a person who didn't even know the situation at the other hospital. What - I thought - Is there something in my chart that says harass the patient about the life of her newborn son and pulling him off of life support? I told her we hadn't made a decision yet. She got the hint and left. It was a good thing because I had enough and may have told her off. I'm guessing the care I was getting wouldn't have gotten any better or for that matter any worse. Kennie made his bed and he went to sleep. Exhausted from the day he seemed to go out quickly. I cried myself to sleep again praying Kevin would still be alive in the morning.

    Breakfast seemed to come early and so did the doctor. He said Kevin did well last night. His breathing was improving, more tests came back normal, but still no trisomy results. A sigh of relief went through us with the good news. You could actually see our shoulders relax and our bodies exhale. The doctor told us about Kevin before we could ask. He started his examination by looking at my incision and announcing that he was going to remove the staples. It seemed early to me. What if I pop open? Was he sure there was enough time for me to have healed from the operation? Before he got started, he had me sit up to look at my back. He reread the report about the numerous attempts to insert the needle into my back for the spinal anesthesia during surgery preparation that had failed. He was there, didn't he notice? I guess he missed that part.

    Good thing he reread the report. Apparently, I had multiple staph infections but due to the pain medications I was taking around the clock I had little to no discomfort. He wiped my back with some kind of antiseptic and helped me lie back down. He prescribed an antibiotic for the infection. He had me lift up my hospital gown, only exposing the bandage and keeping my modesty intact. The doctor peeled off the bandage of gauze and clear tape and placed the discards on a metal tray. He unwrapped a small pair of clippers and began clipping each staple in my abdomen. I told him that I knew he was clipping the staples in two but it was strange that I couldn't feel it.

    He informed me that the lack of pain was because the nerves had been severed in my abdomen during surgery. "You'll get the feeling back later." He then pulled each broken half of the staple out one half at a time, placing them on the metal tray until they were all out.

    He began to wipe clean the incision and said, "Did you know you're allergic to iodine?"

    "No," was my reply.

    "Well, there was a reaction in surgery while you were out. We treated you for the reaction, but don't let anyone use iodine on you in the future." He placed a new gauze dressing on my incision, warned me not to get it wet for about a week, pulled down my gown, and pulled up a chair.

He started to counsel us again on Kevin being on life support and how now is a good time to make the decision to remove him from it.

What? I couldn't believe it. Everybody in the medical field who came in contact with us was pressuring us to pull the plug and let Kevin die. Why? Didn't he just say, Kevin did well last night?

I replied with, "We don't have enough information to make that decision. The trisomy results weren't back yet and the nurse at Kevin's hospital said that the oxygen levels were starting to go down, which meant Kevin was showing signs of starting to breathe on his own." I added, "If trisomy babies are not compatible with life, why not let Kevin die on his own? Why do Kennie and I have to make a decision like that?"

When our answer was no, the doctor abruptly stood up, picked up my chart (like the day before) and asked if I want to go home today. He clearly wanted to discharge me to get rid of me. I got the instant cold shoulder.

I told him that it was my understanding that after a C-section you have so many days until you're discharged, which would take me to the 28th and discharging me today would be a day too early. I really could benefit from another day to make sure I didn't have any more complications with my back infection and my incision. I knew there was a law that was going to change a C-section birth to a mandatory three day stay and just because it wasn't law yet he was sending me home early? He agreed to let me stay the last day. He filled out the discharge papers for the morning and then he left. It occurred to me that he was starting his vacation. Me and my little family were holding him up, an inconvenience. Maybe that's why he removed the staples today. I got to thinking that he wanted to close the books on Kevin by taking him off life support and discharging me so he didn't have to think about us while he was on vacation. Closure - at least for him. I also felt it was safe to assume I didn't need a pass with a time limit on it to go to Kevin's hospital for a visit.

    We called our parents and told them about the plan to go to the cemetery just to check it out. This was a very difficult decision. We invited them to join us. We weren't sure what we were to do with the information we just knew we need to look into it. What a way to start our morning, but we wanted to get it over with. The nurse came in to give me medication and some to hold onto for later. Seemed a bit out of protocol, but my doctor wasn't going to be able to call it in anyhow, he was on vacation. I was given my clothes to change into and put them on with Kennie's help. The nurse didn't stick around to help. I was starting to move around better but still not back to normal. I was unable to get out of bed on my own, but Kennie was there to help.

    I called the nurse who had once again disappeared, so we could get a wheelchair and leave. No response. Kennie left and returned with one. I grabbed a pillow and out the door we went. Still no eye contact from the nurses. This time I knew it was intentional. It felt like no one cared. I started to ask myself why we chose this hospital. Oh, that's right, the doctor and the insurance company chose it for me. I had no other options. Kennie went to get the car while I waited in the sunshine by myself trying to hold back tears. Thoughts starting to race through my mind uncontrollably about what had happened to me: losing four babies; doing everything I could to prevent another loss; Kennie being knocked out during delivery; having Kevin - who's fighting to stay alive at another hospital; rude nurses and doctors at my hospital who don't care about what Kennie and I are going through, only trying to go on vacation and avoiding us at every cost; both hospitals counseling us, almost harassing us to remove Kevin from the ventilator. Do they really know what they are talking about? I have serious doubts.

Kennie pulled up and saved me from my thoughts and a face full of tears. The cemetery was close to the hospital. The entry to the cemetery was beautiful with big iron gates, lush green lawn, ponds with ducks.

Slowly and in some discomfort with no wheelchair I made it to a private room. As our parents arrived, they were shown to the room too. We told the director about our possible need for a cemetery plot for my son who was still alive. This all seemed so wrong. I was crying all the way through it. The director spoke to Kennie and our parents and then offered to cover the costs of the service and the spot in the baby garden. He assured me that there were funds set aside for such needs. He could see how much pain I was in both physically and emotionally. I got more compassion from him than I did my own nurses and doctors at my hospital. A stranger I just met. Sad, I thought. He also knew I needed to hurry things up so that I could go see Kevin. Every minute counted. We were once again handed literature. Getting into the car I could tell it was almost time for the pain medication. Kennie pulled up to the hospital and there was an orderly with a wheelchair who offered me a ride. How kind. This was like night and day compared to my hospital. Just couldn't get over it.

The bumps weren't that bad, but the elevator, ugh still painful. The orderly stopped pushing me at the isolation room and Kennie took over. We got gowned up and slowly I made it into the NICU. We were greeted by Kevin's nurse who quickly got chairs for Kennie and me and removed the wheelchair. I'm guessing it was taking up too much room. She brought us up to date with Kevin - vitals, returned test reports, test that were being performed, and his improved breathing.

Having my thoughts a bit more together than yesterday, I asked about Kevin and his eating ability. She said that Kevin was getting what he needed through his IV. It was an answer but not a good one in my book. Doctor #10 (one that we liked) came up to talk with us about removing Kevin from life support again. His timing was bad in that we just came from the cemetery and it was definitely not gonna happen right now.

Again, our answer was no. We needed more time and information.

"When all the tests come back, we will make an educated decision, but not now."

The nurse told us that Kevin's need for the ventilator was decreasing and reaching close to normal levels. This meant Kevin would be breathing on his own soon. This made me smile. I keep trying to tell myself that the doctors meant well, but continually asking us to remove Kevin from life support was borderline bullying and it was getting old. Another nurse who, was not Kevin's nurse, chimed in and added, "Think about it, if it wasn't for the ventilator Kevin wouldn't be alive right now." Okay, what? Isn't that what a ventilators job supposed to do? Keep you alive. Where did she come from and who was she to add in her two cents? She made no sense. Our answer was there. We will wait it out.

The social worker had done her job. A pastor from the local Presbyterian church came by and renewed our faith. He prayed for Kevin, Kennie and me. It was short but it meant a lot to me.

Kevin had two main nurses who requested him as their patient. I was comforted knowing that he was wanted. The nurses very quickly became as close as family. One was a great sounding board. She knew our story inside and out. She took the time to hear and listen to the story. Most people hear but do not listen. There is a difference between hearing, giving to give the person time to talk and listening, engaging in a person's story to really understand what he went through or is going through. She also knew, because she was listening, that we were not giving up on Kevin. She asked if I was discharged from the other hospital yet. I told her that it was my last night. I just couldn't imagine going home without Kevin, but I knew it was going to happen and I dreaded it. I was almost to the point of crying when I thought of it. My hospital was supposed to have a family dinner. Finally, something good and bad: dinner with Kennie but no Kevin. Another normal family dream I had that was shattered.

  We became very familiar with Kevin's hospital, its waiting areas, visiting hours, nurses shift changes, and food. Visiting hours and shift changes were not enforced on Kennie and me. Family and friends would still come and go. Kennie would sit with them in the cafeteria and bring me back something to eat. I never left Kevin's side - I just couldn't. Every moment was so precious to me. I was starting to move around a bit more. Walking very slowly to the restroom and around the NICU. Still on pain medication, but using less around the clock.

  The night came and once again it was time to leave. Much later than the night before, but I was no longer on the doctor's schedule. I was still feeling a bit insecure about leaving, not knowing Kevin's future. I kissed Kevin on the hand and told him once again, "I love you, Kevin. Mommy loves you." Tired, just going through the motions and kind of numb to the whole thing…I was hoping this is all a bad dream.

As I sat down in the wheelchair that Kennie had brought me I was thinking, how… how can this be the outcome of all of our/my efforts? What did we/I do wrong? Everything was still flashing though my brain, trying to find an answer or some reasonable solution and yet there wasn't any. Out the door and down the hall we went. The bells and alarms from the NICU getting softer and softer until they were gone.

On the drive back to my hospital I started to feel sorry for myself. Why is it so hard for me to have a baby? Why are we going through this? Why was Kevin born with problems? Is it because I forced myself to have a baby and never gave up on having a baby? Because I believed I could have a baby? Now I have one and he's mine. Now all he has to do is keep improving and live.

In no time we were back at my hospital. As usual, no eye contact, no smiles, no welcome back and then the big kicker, no romantic family dinner. They told us it was because we were too late for dinner. I think it was because we didn't have our baby, they thought he would be dead by now, I would be discharged and no longer a concern of theirs. I don't think they even ordered us a meal to share. Another night of crying myself to sleep. I'm sure it didn't last as long, we were both exhausted. These stressful long days were getting to us. In some ways I was thankful this was my last night at my horrible hospital.

The morning came. I knew the doctor had already discharged me in advance and was enjoying his vacation somewhere. No doctor came to see me before I left the hospital. A nurse gave a quick glance at my back to check the staph infections. No breakfast was provided. Not sure what happened there, but not a surprise. Still unable to get up out of bed, but from a sitting position I could manage, I slowly got dressed.

Kennie packed everything and went to get the car. He returned after some time to find me still sitting on the bed/couch.

He asked, "Why didn't the nurse come and get you? I told the nurse at the front desk to get you a wheelchair and I would go get the car. I've been waiting outside in the driveway with the car for you." Disgusted with the whole situation I stood up and walked out of the hospital on my own. No wheelchair, not one goodbye, smile or "wishing us well" from the nurse's station and I think every one of the nurses was standing there watching me leave. The only moment of contentment was when I realized that I was done with this hospital.

We went straight to Kevin's hospital. It's funny what goes through your mind when you have time to sit and think. All of the new moms get a wheelchair and wheeled out of the hospital, holding their new baby, but didn't I deserve the same quality of care from the hospital nurses? So sad I didn't have my baby in my arms. It didn't matter to any of the nurses, but it did affect me emotionally. Something I'll never forget. I also thought about how impressed I was with the facility at first. Yet all the money they put into making the birthing suites beautiful didn't help me. They should have put the money into training the nurses to be more compassionate. I tried to deal with it by telling myself I didn't have to go back there anymore. Done. I was crying most of the time. Puffy eyes and tears were something Kennie was getting used to. Oh, I shared my thoughts, but we had to focus on what was to come and not the things that had happened.

Kevin's hospital what a sight for changing the mood. This time I decided to try walking in. Kennie and I walked through the NICU and I saw another parent standing over a baby. Excited that there was another parent in the room, I walked over to her and asked her what she named her baby? She quickly informed me that she was a social worker and not the parent. My heart sunk.

I made my way over to Kevin. He looked pink. This made me smile. He was starting to move a bit which caused concern for the oxygen and IV tubes. No, this was Kevin's way of letting me know he was alive and wanting to live. I asked about the lab results for the trisomy outcome. Nothing yet. He had lost weight since birth. I was told this was normal, most babies lose weight after birth. He had urine diapers but only one little tar like dirty diaper.

She then asked the question that made me fill with emotions, "Would you like to hold Kevin?"

My breath fluttered as I exhaled. "Of course!"

He was officially three days old and I haven't even got to hold him yet.

I said, "I thought with the ventilation tubes that it wasn't possible?"

She explained that she can manage the tubes and assured me this wouldn't be a problem and Kevin wouldn't be harmed in the process.

As she went about getting a recliner and preparing Kevin, another thought entered my mind. I could have been holding Kevin from day one? I corrected my sad thought quickly. Focus on the here and now.

I sat down in the chair and Kevin's little body was gently moved from the incubator to my arms. This was the best, most indescribable feeling I have ever had. I just sat there in awe of the whole experience, letting the happy tears run down my face. This was my baby.

Kevin seemed so relaxed. It was as if he knew he was home in my arms. I instinctively started to sing to him. His eyes tried to focus on my face as if he was seeking out my voice with his eyes. I really got to see him for the first time. No equipment or lights in my way. I could look down on his whole little body. He had so much black curly hair that cuffed around his tiny ear. I got to feel his weight and see how incredibly tiny he was. His little three and a half pound body was so light. His hands were so tiny and holding a little rolled up gauze to keep his hands shaped since he wasn't moving them that much. His face also tiny with the opening of his cleft lip and palate. There was the ventilator tube sticking out of his nose opening and tape to his cheek to hold it in place.

Continuing to sing to him, I saw him smile. The moment Kevin smiled someone said, "It's gas, he's too little to show an emotion" (people always say it's gas). I don't even know who said it but I know he smiled at me. This made it all worth it. I felt complete. The nurse took a polaroid camera out of a cupboard and took a picture of me holding Kevin. Then Kennie leaned in and another picture was taken. I was so proud. My first family portrait.

Even though I held him for hours and wanted to continue holding him I knew it was time for Kennie to hold him. He had been hovering around my shoulders, looking at Kevin, making memories, and taking note.

I asked Kennie, "Do you want to hold Kevin now?"

That deer in the headlight look was all over his face. He went white, but I knew he couldn't say no. Most men I know are uncomfortable holding "wobbly headed babies" unless they are their own. Kevin was less than four pounds and came with a bunch of intimidating tubes. A little uncomfortable at first but it didn't take long before Kennie was talking to Kevin and becoming more relaxed. More pictures were taken. Looking at the pictures that were taken I noticed how tired and sleep deprived we were, but aren't all new parents sleep deprived? Finally, a feeling of normalcy. A few more pictures were taken with Kennie holding Kevin and our extended family started walking through the door. They were also surprised that we were able to hold Kevin. After a bit of a visit and finding out that we didn't get breakfast, we were encouraged by the nurse to go to lunch with everybody at the cafeteria.

Kennie walked into the cafeteria like he owned the place. This was my first time actually in the cafeteria. Getting a tray for both of us Kennie noticed that we were in the company of a lot of doctors who were ordering an obnoxious amount of broccoli for lunch. It did look good. Having no appetite myself I got the soup, left it with Kennie and went to find a table for all of us. Kennie was the last to arrive at the table. He had my soup and a big mound of broccoli. He said it made him fit in with the doctors and made him look smart. I just laughed. Another moment of normalcy.

Some family went home, some stayed and returned to the room with Kennie and me after lunch. I needed to use the restroom and told them I would see them up there. I was actually having an almost normal day - well what was a normal day to me. On my way back up to see Kevin got in the empty elevator and I hear someone yell, "Hold the door!" So I did. It was a team of firemen with a patient on the gurney. The patient looked out of it. It was very obvious when the doors closed that she hadn't had a bath in a while. The odor filled the room.

"What floor?" I asked. We were all going to the same floor.

The fireman in charge asked the woman on the gurney, "Tell me again what happened?"

The woman on the gurney, in a groggy voice replied, "Well at the first pain I grabbed my flask and took a swig and continued until it was all gone. Then the pain got worse and the alcohol wasn't enough. So, I cut me some snort and honestly, I don't know how much I did, because I passed out. Next thing I knew you all were there."

Then the fireman asked, "Did you know you had your baby?"

She paused a moment to think and said, "Yes. I saw it hanging out of me and that's when I must have passed out."

I couldn't wait for the elevator doors to open. For a moment I thought I could pry them open with my fingers and crawl through whatever opening was there. Finally, they opened and I was the first one out. Never looking back, crying, and as fast as my painful C-sectioned body would get me there I made it into the NICU. I gowned up and walked into the room with a sigh of relief. I noticed the new baby in the room. Unmistakably, it was the woman in the elevator's baby. The poor little baby was shaking, crying, and alive. Later that afternoon the baby was visited by the social worker I mistook earlier for a parent.

When I arrived at Kevin's bedside, I couldn't wait to hold him. I regretted not going up with my family, I could have avoided that experience in the elevator. My family noticed that I was obviously shaken up. Briefly and quietly I told them all what happened to me in the elevator. Why, when I did everything I supposed to and followed everything that was asked of me, did Kevin turn out like he did? I was thankful that I never did drugs. There was nothing in my past that I could feel guilty about, but my question still went unanswered. Trying to move on we continued to hold and bond with Kevin. Family continued to come and go. It was late and time to go home. Part of me was scared to go home without Kevin. We turned onto our street and the tears started to flow. Hell, I couldn't stop the tears even if I wanted to. We pulled into the drive and opened the garage. This was a horrible feeling. Every step was agonizing without Kevin. As I made my way to my bedroom, I had to pass the nursery. With a face full of tears, I gently reached for the door handle and quietly closed the door. I continued to my room, changed, crawled into bed, and cried myself to sleep. It had become a routine for me now.

Saturday started out relatively uneventful. We called the hospital. Kevin had a good night and was doing well. I decided to take a shower, mindful not to get the bandage wet. I taped a plastic bag over it and I got into the warm shower, took a deep breath in the steam filled room, and relaxed. That's when it hit. My breastmilk. It was squirting everywhere in the shower. What do I do with this? Kevin was being fed through his IV. Shouldn't this have gotten here when I gave birth? Kennie thought it was amusing. We both forgot about this step. Kennie got the pamphlet about breastfeeding and started reading. There was nothing to suppress breastmilk, the pamphlet just said not to encourage it. That wasn't helpful. I was given some disposable pads that you place in the inside of your bra to absorb the milk and decided this would help remedy the problem for the moment. But how do I get rid of the milk? Pills? Shot? I guess I needed to ask someone at the hospital.

When we finally made it to the hospital and were at Kevin's bedside, we instantly noticed Kevin's breathing was improving. I looked at his chart. His weight was still going down and there was no news on the trisomy labs. I told the nurse about my breastmilk coming in. She said it wasn't uncommon for a C-section delivery to have delayed breastmilk because your body didn't go through the natural process of birth. She confirmed that the pills and shots that women used to get if they chose not to breastfeed were no longer available. She suggested that I used cabbage to suppress the milk. Okay, what? Cabbage why and how? She said the cabbage has a natural suppressant in it. She told me to break off a leaf, place it over my breast and put my bra on as normal. She also said the tighter the bra the better to keep the supply and demand down. It took me a minute to understand but I got it. I'm glad we had a moment to ourselves to discuss this.

Extended family that couldn't visit during the week due to work and school schedules were starting to show up for a visit. Just like when Kennie was in the hospital, the show of love from family was definitely present once again. Kevin's hospital was becoming our temporary home. It's amazing what becomes comfortable to you.

About midday the nurse told us that the team of doctors wanted to talk to Kennie and me. I told Kennie this can't be good. With all of the doctors and nurses trying one at a time to get us to remove Kevin from the ventilator, they are now going to team up on us all at once. Kennie assured me we would stay strong and support each other as he gave me a hug.

Around 4:00 p.m. we were taken to a conference room where every chair around a large table was already filled with white jacketed person, except the two closest to us. The nurse who I had bonded with had walked us there. She left and I thought, Oh no. Don't leave us. To my relief she returned with a chair for herself. I would guess there were around 13 people, plus Kennie and me.

The group started by telling us that the lab results came back and Kevin was not a trisomy baby. I looked at Kennie, smiled and squeezed his hand. The nurse sitting behind me patted my back and smiled. She might have been pre-informed. We were relieved and excited. This meant Kevin was not terminally ill.

The second thing on the doctor's agenda was getting us to remove Kevin from the ventilator. I asked what normal oxygen levels were for removing someone, specifically a baby, off of a ventilator?

When I got my answer I said, "That's when we will remove him, then and not any sooner. If Kevin is not a trisomy baby then he is normal and should be weaned like a normal baby."

One of the other white coats spoke up. I think he was an intern. In a loud voice and shaking his head in the "no" motion he abruptly said, "Kevin is far from a normal baby with all of his anomalies." This white coat was rude and abrupt with us.

That struck a nerve with me. I replied, "Yes, but babies can go on to live normal lives with cleft lips, clubfeet and other birth defects."

He had to agree.

That was when I said, "I want the DNR removed." Eyebrows were raised on this statement. Several doctors tried to speak out against this decision.

Kennie jumped in, "Look we signed your DNR when there was a chance that Kevin was terminally ill. The tests proved he's not and we don't want it anymore. So, remove it." Not one person said a word to him. It was as if they could talk over me - my mommy thoughts didn't matter - but Kennie stepping in validated my request.

I added, "That also means that in the event of an emergency, CPR would be performed, right?"

Heads at the table were now nodding up and down to assure me Kevin would be saved. This had been adding to my sleepless nights.

Since we had some renown specialist at the big table, I had to ask a troubling question, "Since Kevin is not a trisomy baby, what happened to him to cause his problem?"

There were many hypothetical answers, but the only one that made sense to me was a stroke in utero that slowed or ceased development of Kevin's body. He also said that if it was a stroke, the stroke may have been caused by uncontrolled, undiagnosed sugar levels, diabetes. There it was. Even though it was hypothetical it was what made sense to me. Inside my head I was screaming! I had told every OBGYN doctor in my path that diabetes ran in my family and I was only treated for the illness the last two months of my pregnancy. Trying to compose myself with these raging thoughts going through my head, I asked if there was anything else we need to discuss. Nothing. The room cleared out except for the nurse, Kennie, and me. The nurse gave us a hug. She assured me that we both acted like protective parents. Another smile went on my face. I really liked this nurse.

    We returned to Kevin's bedside and informed the family of the good news; that Kevin was not a trisomy baby. It was as if the anxious stress was gone. Oh we still had a long way to go but the first big hurdle was jumped. I started monitoring Kevin's oxygen levels much closer, starting with the current levels which were still far from the objective. After spending more time with Kevin and the family discussing the news, I found our mindsets were changing. We went from thinking Kevin was going to die and planning funeral services, to once again planning for life. The first thing I did when I got home was take the cemetery and the dead baby support group packets and chucked them in a drawer. I should have chucked them in the trash. I didn't want to see them again.

    I went over to the nursery and opened the door and announced, "Kevin will be coming home soon." The faded dreams were starting to materialize again. Kennie and I had the best night's sleep since long before Kevin's birth. Not being a trisomy baby meant he would be alive in the morning. No terminal illness or DNR to take his life.

The next day was pleasant. As hard as it is to believe that spending all day in a hospital could be pleasant, it was. Lightweight, upbeat conversations, and keeping an eye on the oxygen levels which were continuing to be less and less. I was hoping that the nurse wasn't under some direction to force his oxygen levels down, but she was the one I trusted. Kevin was pink and starting to take big deep breaths for his little body. I asked again about feeding Kevin and was told that the IV with glucose was enough for now. It still didn't seem right and was probably the reason for his weight loss. Kevin was almost a week old now. Not much more happened on Sunday and we went home feeling pretty good about the day. It was Kennie's final day for vacation. This was a problem for me. How was I going to get out of bed? This was something I couldn't do on my own yet and I still needed Kennie's help.

It was hard but Kennie returned to work. Before he left, he helped me up and I sat in the recliner until it was time to go to the hospital. I drove to the hospital for the first time by myself. I had so many insecurities. I can't even get out of bed by myself and I'm behind the wheel of a car. I had to park in the tiered garage and walk a bit farther, but I made it. I went to Kevin's spot but he wasn't there. The blissful day we had yesterday suddenly disappeared. I had a major fright race through me. What happened to Kevin?

"Mrs. Johnson!" a nurse called my name. A voice I didn't recognize. A new nurse had him and he was moved to another area of the NICU. Oh, thank God! The first things I noticed were the oxygen levels and his color. Kevin was pink and the oxygen numbers were just barely on. When the nurse noticed I was looking at the machine, she informed me that today was the day to remove Kevin from the ventilator. Wait? What? I thought it would take more time to get the levels lower and I needed more time. Kevin had a different agenda. He was almost breathing on his own now. A bit panicked that I was all by myself, I called Kennie and told him he picked the wrong day to go back to work. We were taking Kevin off of the oxygen today. Needless to say, Kennie found a way to finish early and come to the hospital. The nurse informed me that removing Kevin could wait until Kennie got there. Good I thought because it wasn't going to happen with me by myself. Not having Kennie and a new nurse would have been an overwhelming thing for me.

    While waiting for Kennie I gave Kevin a sponge bath. For a little guy he had a broad chest. He seemed to enjoy the bath. I dressed him in the clothes that the hospital provided me. That was another thing we needed to do, buy Kevin preemie-sized clothing. The clothes that we got from the baby shower for a large baby. The doctor told me I would have a ten-pound baby. Shopping for baby clothes was a project for my mother-in-law Ruth. She loved to solve problems like this and she was good at it. In fact, Ruth had already shopped that morning. She was way ahead of the game. She brought me the clothes she had purchased and we changed Kevin before Kennie arrived. Kevin looked adorable. Real baby clothes that fit.

    Kennie finally arrived and walked into the NICU with a smile on his face. He was excited to get Kevin off of the ventilator. Me on the other hand, I realized the possible outcome may not be so good. I drew from Kennie's positive nature telling myself that it was going to be just fine. Kennie and I talked with the nurse about the oxygen levels to assure ourselves we were making the right decision at the right time. Kevin's oxygen stats were between 90 and 98 and 20% oxygen being fed to him. This meant he was breathing mostly on his own. Feeling a little reassured we agreed to go forth with removing the oxygen tube. Partitions were put up around Kevin's incubator to give us privacy.

The doctor explained how he would pull all of the equipment off of Kevin and how the tube that was down in his lungs would come out. After all I had gone through with Kennie I couldn't believe I found my knees shaking. The nurse suggested we wait in the family room and she would bring Kevin to me once the ventilator was removed.

I asked what we should expect?

She said, "All babies are different. Some gasp for air, some barely breathe or take shallow breaths. There is the possibility that he could fail to breath on his own."

That didn't help, but we knew it was time. If Kevin was going to live this was his moment to show us. She also said that morphine could be given to him to help him relax and we quickly declined the offer. My dad stayed and watched the removal of the equipment from Kevin. We were instructed to wait in the family room on the little love seat and the nurse would bring Kevin to us.

The family room was just outside the double door exit from the NICU. The room was incredibly small and didn't hold many chairs, so most of the family waited in the hall. The room was about six feet by seven feet. There were three chairs, a love seat and a small table with a lamp hanging above it from the wall. I went in and sat down in the chair right next to the door. I wanted to hold him the minute he came through the door. I was fearing the worst. Kennie sat next to me. Ruth and Roger were on the love seat and my dad had a chair sitting up against the opposite wall from Kennie when he joined us. We all had bewildered looks on our faces, but it didn't last long because we could all hear the much-anticipated double doors open and see the nurse coming quickly through them holding

Kevin. He looked like a normal baby, not hooked up to anything - IV, oxygen, heart monitor - nothing. I started to tear up then quickly dismissed the idea of crying. He was quickly handed to me and I couldn't take my eyes off of him. I was watching every breath. The nurse stood there for a few minutes talking me through the breathing normalcy. A little gasping, color changing, but still breathing. After a while she excused herself and left. The emotions were overwhelming. I was watching every gasping and shallow breath he took, wondering if it was his last. I noticed his color. He wasn't as pink as he should have been. Was he going to pink up? He seemed to have dark skin, but I also wondered if it was the lighting in the room. As every moment passed Kevin's breaths got deeper and I drew comfort from it. At one point his breath was so deep that it was a while before he drew his next one and I began to panic. Just before I started to react to it Kevin took a breath and so did I. Kevin continuing to breathe was the blessing we were praying for. His gasping for a breath wasn't as bad as I was told it might be. It was more like when you swim from the bottom to the top of a pool and take a gasping breath. Maybe my imagination was worse than reality. I noticed that his IV was capped off but still in his little arm. He looked up at me. He seemed to smile as if to say, "See mommy, I got this." I began to cry happy tears. I knew he was going to make it. My son was breathing on his own. Ten minutes passed and the nurse came in to check on us. She placed a knitted hat on his head.

  The nurse smiled and said, "Kevin seems to be doing fine." She checked his vitals and then left us again. After the stressful moments passed the family started rotating in and out of the tiny room. There was never an empty seat. I'm sure it was nerves, but I started playing, singing and giggling with

Kevin. He seemed to respond. My little tiny baby boy was so strong. Just six days old. He survived a traumatic birth, all the poking and prodding, not being able to be held by his mom or dad for days, being yanked off of his breathing machine, but somehow, he had the will to live and he did.

After sitting there holding Kevin for seven hours we finally felt comfortable enough to go get something to eat in the cafeteria. I walked out of the family room carrying Kevin into the NICU and I placed him into his incubator. He looked up at me, and like the rest of the babies in the nursery, he was no longer hooked up to all of the machines.

He still had his IV, which prompted the question, "When will Kevin be able to eat?"

The nurse said she would ask and get back to me. He was unable to suckle because of his cleft lip and palate. She said if he can eat it would be through an NG tube. I knew instantly what that was. It brought back memories from the days Kennie spent in the hospital and had green baby food fed to him through his nose. What were the odds that my husband *and* son would have to be fed by an NG tube? I was concerned that Kevin wouldn't be able to be fed through the NG tube because he didn't have a closed nose. The nurse assured me it could be done. Then encouraged us to go to dinner by telling us that Kevin is in good hands. She knew I had been there all day with very little to eat.

When we returned to the NICU Kevin was doing fine. It seemed Kevin found some comfort in wiggling a bit, which was an impossibility before with the breathing tube. Without the tubes it was easy to just pick him up. Things were starting to have a normal feel. Even though we had some reservations, we called it a night. The nurse assured us that she would call us if something happened.

When we got home Kennie and I had a conversation about the stressful day we had. We both suspected that the staff at the hospital thought Kevin wouldn't make it. The medical staff probably thought when Kevin was placed in my arms he would die but he lived! Now the game plan for Kevin was going to change for all of us. Kevin was alive and the scary unknowns of him dying from a trisomy illness was gone. Aside from his physical problems, which could be corrected over time, there was nothing life threatening about him.

The next morning was Tuesday. Kevin was a week old. A milestone for all of us. Kennie went to work assured that I would keep him informed of any changes in Kevin's health. Once again Kennie helped me up and then I drove myself to the hospital. This was really a big deal in itself for me. I was still healing from my C-section. The drive was about 40 minutes and the walk from the parking lot was not guaranteed to be close, but I did it again. I guess with the average, no complication C-section birth, the mother would be still in bed taking it easy at home. I didn't have that luxury. I couldn't concern myself of my needs. My focus was on Kevin.

I made it into the NICU Kevin was moved yet again and I had to find him this time. I noticed a familiar face. The nurse I trusted was back and Kevin was her patient. She was smiling as I walked up to Kevin's incubator. There was a change. Kevin was being NG gavage fed. He had a tube coming out of his cleft lip that was gavage feeding him, just like Kennie's feeding tube when he was in the hospital, except much smaller. The NG tube was placed through his nose and lip area where it didn't grow together and it went down into his stomach. The other end of the tube was taped to his little face to hold the tube in place. When it was time to feed him a gavage tube (2-4 ounces) was connected to the end of the tube line and filled with the appropriate amount of formula. The formula could vary in calories based on Kevin's needs. The gavage tube is held into the air and gravity takes over as food is drained into Kevin's stomach.

This answered my question about breastfeeding. He couldn't suck anyway with his cleft lip. I felt as if Kevin and I were deprived of yet another natural aspect of life. I asked about pumping my breast milk and NG feeding him. I was told that it was too much of a hassle. Didn't quite understand "too much of a hassle" and the cabbage had almost gotten rid of the breastmilk, plus I had too much on my mind to question it. Kevin was getting real food and that was the important part. I was also told that they had no problem placing the tube and the first bit of formula he got clearly satisfied his stomach. Kevin was full for the first time, he went fast asleep and slept longer than his usual time. This was very comforting to me and I wished Kennie was here to share in this.

The nurse told me that when she arrived for her shift she was surprised to see Kevin off of the ventilator and was sorry she wasn't here when it happened. It was reassuring that she was invested in Kevin's well-being too.

The nurse told me that Kevin would be going back to the hospital he was born in because he no longer needed a high level NICU since he was off the ventilator and IV. Wait, what? Can they do that? Who's making this decision? She then informed me that our insurance provider was calling the shots. They wouldn't pay for the higher level NICU because it's more expensive. Are you kidding me? Go back to the hospital that neglected me with a son that has special needs? The shock that I was feeling was unbelievable. At the very least I thought I would never have to step foot in the other hospital again. We have been through so much, now the insurance company is calling the shots? The insurance company has never even seen Kevin and they are dictating to the team of doctors what kind of care Kevin is going to get. Looking back, I believe the insurance company was partially to blame for Kevin's condition. If the insurance company is dictating to the doctor (and had been all along) the insurance company and the doctor should have done a glucose/A1C test on me early to find the diabetes. Oh, but that would cost the insurance company money. Thinking again to myself, I told everyone including my current OBGYN about my long family history of diabetes. I should have gotten a few more sonograms earlier in my pregnancy too because I was high risk. We probably would have known in advance about Kevin's condition.

    The reality of the whole thing was overwhelming. Knowing that I was neglected at the other hospital, how was I going to learn how to care for Kevin from them? Feedings alone were something I literally just found out about. I hadn't even tried to feed him yet. I'm sure there was much more I need to know and learn. The nurse apologized for hitting me with this news all at once, but she explained that the move would happen quickly. I shared with her my experience at the other hospital and she said she would see what she could do about delaying the move. She knew she couldn't stop it.

    I decided to make the most of the time I still had in the NICU with the nurse I liked. I was visited by the hospital social worker once again. Nice lady. Seemed to be very knowledgeable. She told me what to expect for the move and tried to assure me that they wouldn't move Kevin unless he was ready to be moved. I knew better and nobody was really listening to me. I wanted my training for Kevin to happen at the current hospital and then send Kevin home with me. It was ridiculous to send Kevin and me back to the uncaring hospital which I knew would be inferior at best. There was nothing I could do. I pleaded with the social worker, the nurse, and the doctors. No good. My pleading didn't change the power that the insurance company had over the medical professionals.

Finally, Kennie called. Holding back the panic I told Kennie the good news about Kevin's feeding tube, then the bad and disturbing news of the move. His first question was, when? He said he was leaving and on his way to the hospital. Thank God. I didn't have much more in me to continue on my own. I returned to Kevin and asked the nurse as many questions as I could, figuring that my time was limited with the people I trusted. The doctors made their rounds but stayed a limited amount of time with me. They probably knew I was not going to give up on my quest of not moving Kevin. Later I saw the nurse and the doctor talking but never was informed about what but suspected it was about us. I just hoped that the nurse was arguing on behalf of Kevin and me.

Kennie arrived and we talked about insurance making us move and Kennie became angry. I knew raising voices and anger wasn't good for the babies in the NICU, including Kevin. We went down to the cafeteria to discuss it further. I told him how the insurance company was the one calling the shots and the doctors at the insurance company weren't even the ones who were seeing us first hand. At least now Kennie was aware of who should get the wrath of his anger. Kennie now had his voice and realized how we were being treated. We returned to the NICU with a game plan and a different focus: get as much training from this hospital as possible. This was already my mindset.

We had been spending 15, 18 and even longer hours at Kevin's bedside since he was born. Later that evening the nurse informed me that she and others had arranged for a room at the hospital for me so I could spend the night. Not knowing when the last day at Kevin's hospital would be, she took it upon herself to start training me right away. The little room was intended for an intern but it would allow me to stay all night with Kevin. The nurses could watch over me while training me to take care of Kevin. The nurse informed me that the room we sat in when Kevin was taken off the ventilator would be converted to a makeshift bedroom. The little couch was able to fold out into a twin sized bed and the chairs were removed. She got me what I needed for my own hygiene and had the room made up for the night. Everything was happening so quickly. As our family arrived, they were told of the move implemented by the insurance company. They were just as uncomfortable as we were. Some even attempted to speak out in our behalf to the staff but to no avail.

    Our family left for the night. Kennie had work in the morning but like me was invested in Kevin's training and decided to stay. Somewhere around midnight I went to the little room on Kennie's suggestion to get some sleep. Lesson one: Take turns. All of us were not required to be there all night with Kevin. Kennie would take the first shift until 3:00 a.m. He looked exhausted.

    I said something like, "You need the sleep."

    The nurse, trying to make us feel better, said, "That's normal. All new parents are exhausted. It's part of having a baby."

    This made sense and seemed to add some comfort to dealing with everything. I kissed Kevin, told them all I would be back at 3:00 a.m. and left for the little room. I went to the room and opened the door. The little bed took up the whole room. The only other thing in the room was a tiny nightstand with a phone on it and a light (scant) hanging above it. There was barely room to walk beside the bed to get in, but I was counting my blessings. I had a bed near Kevin all night long. I crawled into bed and stretched out. Finally, some sort of relaxation. At that moment I realized my mistake, I left the light on. I couldn't roll over, sit up and turn out the light due to the incision from the C-section. I had no ability to tighten my abs and sit up on my own yet. I had to try to sleep with the light on until three in the morning. How will I get out of bed to relieve Kennie at three? I managed to fall asleep, it really wasn't that hard. The door opened and an extremely tired Kennie was peeking in. The clock on the wall said almost 4:00.

"Why didn't you come out?"

I told him that I couldn't get out of bed. I pointed out that I couldn't even turn off the light. Kennie somehow squeezed through the side of the bed and helped me up. I thought he was going to crawl into the bed that I just left. Instead he said he was going home, maybe sleep, feed the dogs and then to work. He asked me if I was going to be all right? I had no choice. I had to do this. It seemed I had to become an expert in a field I didn't choose. I had less than a week to learn what nurses get two years to learn. Choosing not to share my insecurities with anyone, including Kennie, from here forward I replied, "Yes. I'll be just fine." A kiss goodbye from Kennie and I was on my own. At least that's how it felt. Knowing Kevin was depending on me and what I learned, I wasted no time. I was thankful for the long shifts the nurses put in. I had a 12-hour shift with my trainer/nurse and I made the most of it.

Gavage feeding was a new thing to me. Every three hours around the clock I watched how the nurse mixed the formula together to get a higher calorie count. Afterwards she would fill the gavage with the right amount of formula, raise it into the air about a foot and let it flow into Kevin's stomach, and then lower it to stop the flow and let Kevin digest it. It was not a quick process. Kevin seemed to be looking around the room while being fed. He was experiencing something new and he liked it. You could see his little belly filling up. When the formula was all in Kevin the nurse would remove the gavage and cap off the tube. Part of the tube was taped to his little face; the remaining part was just left to hang. It was maybe eight inches or so extra. She took his temperature often and explained to me that premature babies have a hard time maintaining a normal 98.6°F temperature. Kevin wasn't a premature baby, but he was of premature weight so he qualified. Kevin required preemie-sized diapers. Another purchase we needed to get. I started making a shopping list and it grew quickly.

After a few feedings it was my turn to try. I did it just like a nurse. Confidence restored. I just smiled. If I wasn't getting a lesson, I was holding Kevin. Cradling Kevin in your arms was normal, but picking him up and moving him into your arms was a bit different from regular weighted babies. When you picked Kevin up you needed to support his head like any newborn, but his size and NG tube were what changed the game. Once again watching how the nurses maneuvered Kevin showed me how to do it. They would place the palm of their hand on his chest, ring finger under his left arm, thumb under his right arm and index finger under his chin to support his head. With their opposite hand behind his back to secure Kevin, they would lift Kevin, carrying most of his weight on the hand holding his chest. That way the NG tube wouldn't get caught on anything and could hang freely. This helped me get comfortable picking Kevin up and getting him into my arms on my own. I knew his airway was protected.

Kevin did his first real poop. Not a newborn tar poop. This was a big deal. It meant that his bowels were working and I had the honor of changing him. I've changed babies before, but not one this small. It's different. Gosh one baby wipe was practically all you needed. There was no smell. The umbilical cord stub was still there, but almost ready to fall off. I was told within a day or two it would be gone. More anatomy teaching and I absorbed every word. Some I already knew, some was new to me, anything I didn't understand I looked up. This was a new education, similar to when Kennie went through his Guillain-Barré syndrome. If I didn't understand something, I was determined to find out about it.

Kevin had testing going on too. Now that he could be transported around the hospital without the ventilator and machines attached, sight, hearing, sonograms, etc. tests were performed. I think at first the doctors thought it would be a waste of time for a terminally ill baby to be tested and now that he wasn't terminally ill, they were behind on their protocol. They knew I didn't trust the inferior hospital we were being transferred to and they were attempting to get it all done before we left.

Kennie came by after work and I filled him in on what I learned every day. I showed Kennie Kevin's chart and all the nurse's entries and how all of the tests came back in normal range. Once again Kennie took the first shift. This time it was earlier in the evening and Kevin had a present for him, another poop. Kennie wasn't exactly a pro at this, but with extra wipes he did a good job on the little poop diaper change. Kennie came and got me from the little room when he needed to go home. I got up to join Kevin. I'm guessing it was around one in the morning.

This time when the nurse change happened at 7:00 a.m. I excused myself to go take a nap. I was mostly in their way. When I got to the little room it was already changed back to a family room, but the couch was still there and so was my pillow. Heck, I still wasn't back to myself and getting up out of bed was still difficult so this kind of solved that problem. I could sit up at an angle and sleep.

I must have been more tired than I thought because it was almost 10:00 a.m. by the time I returned to the NICU. I immediately noticed there was no NG tube hanging on Kevin's face. This was really the first time I saw his entire face. The ventilator covered most of his face at the beginning and when it was removed, I was so afraid of him dying I wasn't really looking at him. Then the NG tube was taped to his face all the time and now there was nothing to hide his little round face from me. I smiled.

Of course, it prompted the question, "What happened? Why is the NG tube missing?"

I was told it had a kink in the line and it had to be replaced. I was just in time to do it. This frightened me. How do you know for sure that you placed it in the stomach and not the lungs? I didn't want to accidentally put formula into his lungs. Well there was a trick to it and I learned the trick. Once the tube is placed, using a stethoscope you listen for a small, faint pop noise to know it's in the stomach. At first, I was very uncomfortable with this. With the nurse watching I picked up the tube and placed it in Kevin's mouth and down into his stomach. It had a measurement on the tube and I was directed when to stop by the dots of measurement. I listened for the pop noise and it was in. I taped the excess tube to his face to hold it in place and I was done. The nurse checked it. I got it right on my first try. I had to get it right or Kevin would suffer. The only thing in question was the base tape on Kevin's face was starting to irritate his skin. The nurse placed a gentler tape on his face, then the tube and more tape on top of the tube to hold the tube in place. The first tape would be stationary and the second on his face could be replaced as much as needed without pulling on Kevin's skin. I also wanted to know how long the tube could stay in. I was told a couple of weeks, unless there is a problem like if the line gets kinked. Satisfied and a bit proud of myself after realizing that I did it, I placed the NG tube correctly and fed my son. I started to wonder if I could do this without a nurse standing next to me. I would have no choice. This was going to be my responsibility with Kevin.

    The nurse then told me that when she was removing the NG tube that morning, the end of the tube passed by Kevin's tongue a small amount of formula came out on to Kevin's tongue and Kevin got his first taste of formula. Apparently, he loved it and even more exciting for us was he was able to swallow it without any problem. This meant maybe NG feeding would not last much longer. She had already placed a phone call to the appropriate therapist to test Kevin's ability to suck and swallow. The nurse said there were special bottle nipples for these situations. Encouraging. The therapist showed for her assessment of Kevin. With a special-nippled bottle she managed feed Kevin over an ounce of formula. Good job Kevin. She continued to come by daily and practice with Kevin bottle feeding, but even though Kevin was capable of sucking and swallowing, she felt at this time that NG feeding was safer. Once Kevin gained weight and got a little older it would be better to introduce a bottle to him.

    I asked, "When that would be?"

"When he is a month old and about six plus pounds, we can contact a therapist and start working on it."

We had to wait. I felt bad for Kevin. His first taste of food and then it was taken away. But I understood why.

Another first for the day was that the grandmas got to hold Kevin for the first time. The nurse or I would pick up Kevin from the incubator and place him in their arms. It was kind of hard to pick him up, but holding him was a piece of cake. He weighed less than four pounds. No fatigue at all. The smiles on the grandma's faces were very soothing for me. I understood the intimidation they must have battled at first, but somehow little Kevin took it all away. The little baby smells, the tender skin and the faces Kevin was starting to make, probably helped win them over too. We were fortunate that the grandparents were mostly retired or had flexible schedules. This made our support team solid.

The rest of the day was fairly uneventful. Heck how could you top that? I spent the day and night practicing what I had learned. I asked questions about what I didn't understand to perfect what I needed to know for Kevin's care. I expected that when I get back to the other hospital, I wasn't going to get this kind of training or any more bottle feeding. At home I really would be by myself with Kevin all day. Except for some flexible grandparent schedules that would offer me some company, most everyone else worked and had a busy life. If I needed something, I could call on any of them, but that wasn't my style.

We spent another night at Kevin's hospital, thankful some sort of routine was in play. I knew it would be ending and I was becoming scared.

Friday morning lots of doctors visited Kevin. Some were interns, some specialist, and the others were the main doctors. I tried to ask the doctors questions and got, "Save it until we are all done."

Not wanting to wait, I asked the nurse "What were the doctors examining Kevin so thoroughly for and why won't they talk to me?"

She told me that I couldn't talk to the doctors while they are doing their examinations, but not to worry I would be able to ask all my questions later. Well later never came, but the evening did. I was told that I no longer had access to the little sleeping room. Heartbreaking. When it was time to go home the nurse suggested that we sleep in. Maybe come in after sharing a normal breakfast at home together and to call her if there were any concerns. Good idea. We were very exhausted and could use the catch up on our sleep. Plus, we knew it was only a matter of time before we would have to put our guarded trust into my old inferior hospital.

We slept in on Saturday as suggested. While having breakfast Kennie and I had a long overdue talk about the future. There was so much to talk about and we needed to come up with our questions before we were home alone with Kevin. Future doctor appointments for Kevin? His nose, cleft lip, cleft palate, club feet, pediatrician, feeding supplies, etc. I was still feeling insecure, I felt I couldn't tell anyone and I needed some reinsurance - like a nurse to check up on me. My insurance wouldn't cover home health care, at least that's what I was told. Hm, this was going to be tough.

We got to the hospital around 11:00 a.m. We visited with Kevin for a while. We never did get our questions answered from the swarm of doctors yesterday. The usual family members came for a visit and showed their support. The excitement was when both of the grandmas took turns holding Kevin while the grandpas watched over their shoulders. The grandpas were joking that they couldn't hold Kevin because they had to supervise the grandmas to make sure they were holding Kevin right. The grandparents were starting to get comfortable around Kevin. That's when I started to notice how many people Kevin was bringing together. Family was a given, but the family members would tell us that a lot of people were asking how we were doing. From little league, extended family, friends that we knew and some we didn't. All were caring. What an amazing little guy Kevin is.

Late afternoon we got a visit from the social worker and in a roundabout way got our answers about the doctors visiting yesterday. Kevin was being released from his hospital and being moved back to my inferior hospital on Monday. A huge disappointing breath left me and my body actually went limp. I didn't want this to happen and no matter what I did I couldn't stop it. In the old "pull yourself up by your bootstraps" manner I started asking the questions that Kennie and I came up with at breakfast.

"Future doctors?" I received names, addresses and phone numbers to make future appointments. "Feeding and other supplies that are needed?" The nurse informed me that the hospital Kevin is going to would supply all that we needed. They should be able to handle that.

"Is there any kind of assistance that I can get while I'm at home by myself?"

"Yes."

This was a surprise. That's when I gave a sigh of relief. She told me that she had been made aware of my experiences at the other hospital and was concerned for me. The social worker explained that she and the nurses were responsible for setting up the little sleeping room for me. This would give me as much time as possible to spend with them for Kevin's and my sake. She also took the initiative to call Hospice and arrange for a Hospice nurse to come out and check on me from time to time.

"Hospice? Isn't that for terminally ill patients? Kevin isn't terminally ill."

She explained that Hospice has some kind of a "Peds-fund" setup for babies in need of special medical assistance. They have the ability to help out in a situation like Kevin's.

"Thank you."

She said there was a Hospice nurse who will be coming out today or tomorrow to assess Kevin and meet Kennie and me. When I get home with Kevin the Hospice nurse would come to help me get comfortable with life at home. Somehow she made it sound so easy to adapt Kevin into our life at home. Not liking the other hospital at all, I was actually thinking that we should skip the process of going back, but no. I was reminded that somebody else was calling the shots. Okay, play the game even though there was no logic to it.

The rest of the day was spent watching and waiting for the Hospice nurse, but she never showed. The social worker said Saturday or Sunday so maybe she would come tomorrow. Goodnight once again.

Sunday was the same, we arrived at the hospital after 11:00 in the morning. I think the nurse was right. A well-rested mom and dad function better and when Kevin comes home, we would have to take turns sleeping and watching Kevin.

When we got to Kevin's bedside the Hospice nurse was waiting. She had already done her assessment of Kevin and was bonding with him by talking to him sweetly and smiling at him. It showed me that she cared. She introduced herself and told us about the care game plan for when Kevin gets home.

She and Kevin's nurse came up with a list of supplies that she would bring to our house. She explained how she would check his vitals twice a week and that if I needed her more than that she was just a phone call away. This was the best scenario I was given and I was thankful. I'll take it! I felt mostly prepared and free from some of my secret anxieties. I had some form of backup. I guess I was ready, but are you ever really ready for something like this? Monday is Kevin's next big car ride in an ambulance. The thought still bothered me and I never let anyone know. The rest of the day was just light prep for the move and visiting with Kevin. Holding him had become Kennie's and my favorite pastime. After the last feeding before Kennie and I left it occurred to us Kennie still hadn't learned how to gavage feed, let alone placing the NG tube, mostly because of timing. He just wasn't there when it was done or someone else (the nurse or myself) was feeding him. I guess he thought that I needed more exposure and experience than he did.

    Monday. The dreaded day. Kennie went to work. I went to the hospital. It was a short visit and I was provided with more reading materials on anything and everything the nurses thought I could use.

    The moment came. Kevin's chauffeur was here for his second ride in life. I don't know why, but I was nervous for Kevin. Kevin was much stronger than the first ambulance ride. Was he going to be all right? The attendants were Emergency Medical Technicians (EMTs). I was then instructed to say my goodbyes and they would have Kevin at the other hospital in no time. I did just that. I profusely thanked Kevin's team of nurses and hugged them. I told them I would never forget the kind and caring way they treated Kevin, Kennie and me and then I had to go. I didn't want Kevin to be over at the other hospital by himself. Before I left Kevin's hospital, I called Kennie to tell him Kevin was in the ambulance on his way to the other hospital. When I arrived at the hospital the ambulance was leaving and it was just as Kennie described. The ambulance had a crawling little baby picture on the side panels.

I had no energy. I imagine it was like visiting a train wreck sight. All the horrible memories of this place were rushing back to me. My only positive thinking was maybe they would treat Kevin better than they did me because he was a baby. Kevin's pediatrician was making his rounds when Kevin was brought in and was there to greet him. Good start. He commented on Kevin's breathing remembering how difficult it was to intubate Kevin at birth. He assessed Kevin and signed him in as his patient. I asked how long he planned to have Kevin in the hospital. His response was about a week. As scared as I was to bring Kevin home, I was already counting the days he had to endure this hospital.

The nurses took over. Not friendly at all. No interaction with me unless it was absolutely necessary. They hardly talked. This was no surprise. The game plan for me was to never leave Kevin's side. A little bit of conversation from the nursing staff was directed to me mostly to see what I knew about NG tubes, temperature checking, etc. I think they decided not to do anymore training with me. Maybe I should have been a little more vague, but then again, I didn't really want them to contradict what I was taught. Nothing further was taught to me at this hospital. Returning to this hospital also sparked the memory of the Lamaze classes and how no one reached out to me, not even the teacher. This made me wonder if the instructor made an announcement on my behalf about Kevin. I guess if I continued to think about it, I could just come up with all kinds of unpleasantries from this place. Time to try to let it go the best I could.

      The second problem happened later that afternoon. This hospital was much closer to our home. Family and friends who were driving by could stop for a visit and offer support for us. Wrong. It was quickly pointed out that there were to be only two visitors at a time and it was strictly enforced. Are you kidding me? When Kennie got there he was pissed, but rules were rules. At first there were people waiting to see Kevin which created a line. Most had other things to do and couldn't visit very long. They would just wave through the window into the nursery, when the blinds were open. After word spread about the enforced two maximum visitors people stopped coming by. We lost family and friends support, but I didn't blame them. Then the worst problem. The visiting hours were enforced and they made no exception for us. Are you kidding me again? Why are we being asked to leave the nursery? The moms and dads who are still here at the hospital are allowed to visit their babies after hours in the nursery. I got some feeble excuse about how they can take them back to their rooms, but that wasn't what we were seeing first hand. They stayed in the nursery with us until late. In fact, they seemed to be annoyed that Kevin was back in their care, almost as annoyed as I was that Kevin and I were back. It was even suggested that we should ask the doctor about leaving their nursery/hospital sooner. Who are they to say when it was appropriate to go home? That's the doctor's call. Kennie and I were promptly kicked out at 8:00 p.m. Visiting hours were over. I had no choice but to kiss Kevin goodbye and leave. I cried all the way home and most of the night. Part of my tears were from being so mad and the part from fear that Kevin would be okay.

Visiting hours didn't start until 11:00 a.m. and I was waiting for them to open the blinds at 11:00 a.m. With the blinds closed it made me wonder what they were hiding. I couldn't get back to Kevin fast enough. Funny, with all of their quirks about rules, the rule about washing up and wearing a yellow gown before entering the nursery was not enforced. Kevin was two weeks old today. Amazing since we were told he wouldn't live through the night when he was born. We were living on pins and needles for two weeks, but we were alive and living!

The rest of the week went pretty much the same day after day. No further training. Family stopped coming to visit for the most part, but they did call to check on us. The hospital repeated all of the tests that Kevin's original hospital did. What a waste of time and money, not to mention making Kevin go through them again. Maybe that was the idea, to make money re-performing the same tests that once again came back negative. Finally, it was Friday, August 11th, Kevin's due date. Another milestone and another visit from the pediatrician. He announced that Kevin was being discharged tomorrow, Saturday. He said there was nothing more the nursery could do for him and it was time for Kevin to go home. He handed me the discharge paperwork and his business card.

"Does this mean Kevin's going home now?"

"No, it's Friday. Get the paperwork prepped today then you don't have to come in on Saturday."

When the doctor left and I looked at the paperwork I read the date again, Friday August 11. I wondered if it would have made a difference if we waited until now to deliver Kevin. I know it wouldn't have changed his health problems, but it just made me think of the possibilities if Kevin had been given more time in the womb.

Saturday came. From the moment we arrived to the time we left went quickly. I picked up Kevin and Kennie met us at the sliding doors. I was so ready to leave this place. It was so uncomfortable there, but that was expected. Kennie motioned for us to stop before exiting the double doors of the hospital. Kennie came in just inside the doors and we all walked out together as a family. He knew this was important to me. We walked out as a family of three.

Kennie opened the door to the car and I put Kevin into his car seat. I was a little intimidated because Kevin was fragile like any preemie-sized baby would be. The first thing I noticed was that the interior of the car seat was way too big. There was a look on my face that said it all and Kennie didn't miss it. Kennie wondered what was concerning me. "Look at the size of the seat verses Kevin. His head is going to wobble around if I leave him in there. It's huge."

Kennie reached into the diaper bag, took out a receiving blanket, rolled it up, and cradled it around Kevin's head to help make the area smaller. It worked. It helped to keep Kevin's head upright and protect his breathing. Success. I buckled myself in next to Kevin in the back seat and we were on our way. Kennie was our chauffeur and he was a very proud chauffeur too. I watched Kevin like a hawk. He did great. When we would come to a stop light Kennie would look back to make sure we were doing okay. There was music playing in the car and Kevin noticed. I could only imagine all the new experiences that Kevin must have been having. Noises that the hospital had like, bells, machines, and unfamiliar voices were replaced by our voices, music, and the car engine. Also smells like oxygen and plastic smells he became accustomed to were being replaced by fresh air coming through the half-opened window and sunshine touching his face. It was also the first time we were in charge. No doctors, no nurses, just us. Less than a ten-minute drive and we were home.

Realization hit as we pulled into the drive and our garage door was opening. We were home. My family was home. We got out of the car and I carried Kevin into the house. We were really home. I couldn't get over it. What an amazing feeling. No anxieties. It was as if the calm was waiting for us to come through the door.

I started talking to Kevin as we made our way through the house. "You are home Kevin. This is your room." Tears of uncontrollable joy were rolling down my face as we toured his well-stocked 10x10 room. We had over five years to prepare for a baby from the time Kennie survived his Guillain-Barré illness. Plus, considering that we closed the door to it and then reopened it this was truly a miracle that Kevin was home and in his room. We had made some adjustments to the house in preparation for Kevin's arrival, but now that he was home, I needed to get things more accessible to me for Kevin's care. The first thing I did was play music. Two CDs were particularly soothing and we played them a lot. We had a portable player with a remote which was perfect for when I couldn't get up with Kevin in my lap. We had a swing for Kevin, but like the car seat it was too big. We put that aside and out of the way. Our family room was about 20x20. There was very little color, mostly beiges and slight variations of browns and other earth colors. There were two leather couches, a recliner, entertainment center, and a rock fireplace in the corner that had never been used. We live in California. The kitchen was small but functional with a counter, cabinets that hung low over it, and three barstools. We had a corded wall phone hanging at the end of it and a big beautiful wooden sliding French door to look out to a perfectly manicured grass and concrete backyard. There was not much grass but enough for our cocker spaniels.

We were home by ourselves for over two hours getting comfortable with Kevin. I took "Ted" the teddy bear and sat it on the floor, placed Kevin up against him and took a picture and the doorbell rang. Our first visitor. Thinking it was family Kennie jumped up with excitement and went to the door. Our entry was quite long, maybe 20x8, leading to a set of double doors at the end. When he opened it there was an unfamiliar face. I was holding Kevin on the couch waiting for whoever it was to appear. It was the lady from Hospice and Kennie didn't recognize her which was understandable she was only there in the hospital for a short time and that was over a week ago. I smiled and was relieved to see her. She sat down next to me, asked how we were all doing, and began assessing Kevin.

She started with Kevin's vitals, which were fine. She then went out to her car and started bringing in equipment for Kennie and me to use on Kevin. The first thing she brought in was the oxygen equipment and accessories. Kevin was size extra small on everything. She explained how to use it. The equipment was conveniently portable on wheels and I could take it from room to room or anywhere we needed. She continued to bring in other things in from her vehicle, suctioning, first aid, gauze, ointments, etc. She explained everything thoroughly, what it was, how to use it, and gave me a number to call 24 hours a day if I had any questions. My confidence was definitely improving. I couldn't believe Hospice was doing all of this for my son, knowing I couldn't pay them back. She was there because our insurance company, who kicked us out of Kevin's hospital early to go to my inferior hospital, wouldn't pay for the necessary equipment to aid in Kevin's care at home. Insurance that we had been paying for years wasn't there for us when we need it most, but Hospice's "Peds-fund" was.

"Thank you so much." was all I kept saying to the nurse. She was my saving grace in my time of need. She had been there for about 30 minutes when I realized Kevin needed to be fed. Kennie prepared the formula, brought it to me and I quickly found out how awkward it was to hold Kevin and gavage feed him. I never did this at either hospital. Kevin was always lying down in the incubator. The Hospice nurse made a makeshift bed on the floor with receiving blankets and suggested that I place Kevin on it. Knowing I had become kind of a clean freak after Kennie came home from surviving Guillain-Barré, I was okay with lying Kevin down on the floor. This would become our normal thing for the future in that it worked well for us. She then reacquainted me with how to connect the gavage to Kevin's tube, filled the formula to the appropriate level and held it up to let it go into Kevin's belly. It wasn't long that Kevin was alert and looking around at us. A little sugar (food) rush. When he was done eating as instructed, I flushed the tube line with a half cc of water. I picked him up and cradled him in my arms. The nurse could tell that we were as set as we were going to be for now. I thanked her again and she left.

Over the next few days somehow all of this started to be normal. Normal routines were formed. We were new parents with a deprived sleep schedule, feedings around the clock, diapers that needed to be changed, and unannounced visitors, which we loved having. Some things were not normal to others, but became "our" normal, like taking Kevin's temperature, dressing him when he was cold even though we were in tank tops and shorts. Suctioning him was easier with the bulb syringe than using the machine. His oxygen was used daily at first; however, it was needed much less than when he was in the hospital. Some days we didn't even use it, but it was always there when we did need it. His changing table was moved into our master bedroom which was never used for a changing table. He was so small changing him was easily done anywhere. Instead of a changing table we used it as a medical supply storage table. It resembled a doctor's office examination table. Sleeping was something different too. A gift from a talented lady at one of the showers was a homemade baby-tube-bedding for our bed. About two feet long by 18 inches wide, stuffed tubes on each side about five inches in diameter, covered in mostly white and colored baby feet print. The main part where Kevin was to sleep was lined with a baby changing pad for wet nights. The idea was to place the baby between the tubes on the center material. At that time it was recommended to put the baby on his side. The tubes allowed you to roll it up to Kevin's back and keep him from rolling on his back, which would be dangerous for him if he had a wet burp. Considering his cleft palate and cleft lip he could choke in the middle of the night, in the dark we might not notice, and Kevin could die. This was not going to happen on my shift. The tube-bedding was placed between Kennie and me so that we could both watch him. At least until Kennie left for work at 2:00 a.m.

    One morning when Kennie's alarm clock went off I turned on the light to see Kennie lying on his side facing me with his left arm over his head covering his left eye. Kevin was in the exact position. A total like father like son, picture perfect moment and I didn't miss it. I started taking pictures whenever I was able to and after a while, I had a full camera. Kennie had the pictures developed and brought them back to me. They were amazing to me. I sat them on the counter with plans to have them convenient to show them off when we had company.

Kevin was fed every three hours around the clock. It took about 30 to 45 minutes for him to take/drink his formula. I had to set him up and watch him for an hour to make sure he didn't have a wet burp. If he did, I would turn him to his side let it drain out of his mouth and suction anything that was left. Like any other mom I knew my baby very well. The cute part for me was when he yawned. His whole face yawned. You could see everything in his mouth and truly understand what didn't grow together during development.

Kevin made noises while he slept. This was actually comforting. If he was making his gurgling noises I could sleep. If the gurgling stopped, I would wake up. Even though we slept with a nightlight on I would still wake up, turn the light on my side of the bed, and look at Kevin to make sure he was still breathing. He was always okay. I'm sure it was me, but I needed to be "safe than sorry". Kennie may have been disturbed by the light, but Kevin never was.

One night at 1:00 a.m. after feeding Kevin putting him to bed, (as you can imagine I was very sleep deprived and got about one or two hours max sleep, at a time around the clock) he was squirming a lot, so I turned on the light just in time to see Kevin take his little index finger and somehow manage to get it under his tube that was taped to his little face, hook it and pull the whole thing out from his stomach. I couldn't believe what I saw. I woke Kennie up and we both were witness to Kevin smiling back at us as if to say "Look what I did." He actually appeared to be proud of himself. In reality I'm sure he had some comfort in that tube being out. I removed the tape and tube from his little face, turned out the light and we all went back to sleep. Kevin, I'm sure, slept the best.

Kennie went to work a few hours later and the time came to feed Kevin. Why didn't I put the tube back in before Kennie left? I went to the bag that my hospital gave us to retrieve a new feeding tube. No NG tubes. The inferior hospital lived up to their reputation. They were supposed to send us home with everything we needed to take care of Kevin. Well this was a big oversight on their part. I then looked in the supply bag that Kevin's hospital sent home with us. Nothing. Lots of oxygen tubes not one feeding tube. I went to the Hospice supplies. Same thing. Panic! There were none. How was I going to feed Kevin? Option: Call the pediatrician's answering service 3:30 a.m. The office was closed. I was told by the doctor on call that I could thoroughly rinse out the tube I had and reinsert the tube for his next feeding. The doctor assured me he would place an order at the pharmacy for the NG tubes in the morning. This reasonable and that's what I did. Rinsing the tube wasn't difficult. I was quite confident about it when I was done. Placing the tube was quite another concern though. I was sleep deprived and now I was in the worst situation I could think of. I was alone, it was after 3:00 a.m., and I had to place an NG tube in my baby's stomach for the first time by myself and hope that I don't insert it into his lungs. I was scared to death, but knowing I couldn't be scared to death I sucked it up. I put my anxieties aside and did what I had to. Kevin was hungry and if he started crying it would add more problems to my situation. I couldn't leave Kevin to get something once I started. I had no one to hand me anything if I missed getting it ahead of time so I thoroughly prepared before I began. I put Kevin on our king-sized bed so that he would be comfortable. I started by preparing the tape to apply to his face at the end and inserted the tube into Kevin's open cleft palate/mouth area. As I put the tube farther down his esophagus, I had serious insecurities if I was getting it right. Kevin's tongue was moving back and forth in his mouth as I put in the tube. He seemed to be pacifying on the tube I was inserting, but his breathing was fine. This reassured me I was not in his lungs. I got to the spot pre-marked on the tube by the nurses on where to stop. This tube was supposed to last for up to two weeks. This is where the nurse I liked said I should tape it to his face. Well it was in. I was given a yellow plastic disposable stethoscope from Kevin's hospital to use at home. I placed it on Kevin's abdomen and pushed a small amount of air from a syringe into the tube and waited for the pop sound which would indicate that the tube was in Kevin's stomach and not his lungs. "POP!" Success. I released the deep breath I was holding. I started to cry and quickly dismissed it. I just told myself to recheck the pop noise to confirm and feed the baby. Kevin's hungry. This was too clinical and was not the way I should have been feeding and caring for my baby. I placed a tiny bit of formula into the gavage and slowly started feeding Kevin. It went in with no problem. I did it all correctly and Kevin seemed happy. As I continued to feed Kevin I told him, "As cute as you were after you pulled the tube out you are never allowed to remove it again." I found myself talking to him a lot. Singing was something that never stopped either. I always had music playing. TV was a luxury. I couldn't allow myself to get involved in a show because it would take my eyes off of watching Kevin.

When I got a chance to talk to Kennie and tell him what happened he was very supportive and proud of what I had accomplished. I hung up the phone and called the pharmacy to see when I could pick up the NG tube prescription. The pharmacy told me they wouldn't fill the prescription because they would have to order 300 preemie-sized NG tubes at three dollars a tube and Kevin's prescription was only for eight. That would leave the pharmacy with a surplus of 292 to store and more than likely would have to throw away them away. The pharmacy was refusing to order them. I called the pediatrician's office and complained. The nurse said she would call the pharmacy and work something out. Time went by with no return phone call from the doctor's office or the pharmacy. Kennie came home, we talked and it occurred to us that there was potentially bigger problem. What if there was a kink or a block in the line? I couldn't reinsert a blocked tube. Kevin wouldn't be able to eat and would start crying for his formula. We didn't think Kevin could do what he did and pull the tube out. What if he did it again tonight? Panic started to bubble. I called the hospital Kevin was discharged from last. I explained the situation and asked if I could come down and pick up a baby NG tube until we could get some ordered. They said no. They explained that Kevin was discharged from the hospital, was no longer covered by the insurance and therefore they would not be reimbursed for the cost of the NG tube. They were the ones who caused this problem by failing to give us one when we left. I know that hate is a strong word, but I really hated them. I knew that yelling at them was not going to help. I had a problem that needed to be solved and I needed all of my energy to solve it. I hung up and made my next phone call. This time to Hospice. Kennie reminded me the nurse was coming to the house tomorrow. Unfortunately, she was in the same boat. She didn't have any preemie-sized NG tubes. All of her patients were adults and the tubes she had were far too big for Kevin. The diameter was thicker and the length was far too long. She said she would bring one anyway and maybe we could improvise by cutting it down to size.

The nurse from the pediatrician's office finally called. She said, "The doctor had worked out a deal with the pharmacy, but the order would take about two weeks to get it from the manufacturer." The pharmacy would fill the prescription and I could go down and pick it up. I know that this is someone just trying to help, but this just wouldn't do. I need a backup NG tube now.

My reply was, "This is not an option. My baby can't go without food for two weeks." We decided to let the order go through and continue to try to get a backup NG tube. In my last ditch effort, I called Kevin's hospital. All the other avenues we tried failed. I asked to talk to my favorite nurse and then held the line. I didn't care if it took hours I would hold. Finally, a familiar voice. I explained my problem in detail.

She put me on hold for a moment then came back on the line with "I have two for you and I'll have them waiting downstairs at the security deck."

I almost went into a full-blown cry. I could hardly speak to thank her before I hung up the phone. The whole thing had finally caught up to me and my emotions took over. Kennie left for the hospital and returned after an hour and a half with the most hard-to-get preemie-sized NG tubes. We were incredibly thankful to have them. The Hospice nurse showed up with the adult NG tubes the next day and we said thank you, but no thank you. They wouldn't have worked anyway they were too big. Two weeks almost to the day we got the prescription for Kevin's eight NG tubes. They were much different than the ones the hospital gave us. They were solid white and you couldn't watch the formula go through the tube or see the line flush at the end. No markings/measurements on the tube to indicate how far the tube was in which made it difficult to know where to stop inserting the tube. I measured the old NG tube before we threw it away and marked the same length measurement on the new NG tube. Problem solved. Kevin was starting to use his NG tube in his mouth in place of a pacifier on a regular basis. Where there's a will there's a way.

We didn't take Kevin out much. His resistance to illnesses was to low and he didn't need to be exposed to even the common cold, as with all newborns. The reactions from people were mixed when we did take him out. Most were caring, but their initial reactions were disturbing to me. That's when I decided I didn't like the word "retard" and never allowed it into my vocabulary again. It made me start to wonder how Kevin was going to do in life, but that was not something for me to worry about right now.

Over the next few weeks we had all kinds of doctor appointments. We saw the Pediatrician to check on Kevin's growth. The Hospice nurse was telling me everything I needed to know like weight, height, vitals, but Kevin was still required to have a checkup. Even though he was gaining weight he was still at preemie-size. The office girls at the pediatricians were amazed that I could place an NG tube. They had all confessed to me that they couldn't do it. They even paid me a compliment and said I must have missed my calling as a nurse. I became somewhat proud of that compliment.

I recalled a thought I had when I started to learn how to care for Kevin and shared it with them, "You chose this profession as a nurse. You went through the education and had years of training. I was thrown into this profession. I don't really mind though. This is my son and I will do whatever it takes."

We were starting to see a specialist (doctor number 11) to assess Kevin's future surgeries like closing his cleft lip and palate, and how to start the process of fixing his clubfeet.

Starting him on a bottle and the therapy he needed for it was something else we discussed. All of it was going to take a great deal of work, money and patience as Kevin grew. The dedication Kennie and I had would see this through and we would hold Kevin's tiny little hand all the way. I was sent to a gastrointestinal doctor with Kevin. I wasn't sure why. He was having regular bowel movements. This doctor did his exam and gave me a small tube to insert into Kevin's rectum. Small to you and me, but not to Kevin. The doctor demonstrated how to use it. The intention was to stretch the rectum opening for easier bowel movements. I didn't like the idea of this, especially since I didn't agree that it was necessary. I tried it once when I got home, Kevin cried and I stopped using it. I felt so bad for putting him through that. I figured I had the tube if Kevin developed any future problems and I could attempt to use it again. Plus, it reminded me of the doctor that performed the rectal examination without my permission.

    We had a growing support group. Friends and family visited often but they didn't stay long. Some brought food to freeze for when we couldn't cook. Ruth bought a soft car seat reducer to be placed in the car seat to cradle a preemie-sized baby. Even though it reduced the area it was something Kevin had to grow into. She bought preemie clothes for Kevin. The clothes at the second-hand store were hard to find and the department stores wanted $25 an outfit. Needless to say, he had only a few outfits. Most of our visitors understood that taking care of Kevin, meant he was never left alone and I was unable to do normal things like cook and clean the way I wanted to without Kennie home. The nurse from Hospice somehow arranged a person to come out for an hour at a time to help me with cleaning or whatever I needed. They were not medically trained, just company for the most part. There was no guarantee that they would be back either. Just a sporadic scheduling of their time. She told me that I should be getting "res-care", which was home health care, for a few hours a month so that I could get out once in a while or just catch up on my sleep. She applied for it for me and said it might take a few days, but assured me that I qualified for it. She submitted the request and checked on it often knowing I was really in need of it. Well like everything else we found out it was going to take some time to get in play.

Kevin's hair was starting to grow just enough to notice. It was jet black and wavy and was beginning to curl around his ears. When I gave him a bath, I was very careful not to get his face wet. I would wash his face with a soft baby washcloth. Oh, he loved his baths. I would support his head and he would stretch out his little body, wiggle his toes and sometimes his fingers. He even made little cooing sounds. He would look up at me and smile. Well a Kevin smile. He didn't have an upper lip, but his cheeks would do the work of smiling and his eyes finished it with a twinkle. One time he was lying on the receiving blanket on the floor with Kennie after he was fed and he rolled over. This seemed impossible given his age. Normal babies at this age can't do this. We put him back on the blanket and it wasn't long before he was off of it again. Somehow, he managed scoot and/or roll on his own. Be it an accident or intentional he could move about two feet all by himself. I didn't have any explanation for how he managed it. Kennie, Ruth, and I watched it happen often.

The lack of sleep was starting to show on me. The typical dark circles under the eyes from lack of sleep were the most obvious. Kennie was helping with the feedings and this helped a lot. Everyone else was understandably still intimidated by Kevin's small size and physical problems. This was obvious with a visit to my mom and dad's house. In a lot of ways, we needed this outing - it brought normalcy back into our lives. I always rode in the backseat with Kevin just to make sure he was okay. Kevin did great. We had a limited amount of time due to Kevin's needs. We visited with aunts, uncles, grandparents. Mom and one uncle were the only ones who held him besides us, but it was still comforting to know we could make trips with Kevin to other homes with little to no problems. The next trip out for fun was to Kennie's grandma's house. She had never seen Kevin. She, like others, didn't want to hold him but she wanted to see for herself how he was doing. Trip worth doing.

The beginning of September our insurance company finally decided to kick in and start paying for Kevin's home health care needs. It took several phone calls from Hospice and myself to get the insurance to pay. They were late, but finally doing what we paid them to do. Kevin was almost six weeks old. It was about time. Hospice was going to have to deliver a new oxygen tank if they didn't. The only one I had was pretty much empty, but Kevin wasn't in need of it much. At first, we used it often, then a couple times a day and now from time to time. It was still a necessity to have on hand.

Late one day, well after five, the doorbell rang. Kennie got up to answer it. It was the delivery of the new oxygen tank from the insurance company I had spoken to earlier that morning. There was young lady at the door who was struggling to hold an oxygen tank, a clipboard and a bag of supplies. He quickly showed her into the house to where I was sitting with Kevin in my arms.

After the initial "hellos", I said, "I wasn't expecting you today. I was told that the tank wouldn't get here until tomorrow because the delivery trucks and vans were all gone for the day."

The young lady said that she lived close to us and volunteered to drop it off on her way home. That helped explain the way she was casually dressed, no uniform or badge. When she appeared to be done and was saying her closing statements, which I'm sure was protocol, I asked her when would the rest of the equipment – the suctioning machine, oxygen tubing, NG tubes –arrive?

She told me that she didn't know anything about the other stuff, just the oxygen, and I would have to call the office tomorrow. We thanked her for making a special trip, said goodbye and we walked her out. As we watched her drive away, Kennie and I both thought it was strange that she wasn't in a company service vehicle but instead a personal old beat-up pickup that blew back smoke out of the tailpipe. We know she was on her way home, but we thought it should be a standard procedure for medical equipment to be delivered in a company vehicle for professionalism alone. Besides what harm would it be to let an employee, who volunteered to make a delivery on her way home use a company vehicle overnight? When we got back into the house, we traded oxygen tanks, comforted that we had a full tank once again. We put the new tank next to the recliner as we always did and put the empty tank next to the front door to return to Hospice on Wednesday when the nurse would come for her regular check on Kevin. She tried to come twice a week; however, this week she could only make it on Wednesday which was two days away.

Kevin was growing and interacting more. I was getting to the point where I could set him down and, as long as I was in the same room with him, he did fine. He liked to sit in his car seat cradle (the part you take out of the car and carry). He could sit up in it and see and hear everything that was going on. Music was still his favorite thing. Certain songs you could tell he recognized. Feedings were something that was no longer a concern. He was getting higher calorie formula and more of it at the doctor's advice. A wet burp was something Kevin could handle on his own. We still watched him for an hour after eating just in case, but there wasn't ever an issue. Housework was something I started to resume little by little. Laundry was not falling behind anymore; it was something that I could do with Kevin next to me. When Kevin would nap, I would nap next to him on the floor. I could hear him the minute he woke up. I figured any sleep I could get would make it easier on me in the long run. Easy was an understatement. Even though we had developed a routine it was still a lot of work, but I got used to it. It was my normal.

I was looking forward to Wednesday and the Hospice nurse's visit. She was starting to become like family. She was always pleasant. She did the routine things first: Kevin's vitals were taken and he weighed in at 5 lbs. 2 oz. I reminded her that he turned six weeks yesterday. It was a milestone. A 5 lbs. 2 oz milestone. I couldn't wait to tell Kennie how much Kevin gained considering his weight loss after birth. I informed her of the insurance company finally paying for and delivering the new oxygen tank. I thought she could take the one she was generous enough to supply us with when she left, but the company who delivered it was going to have to come by and get it. She said she would call and arrange it. I told her I didn't want to give up the suctioning equipment yet even though we never had to use it. The insurance company was supposed to deliver one on Friday. We hadn't even used the new oxygen tank yet, there wasn't a need to.

    The nurse gave me a vote of confidence by saying, "Kevin is growing, getting bigger and won't even need it one day."

This brought a smile to my face as I looked at Kevin. About the time she was getting ready to leave Kennie came home. This was the first time in a while that their paths crossed. We told him of Kevin's weight gain.

He picked Kevin up and said, "My boy's becoming a little heifer."

She gave us all hugs, told us to keep up the good work and that Kevin looked great as she said goodbye.

Kennie and I fixed dinner while we talked about next week's doctor appointments. Family planned to drop by next week; we needed to make a grocery list and Kennie needed to go shopping for it. My work had called. My boss was informing me that my six weeks was up and wanted me back to work on Monday. I told her what happened. She seemed to already know, but didn't care. I told her I would have to get back with her on Friday. I honestly didn't even think about my work this whole time. It was the furthest thing from my mind. Our finances were doing okay and I had more important things, like my son's life, to concern myself with. Kennie told me not to worry about it suggesting that maybe we could get some kind of help to take care of Kevin and I could go back to work part time if needed. Maybe there is some kind of financial aid out there so I didn't have to go back to work right now. We had five days to figure it out.

The next morning was wonderful. The sun was shining and it was somewhat cool. I opened the windows to let in the fresh air. We had an old consul TV in our room. I turned it on to watch the news while I fed Kevin. I had laundry to do, but after I fed Kevin he was so relaxed, I stretched out on the bed and put Kevin belly down on my chest. We were there for some time when I remembered my boss's concerns. I needed to find out what options I had.

The person who would come in and watch Kevin could really only be a trained nurse. This I knew. Part time? Maybe but only after Kennie got off work. More than likely that wouldn't work. I needed to start making phone calls and start laundry. I looked down at my precious little angel fast asleep on me. He was so peaceful and I loved moments like this, but I needed to get things done while Kevin was sleeping. I picked up his little sleepy limp body and started laundry. I moved everything as usual to the family room; diapers, feeding stuff, and the oxygen tank. I made several phone calls. I was left on hold a lot. I left a lot of messages. I even called Hospice and Kevin's social worker at his hospital. They both offered up "res-care" said that it was in the works and should happen any day. They told me that I could get a few hours a week or a month. I could split it up any way I wanted. This was not enough to trade for going back to work. I didn't think it was intended for babysitting either, only for my personal down time. My gut feeling was that I needed to be with Kevin.

Kevin was starting to wake up. I had been on the phone for hours. It was time for Kevin to eat again. I got the car seat carrier, sat it on the floor and sat Kevin in it. He looked cute. I prepped the formula, filled the gavage and started feeding him slowly, we were in no hurry. There was nothing on the agenda except Kevin today. When he finished eating, I just sat with him on the floor, as usual, with music playing. Kevin started to clamp down almost like holding his breath. I knew instantly that there was something wrong and he needed oxygen. This was something he used to do, but hadn't done in a while. I picked Kevin up and carried him to the recliner. The oxygen tank was the same as the other one we had used for this kind of need. I went to turn it on and a part sprung off into my hand. I was aware there was a limited amount of time to get oxygen into Kevin. I tried to put the knob back on the tank. It wouldn't go. I knew I was in trouble when I looked down at Kevin and he was as blue/purple as an eggplant. SHOCK! Are you kidding me? This is a new tank, never used. I got a grip on myself, jumped up with Kevin and ran to the phone about five feet away. I dialed "911". I placed Kevin on the counter, pulled his NG tube out and started cardiopulmonary resuscitation (CPR).

The operator answered, "911 what is your emergency?"
"My son can't breathe! He's turning blue!"
She started giving me instructions on how to perform CPR. I was already doing CPR, but to make sure I was doing it right, considering the intense moment, I let her continue.

When she got to the part of pinching his nose I started to tear up and said, "He doesn't have a nose." I tried to explain Kevin's condition, but she seemed to be confused. She informed me an ambulance was on its way and to continue with the little breaths from the CPR procedure that I was doing.

Kevin was starting to turn to his normal color when there was a knock - more like a bang - at the door. I remembered the door was locked. I had no choice but to leave Kevin on the counter run to the door and let them in. It wasn't an ambulance it was a police officer. I was thankful to see him and starting to tear up as I ran back to Kevin. The police officer followed. He realized that Kevin wasn't breathing. He scooped Kevin's little body up with no hesitation and started his own CPR as he down sat on the couch. His two-way radio was going off, but he never stopped helping Kevin. In the distance I heard the sirens from the ambulance. We had left the front door open when the police officer arrived. The EMTs made their way into the entry. The officer still helping Kevin got up and met them half way. He handed Kevin to the EMTs and they took over making their way out the door. Outside the front door was a gurney being wheeled by two firemen towards them. Kevin was too small for such a large gurney. They quickly realized that when they saw their coworker carrying Kevin and still performing CPR on him. They quickly put the gurney back into the ambulance, handed Kevin to an EMT already in the ambulance, then they all crawled in and closed the door. The sirens were turned on and they pulled away. I then noticed how many emergency vehicles had responded to my baby's need. There was of course the police cruiser, an ambulance, two firetrucks, a fire chief pickup, two more police cruisers, and all my neighbors that were home were outside watching. A fireman came up to me as I was standing on the driveway in disbelief and said I needed to change out of my night clothes and get dressed. He offered to help me lock up my house and told me I needed to meet them at the hospital.

I asked, "What hospital?"

He said the closest one, which was a new hospital to Kevin.

People standing in their driveways watching made me insecure and I looked down to realize I was in a short, baby doll, tank top night gown. Following the Fireman's suggestion, I went inside and started to lock the doors and windows I had opened. He said that he would continue closing them and I could get dressed. I was having such a good day with Kevin. I would have never expected that this would happen. I wanted my moment back when Kevin and I were relaxing on my bed. I went to my bedroom and I couldn't get my brain to work. I put on a bra and for some reason I put my short nightgown back on. I grabbed a pair of shorts and slid them on. The fireman knocked on the bedroom door and came into the room. I realized I was running out of time when he asked me if I wanted to drive myself or let the police officer drive me over. He probably assessed my inability to match my outfit, recognizing that I was still wearing my nightgown as a top and offered up the officer as a chauffeur. Clearly I was not myself or capable of making rational decisions. Knowing it was the best idea I agreed to let the police officers drive me to the hospital. While I was trying to slide my feet into my flip flops the fireman told me the house was all locked up and then he left. A house that was full of emergency people was now vacant, except for my chauffeur.

    I grabbed my sweater, purse and keys to lock the door on my way out. The police officer was apologizing for his cruiser being a mess. The front seat was full of files and other official business stuff. He asked if I didn't mind riding in the back seat? Heck, the back seat was where Kevin and I had been riding for the past six weeks. I was so thankful for him waiting for me and of course giving me a ride to the hospital, I didn't care where I sat. When he opened the door for me, I took a look in, it looked like a cage. The seat looked like it had been mauled, like a wild animal had been back there. Oh, don't get me wrong I was thankful for my ride, even if I was sitting in the backseat like a criminal.

    When we arrived at the hospital emergency room, I had to wait for the police officer to open my door and let me out.

    When he did my thank you was short and I ran into the ER where I was greeted by a lady who said, "You must be Kevin's mother, Carol?"

    She took me back to where Kevin was so I could see him. Kevin's 15-inch body was on what looked like a ten-foot bed. They were still performing CPR on him only somewhere along the line they switched to a little squeezable bottle that worked as a hand pump for air. Seeing my somewhat stunned look the lady informed me that she was the one I was talking to on the "911" call. She was the one who gave me instructions for CPR.

She complimented me by saying, "You did very well at keeping calm. Some people can't and you followed me until the officer took over. Even after that I'm told you never lost it." She asked if there was anyone that I wanted her to call.

I said, "Kennie, my husband. My mom and dad, and my in-laws. Please." I gave her their numbers.

She informed me that I couldn't go in to where Kevin was until the doctors said it was okay. She brought me a chair placed it just outside of Kevin's door. Every now and then I stood up to watch Kevin in the room. They were trying to intubate him. Oh no. We just weaned him off of life support. For some reason I thought "we can do it again," hitting my leg as I sat down. The nurse I talked to earlier came over to tell me my husband was on his way.

She said, "Your dad is in jury duty and the judge will be dismissing him. Your mom is at work and is heading home to meet your dad. Haven't got ahold of your in-laws yet, but I did leave a message."

I was there by myself outside Kevin's door for such a long time. The first person to walk through the door down the long hall was the last person I thought would get there. It was Kennie. He had the longest drive and what should have taken over 50 minutes he did in 20 minutes. Someone was watching over him because I'm guessing that his mind was probably like mine, focused on Kevin. Kennie asked what happened and where was Kevin? I briefly told him and pointed into the room as my voice left me and my face exploded with tears. He then looked into where I was pointing and saw Kevin. The medical team had successfully intubated Kevin. The ventilator was back. Kennie told me he was just heading out for a delivery and his boss ran out and stopped him in the driveway. He backed the truck up to the dock in one shot, jumped out of the big-rig and into his pickup truck. Five more minutes and I would have missed him.

    My folks were the next to arrive, but much later than Kennie. Dad said he was in jury duty, in the jury box when the judge stopped the procedure and called him by name to come up to the bench. The judge then explained that he was excused for a family emergency. Dad immediately left and went home.

    Kennie informed me that his mom and dad were camping in their motor home and he would try to somehow get ahold of them. After sitting in the hall next to Kevin's room for hours, the nurse came out to talk to me. I introduced her to Kennie, mom and dad. She said a transport ambulance was on its way to take Kevin to the local level three NICU. It was not the NICU I was familiar with. I asked if Kevin could return to where we knew everyone, even if it was farther away. She checked it out and came back with a "Yes." It wasn't much longer and we were on our way back to Kevin's hospital. The good one.

    Riding with Kennie back to the hospital gave me time to fill him in on the details of the day and collect my thoughts. Of course, I was crying all the way through the details. There was so much that happened and it seemed like it started so early in the morning. When we arrived at the NICU it was still daylight. After suiting up to go into the NICU, I was greeted by my favorite nurse with a hug. She said that she was sorry this happened. She led me to Kevin's incubator. They had to shave half of his beautiful black hair to place an IV. I had a hard time with it and the nurse apologized and explained why. I didn't hear the explanation because that's when I noticed that

Kevin was crying without making a sound. His face was screaming. My instinct was to reach in and grab him, but looking at all of the equipment I stopped short and thought I might hurt him.

I put my face and chest next to his little body as if I was holding him tight. It seemed to help, his crying was not as hard. I'm sure he was in pain and this time he and I knew the difference (having been at home and not poked every day). How did we get here? I wanted again to go back to the moment when we were on the bed and Kevin was sleeping soundly on top of me. I want that moment back! I couldn't get it back and I knew it. Things were not looking good. It was not like last time. We were told that a meeting with the doctors was being arranged for us to discuss Kevin's current condition.

The nurse waited for everyone to leave and asked me what happened. I told her everything from the time we went back to my inferior hospital, Hospice, how well Kevin was doing, that he weighed in at five pounds two ounces, his doctor visits for reconstruction of his cleft lip and cleft palate, how the oxygen equipment fell apart in my hands and the "911" phone call was made. Her face showed a surprised look when I said the oxygen equipment fell apart in my hands. Apparently, that was missed in the medical notes of the day's events. She and the hospital knew nothing about it. When I finished telling her everything, there was someone at Kevin's bedside announcing that the doctors were waiting for Kennie and me. The nurse asked her coworker and the charge nurse if they could take care of Kevin for her. She explained that it was important that she accompany Kennie and me to the meeting. God knows I didn't want to leave Kevin's side, but once again I wasn't given a choice.

This was a different room. A much bigger room, bigger table, more doctors and I think every intern that was available to join us was there. Once again there wasn't an empty seat after Kennie and I were seated at the end of the table. To the left of us was our favorite nurse, continuing clockwise familiar doctors, number nine and ten (the pediatric neurologist and genetic doctor), then the unfamiliar interns, some nurses who cared for Kevin at one point, then an intern/doctor, given her white jacket. She was very young; her ponytail gave her age away. She was directly to my right. I didn't think it was by chance. The conversation opened with a description of Kevin's condition from doctor #9. He was sincere, but I didn't feel good about his tone of voice. We were informed that Kevin had been having seizures, one every four minutes, since he arrived. The doctors were doing their best to stop them he said, but so far unsuccessful. Doctor #10 was quiet for the most part. An intern sitting at the other end of the table foolishly spoke up.

    Having only read some and not all of Kevin's file he said, "You knew Kevin was going to die. He was a trisomy 13 baby and that's not compatible with life."

    Something inside of me sparked and the nurse next to us saw it. I quickly moved my butt to the edge of my seat, made eye contact with the foolishly outspoken intern and firmly said, "Kevin was not a trisomy 13 baby and if you could read, you would have read that the lab results came back proving it!"

    Doctor #9, trying to defend his intern and knowing he just screwed up said, "Well Kevin's condition was very guarded."

    What does that mean? I thought.

    The nurse I liked spoke up before anyone else in the room could say something stupid to me. She informed the room of what happened to Kevin this morning. She explained that it was not Kevin's condition that caused this outcome. That it was in fact the oxygen tank that malfunctioned and Kevin was unable to get the necessary oxygen he needed. She was trying to save the room from further embarrassment. She added that this could have all been prevented if the oxygen machine would have functioned properly.

Not everyone pays attention to the warning signs, because the ponytail intern to the right of me adjusted her chair towards me and said the one thing that I had enough of, "Kevin's condition is not going to get any better and you need to take him off life support. You need to remove him from the ventilator."

I took a deep breath, sat for a moment, and assessed the situation. While everyone was staring at me trying to regroup, including the ponytail intern. Kennie started to say a few things in our defense and was drowned out by the voices coming from the interns. He kinda figured if I couldn't speak up to make a point, he would step in to help. Unfortunately, I had to agree with the ponytail intern. I still had hope and faith that Kevin could pull out of this, but the facts were the facts. What she and the rest of the room didn't know was I had only one card to play right now. I looked the ponytail intern straight in the eye, my eyes swollen from crying off and on all day, tired from everything I had been through in the last six weeks, let alone the days event, and with a calm voice I said, "Do you have any idea what you're asking me to do?" I got one of those condescending shaking of the head, no. I continued with, "I've been trying for over five years to have a baby. I've lost four babies in miscarriage, I finally brought one to full term and now after everything I've been though, you're telling me to take my only living baby off of life-support."

Still looking her straight in the eyes I finally got a human reaction. She had a sudden shift from the task I believed she was sent by her superiors to do, to seeing me as a person. As she pulled her eyes away from me, she glanced around the room. No one made eye contact with her. She looked back at me and said she was sorry, then looked straight across the table, put her head on the table and cried for Kevin's and my situation. No one said a word but undoubtedly they all heard what I said. I then turned to the nurse and asked her to hand me the trashcan on the other side of her, so I could throw up. She handed me the trashcan and I puked. What a way to clear a room. Needless to say, that ended the meeting. I had been though a lot and the fact that I held my composure that long surprised me.

What was left of the night was spent with Kevin. He seemed to be getting tired. His crying was taking a lot out of him and his little body. I was hoping that I didn't have to leave him but when I asked about the little room for the night, I was told it was in use and unavailable. We waited until we just couldn't stay anymore. We knew we had some tough decisions to make soon and needed our rest. Our nurse encouraged us to go home and get some rest. She assured us that if there was even the slightest change in Kevin, she would call us. She was someone I trusted and believed her word was good. What a car ride home. Crying, anger and sadness. I think every emotion you could come up with went through me with a passion. I was exhausted, but somehow, I still had surges of energy followed by complete lack of strength. I had never felt like this.

When we got home, we found that Kennie's boss had called and left a message telling Kennie to go on his 2:00 a.m. run and pick up a load and bring it back to the warehouse. He guaranteed that Kennie would be home by 7:00 a.m. He had no idea the sacrifice Kennie made that night by calling him back and assuring him it would get done. I really needed him with me, but he also needed his job. I crawled into bed, somehow managed to close my eyes, tossed and turned as the memories of the day continued to play in in my mind. What could I have done differently? I know the facts say I did everything in my power right, but the doubt was still there. I realized that no matter how Kevin's life turns out I would always hold myself responsible.

Friday morning started the moment Kennie went to work. Still on Kevin's schedule of feedings every three hours, I watched the clock tick away. I guess that from time to time my brain shut off, but not much. The reality was our world was crashing all around us and I had a front row seat. Kennie was home as promised and off to the hospital we went. We were greeted by a nurse. She informed us that Kevin's seizures were never able to be controlled, something about the lack of oxygen at some point and he had been having the seizures one every four minutes around the clock. She said the test indicated that there was very little brain activity and Kevin was almost brain dead. She informed us that they planned to repeat the test later and that the doctor (#9) would be in to talk to us. I leaned in close to Kevin immediately. I put my upper body over him and my face up to his, there wasn't much response from him. I think he knew I was there. Maybe my touch, my voice or my smell. He had a Kevin smell, maybe I had a mommy smell. I finally sat down and held Kevin's little hand, talking and singing to him. Family was starting to arrive around lunch. The technician arrived to perform the test again. We were asked to go to lunch so the technician could do his job. Lunch was somber. People were talking but nothing was really being said, they were ignoring the elephant in the room.

Unlike the night with trying to sleep and the clock ticking so slow, the morning and day was going by quickly. Before we knew it, it was 5:00 p.m. and the doctor was standing with us at Kevin's bedside with an expressionless face. He gave us a speech about how I did everything I could yesterday, that what happened to Kevin was not in any way my fault, but that Kevin is now brain dead. There was no activity at all on the scan and at this time the only thing keeping Kevin alive was the ventilator. He would never be able to come off the ventilator and breathe on his own again. Of course, we questioned this over and over. Nope, can't make this decision tonight. Maybe tomorrow. I'm sure based on the doctor's show of emotion after he did his job, it must have been difficult to tell us and be professional about it. My heart went out to him too.

I looked at Kennie. His face was full of tears and he was fighting it. I stood up and just hugged him. Holding on to him was what was keeping me going all this time. He seemed to be so much stronger than I was, but right now he was on equal ground. I think I was holding him up as much as he was holding me up.

The doctor said, "You take all the time you need to think about it and let us know." He gave us his condolences and left us.

The room had the familiar family support, with tears. All the grandparents were there tearing up the same as we were. They had a double hit. They were losing their grandson and had the added worry about us, their kids.

Again, no little room for the night. The same advice given the night before about big decisions was more intense tonight. It was to the point that I was falling asleep holding Kevin's hand and almost falling off the chair when I consented to going home. I had no idea what time it was. I know Kennie had been up well over 24 hours with little to no sleep when we left. Lord only knows how we got home safely. Sleeping was not much of a problem this night even though it should have been. The worst thing in our entire life was going to happen even though we hadn't consented to it yet. I guess there is a point where your body with or without your permission gives in. Lack of sleep, stress, crying eyes, and pure exhaustion kicks in. And you sleep.

    I was lying on the bed as the moonlight came into the room. I tried not to disturb Kennie, he was sleeping so soundly. My eyes were looking directly at the changing table that had morphed into Kevin's medical station. It had Kevin's tiny diapers, tube-bedding, his little powder blue blanket and booties. I started thinking about how Kevin changed our lives for the good and forever. I didn't want to lose Kevin. He had become my world. No matter how hard I tried to hide and keep my tears silent Kennie heard them and woke up. We discussed Kevin and agreed that we would go and spend the day with him. In some ways I guess we were fortunate. He wasn't just all of a sudden gone. We had a chance to let it sink in and accept it. I guess some people would rather have the sudden "gone". Ripped off like a bandage. We weren't given that choice, but to accept what cards were dealt to us. We got to spend one more day with Kevin. Somehow, I felt fortunate.

    Not knowing what we would be like when we came home, we decided to move all of Kevin's things into the nursery that morning. The morphed changing table with all of the un-replaceable Kevin things was the first to be moved back into Kevin's nursery. We next went to the family room, which was where we spent most of the time with Kevin. Of course, it held the most things. Kevin's bedding was on the floor, the car seat where the horrible day started, the oxygen tank that didn't work, the swing he was just starting to use, the big teddy bear he sat up next to, all the unopened formula, bulb syringe and all of the other little things were moved into Kevin's nursery as well. Looking around, we had gotten everything, and it was time to go.

Kennie gave me a hug with uncontrollable tears and said, "Let's go spend some time with Kevin."

The day felt like I was in a cloud of fog. I was going through the motions, but I wasn't really there. It was like Kevin was taking a nap. We had a strong show of family support during the day. Somewhere in my fog Kennie told the nurse of our heart wrenching decision and she told him to just let her know when. I'm sure we were not the first family to spend the day with their baby who was going to no longer be living at the end of the day. It must be difficult for the nurses to watch us, just as difficult as we were walking the steps. We were thankful that they were there to walk with us.

The evening had come. Kevin was lying peacefully and nope, we couldn't do it yet. Maybe I was torturing myself, but I needed more time. We went down to the cafeteria. I couldn't eat. We chose to say goodbye to Kevin when we returned. It was getting late. We made the agonizing walk back. I passed one of my nieces and her mom sitting on the floor waiting for us outside the little family room.

I heard her ask her mom, "Are Uncle Kennie and Aunt Carol going to take Kevin off of the ventilator? Will baby Kevin die?"

Her answer was, "Whatever Uncle Kennie and Aunt Carol choose to do is the right choice."

This was something that, at that moment, helped me cope. I had been asking myself if we were doing the right thing. I think I just got the answer.

The nurse said we didn't have to be there when he was removed from the ventilator. My reaction was, "No. I brought him into this world and I will be there when he leaves." I was scared and shaking as the nurse helped me bathe Kevin. I dressed him in my favorite little preemie clothes. The family that wanted to say their goodbye to Kevin did. Most kissed him goodbye. Kennie was one of the last, you could tell how hard it was just by the length of time he took.

The moment I was dreading was here. I leaned in and kissed his little cheek. I hugged him the best I could and whispered to him, "I love you. Come back to me. I love you Kevin." The whole time I was crying and shaking. Kennie was asked to carry Kevin to me after they removed the tubes and ventilator. I was then led to the little family room where there was an empty couch waiting for Kennie and me. The rest of the chairs were filled with my dad, Ruth and Roger. I was told that my mom was having trouble dealing with it all and was waiting downstairs. I had just sat down on the couch when Kennie came rushing into the room, arms stretched out holding Kevin. The tubes and ventilator were gone. He quickly handed him to me. I think Kennie didn't want to chance that Kevin would take his last breath in his arms. I cradled Kevin like I always did while Kennie sat down close to me on the couch. Kevin's tiny little body was going limp. I knew he was gone, but it wasn't official. I just kept staring at him thinking he would gasp for air. He never did. He went peacefully. The nurse entered the room, knelt down next to me to checked that Kevin's heart had stopped, and noted time of death.

I said, "I think I might be crazy, but his diaper feels full."

She said with a soft voice, that your bowels empty when you die and Kevin's diaper was full. She pointed out how peaceful he looked and then said, "You can stay here as long as you want. No one will disturb you." And she left.

Kennie's arm was around my shoulder. He gave me a tight squeeze and didn't let go. I then made eye contact with my dad who was wiping away tears. He put his hand on my knee to try and comfort me.

In a whisper he said "It just isn't fair. Life isn't fair."

Nothing was being said out loud, the eyes were saying it all. Ruth was sitting across from me, crying. Roger was standing next to her rubbing her back with a face full of tears. Dad got it right. Life wasn't fair! Just not fair! We did everything right. We followed all of the rules and directions. When we knew Kevin had problems we didn't back down. We were very proactive with his care. Why? Why did this happen to all of us? I knew that this was the last time I would hold Kevin and I didn't want to let go. Roger let everyone waiting in the hall know Kevin was gone. Hours went by. Some people went home, understandably. How crazy it must have been from the outside looking in. My baby is dead and I was still holding him. The precious moments came to an end. It was time to let Kevin go. Roger went and informed the nurse. When the nurse came into the room dad and Ruth got up and stepped out into the hall with Roger. The nurse gently and with care took Kevin from my arms and placed him on her shoulder like she was going to burp him or something. She was so caring. Until I saw Kevin's little head flop, and that sight was something that kept haunting me. It wasn't intentional, but my mind wouldn't let me forget it. I watched the nurse carry Kevin through the double doors and then Kevin was truly gone.

    There were tears and hugs with a total show of emotion from everyone. What do we do now? Leave. We made our way to the elevators, to the glass windowed vaulted ceiling lobby, where my mom was waiting and crying. Someone must have informed her about Kevin passing. There was a quick hug from all and we left.

CHAPTER SEVEN: TRYING TO COPE

The son I had waited a lifetime for was gone. I wanted to just sit and cry, which I did. I also knew I needed to go to that dreaded drawer, pull the cemetery paperwork out, and make a phone call. It had only been a day and I felt like my life was over. My daily routine was no longer. It was as if my life stopped. Kennie was there holding my hand and crying with me. How do you go on? How do you go on from something like this? It wasn't like I lost a baseball game. I had a life in my arms and now he's gone. Even though you are filled with grief when you lose your grandparent, mom, dad, or sibling, you can somehow justify an adult dying. At the memorial you have a celebration of life with longtime friends, family, children, and a spouse. You can't justify a baby's life. You can't justify a baby's death. The baby didn't get to live. You grieve for the life you missed out on.

I was a mom for 47 short days. Was I still a mom? Is Kennie still a dad? Did we just lose our identity? If you don't have your baby and there is no one to call you mom, are you still a mom? Our parents have other grandkids so they didn't lose their identity. Nor did the aunts and uncles.

I knew I couldn't leave Kevin's little body at the hospital all by himself. He was in a refrigerated drawer at the hospital and this was playing hard on me. I managed to get up and get the paperwork out of the kitchen. I was reminded of the paperwork about the support group for parents who have lost babies. I gave it another glance - I can't worry about me right now. I picked up the cemetery paperwork and the business cards. The phone call was a disaster. I could hardly speak. The only thing I accomplished was making an appointment for later that day.

Arriving at the cemetery gave me a cold chill. I was reliving the nightmare. We even pulled into the same parking spot. It was another realization of this being a reality. Kevin was dead. I felt like I was just going through the motions and Kennie was leading me by holding my hand. Walking into a conference room with the table and chairs was too familiar as well. The antique smell, as well as the lower temperature in the room, gave me chills. Usually I'm the vocal one, but not this trip. Fortunately, we had already discussed a plan of action and the rest was just putting it into play. Even though the people there were nice, I hated being there.

The first thing to do was to get a car over to the hospital as soon as possible to retrieve Kevin. He was so small they didn't even need a hearse. The second task was to pick a date for his service. Kevin died on a Saturday. Today was Sunday. That left Monday for the service. Service. Who are you going to invite? His best friends? His siblings? His wife and kids? Memory cards about Kevin's life were obsolete and maybe a handful of people would attend. Our moms were going to do the calling for us to inform people of Kevin's passing and his services. My mom and dad opened their house for us to congregate after the service was over. An arrangement of flowers was ordered. Why does a baby need flowers? They are supposed to need toys. Baby's breath in the flower arrangement was a must in my thoughts. Somehow it seemed appropriate. The funeral director said he wouldn't charge us for a closed casket grave site service. Kennie and I wanted a little room for viewing and he threw that in at no cost. It was simple. We needed time to say goodbye.

Ruth and Roger had purchased the plots next to Kennie's grandpa at the cemetery and they made the plot space available for Kevin's final resting place. That took a load off of our list of concerns. This was all so horrible. I literally had to pinch myself, thinking this is not real. But I felt the pinch and reality set in.

I was asked to bring some clothes to bury Kevin in. It was suggested by the funeral director that some people write letters to be buried with the deceased as a way of letting go. They can be sealed. No one needs to read them. Just a way of saying what you need to, one final time. Final. That word stuck with me. It's funny how something so simple and used every day, said at the right moment and the right state of mind sticks with you forever. Final. The end of my son's little life.

The funeral director showed us to the casket room just down the hall. They had all kinds of beautiful caskets and memorabilia you could purchase. Blankets with the loved one's picture on it. Necklaces that you can have the loved one's ashes put into. Kevin was not being cremated so this didn't apply. The caskets were adult size. Kevin was only 15 inches long. Even the smallest of caskets were too big. Gosh, you didn't even need more than one pallbearer to carry it. It was all getting to me and the director picked up on it and started to help us make decisions. A small but soft looking casket was picked out and we were done.

The funeral director was absorbing some of the cost. We never did see a final bill. Kennie and I understood that our parents split the remainder of the bill and we were very thankful. At a time when we spent all of our money preparing for our new born, we didn't have anything left for paying for a funeral and our folks knew it. I wasn't working and Kennie was our only income. We didn't know when we could pay them back. We promised to pay them back when we could but they all said no. All they wanted was to make it easier on us. Thank you was all they would accept.

We went home with tasks. This turned out to be a good thing. Something to do to keep our minds focused. Kennie called his work regarding Monday. Clearly, he was not going to be there. I picked out something for Kevin to wear. That was the easy part. There wasn't much to choose from. There was only one outfit that fit him well and it was my favorite: a powder blue button up sleeper with a yellow half-moon on the upper left chest with a black and white dog cradled in the half moon. It occurred to Kennie and me that we didn't know what we would wear. Kennie was easy – he had a whole closet to choose from. Me – I was a problem. I had ballooned in size considering the toxemia and diabetes. I had no idea what size I was. I had nothing appropriate to wear.

We drove back to the cemetery and dropped off Kevin's outfit and Kennie took me to the mall. Oh, this is NOT where I wanted to go. Really? My eyes were full of tears, my face was swollen. I was out in public trying to find something to wear to my baby's funeral and trying not to be noticed.

I was dreading the possibility that a sales person would ask me, "Are you looking for something for a special occasion?" It was difficult to look for clothes and avoid people at the same time. I found a dark blue, two-piece outfit, reasonably priced and we went home. It will have to do. Someone must have been watching over me because usually when you need to find something specific to wear, you can't find anything and you're there all day.

When we got home, we only had one more thing to do; write the letters. I sat down on the recliner and Kennie was on the couch. We both had stationery and envelopes. I was crying all the way through the writing of my letter. I finished my letter and looked over at Kennie. He had a harder time with the task. He was crying pretty hard, more than I was. This turned out to be a good release. Even though the funeral director said no one else needs to read the letters we shared ours with each other and then sealed them. I gathered up a few things I wanted to bury with Kevin. Of course, the letters, a picture of Kennie and me, and the little stuffed dog Grandma Donna gave him in the hospital at birth. I didn't want Kevin to be all alone. Somehow the little stuffed dog made me feel better about him not being alone.

It was late when we finally went to bed. I leaned over to turn out the light over the nightstand and noticed that Kevin's little blue knitted blanket given to him in the hospital was on the floor. I picked it up and crawled into bed with it. I turned out the light and of course I didn't sleep. I was mostly tossing, turning and continually waking up looking for Kevin. I was clutching the little blue blanket and remembering the reality of it all, crying and trying to fall back to sleep. I was still on Kevin's schedule, waking every two to three hours.

The next morning felt like everything moved in slow motion. I was moving and things were getting done, but it was as if I was not really functioning. Next thing I knew we were at the cemetery. The director met us at the reception desk and escorted us back to the viewing room. The hall seemed narrower and even colder. When we walked into the room it was mostly shades of beige and had long drapes from ceiling to floor. There were two couches and a couple of high back chairs. At the other end of the room was the flower arrangement, the small coffin we picked out and in the coffin was Kevin. I hadn't seen him since he died in my arms and was carried away through the double doors. I walked over to him with Kennie right behind me. Kevin was lying face up with his little blue jumpsuit on.

I leaned in over him and told him, "I love you" and kissed his little forehead. My lip instantly felt the unexpected cold. A reminder that Kevin was kept in the vault, which was really a freezer. Attempting to fight the tears, which were coming like a freight train, I reached into the bag that Kennie was carrying and pulled out the letters, our picture, and his little stuffed dog. I placed them into the coffin with Kevin. This somehow really did help with the mental part of dealing with this. Maybe it was the sheer fact that it gave me something to do. Family and friends started arriving. The first to arrive were the grandparents, then Kennie's brother, sisters, and families. One of my nephews brought Kevin a teddy bear from his own collection and placed it into the foot of the coffin with Kevin. I hugged him and told him that it was a very thoughtful gift. It seemed to fill the other half of the coffin. My sisters arrived. My sisters chose not to bring their children. They thought it would be too much for them. Some of Ruth's close friends came. One friend brought Kevin and me matching guardian angel pins to wear. She pinned one on Kevin and gave Kevin a kiss. The other angel she pinned on me and she gave me a hug. A very thoughtful gift. Amazingly the couches and the chairs filled up quickly. I saw the funeral attendant bringing more chairs into the room for us. The thought crossed my mind that this was a weekday and just before lunch. People took the time off work to say goodbye to baby Kevin. A baby that only lived six weeks, but touched everyone who knew about him. My original thought was we didn't need all this room, who's going to say goodbye to a baby? Somehow, we filled every seat.

Everyone said their goodbyes to Kevin and hugged Kennie and me. Some had never seen him before today, but they knew Kevin's story. We sat in the little room for a long time talking. For some reason my tears had stopped. It was as if I had become a host trying to make people comfortable with the awkward situation. My sister-in-law's mother came up to me and gave me a hug. This was an important hug. She had lost her husband a few months earlier and I didn't know what to say to her then but now I did.

I hugged her back and told her, "I didn't know what to say to you when Bob died and now I do. I'm so sorry for your loss." I now knew first-hand what I was saying and how sincerely I was saying it. Even though we were told that we could use the room as long as we wanted, the time had come to move the service to the gravesite. I was told there were chairs waiting for Kennie and me at the gravesite. The cemetery plot was a short walk from the hall. It was right at the curb. I was informed that the pallbearers would carry Kevin to the site. It was a small coffin and very light weight.

Kennie and I gave Kevin one last kiss goodbye and walked out of the hall and down to the site. I was informed that Roger, Kennie's dad, closed the coffin and locked it. Everything started to fog up for me. I think the grandfathers carried Kevin to the site, but I'm not sure. I'm not even sure how I got to my chair. The pastor started speaking and my eyes were filled with tears again. I'm sure he spoke beautifully. Then it was over. I watched as the little coffin, with Kevin in it, was lowered into the ground. I was asked not to watch as the grave workers finished. Something about the sounds of the dirt hitting the casket was a memory I didn't need. Everyone was making their way to their cars when Kennie pulled up to the curb and opened the door to our red Camaro. His friend, who also drove a red Camaro, pulled up behind him. Kevin's death and funeral was hard on our friend too. He had lost his infant daughter to SIDS not that long ago. He knew what we were going through first hand. I got into the car and the line of cars followed us out of the cemetery gates. There seemed to be an endless amount of cars. We were headed to my mom and dad's. When we got on the freeway a range of feelings hit me. The freeway was wide-open; there was no one in front of us and a line of cars behind us. I never do anything disruptive or unsafe, but not this time. I looked over at Kennie driving and I told him to floor it. Without hesitation his foot went down on the gas pedal. He must have needed a release too. Our Camaro took off with everybody behind us getting smaller and disappearing in the rearview mirror. Every car except for the other red Camaro. We were going as fast as the Camaro could go (around 120 miles per hour) when we heard a huge pop noise and the engine cut off. I don't know if Kennie turned the ignition switch on or if it started up again on its own but the engine was running as we continued at the posted speed limit.

    Of course, we were the first to arrive at my mom and dad's. Kennie's friend was right behind us, got out of his car and came over to Kennie and me.

    The first thing he said was, "Are you both all right?"

    Our answer was no, but it was better now. Needless to say, it was something we shouldn't have done. I wouldn't recommend anybody trying it, but for that moment we didn't care. I guess I needed something reckless in my life. I did everything I was supposed to and it still didn't go right. This was a moment to let go.

People started arriving. Some saw what we did, some didn't.

One friend said, "I saw one little red car take off and disappear. Then a second little red car race by and the two little red cars were gone."

That's the way she described it. I'm glad Kennie was behind the wheel and not me. Most people stayed long enough for a quick chat, said how sorry they were, offered help when we needed it, and it was over.

Once again, we were going home without a baby and very little hope for the future. When we got home and checked the answering machine there were apology and sympathy messages on the machine. There was an announcement that Kevin and I had just been approved for res-care - a total of 40 hours a month.

Upset and slightly disgusted I said, "You are too late, my son is dead." Kennie's boss left a message that he had a load to run tomorrow. Are you kidding me? You just buried your baby son and you don't get to take tomorrow off to grieve and recoup from the whole thing? This is going to sound selfish, but what about being there for me? I need a shoulder to lean on. I don't want to be here alone, but there wasn't a choice in the matter. Two a.m. came, Kennie was gone and the loneliness was in his place. It was as if my eyes couldn't shut. This was the beginning of insomnia, nonstop crying, and no makeup. I tried lying on the bed in the dark but it didn't work. Music reminded me of Kevin and I cried harder. I turned on the television for company. Infomercials were all that were on. I learned about cleaning products, cooking products, slicing and dicing, weight loss ideas, and makeup. Like I would ever wear makeup again. Even if I put makeup on it would just run down my face. It's also amazing how I was able to memorize the phone numbers too, without even trying. Stupid jingles that stick with you like "It's a Small World" from Disneyland. You leave the park and that song stays with you for days. The other thing that was on television was the news. So much tragic stuff. I guess misery does like company. It did seem to help take my mind off of my worries for a moment. No matter what it was, if there was a tragic story about a baby it found its way to my eyes and ears. Babies left in dumpsters, trash cans, discarded like trash. Give them to me. Adoption was a thought I would entertain in the future, but not now. We got so close with Kevin.

    Crying when I wasn't distracted and a day without Kennie meant I had time for my thoughts. I was blaming myself for Kevin's death and replaying in my mind every detail about what happened that day. I wondered why Kennie wasn't verbally blaming me. I was home alone with Kevin. I was in charge of taking care of him. I finally got out of bed around 10:00 a.m., but never made the bed. That's definitely not like me. Some things I knew I needed to take care of. I was told a while back by someone that I needed to follow up with my primary doctor for a diabetes check, to make sure my diabetes was gone and to check my overall health, so I made an appointment to see my doctor.

    I looked at the stack of stuff on the counter. Papers for the cemetery, the support group (not ready for that yet) and developed pictures of Kevin still in the envelope from the store. I took the pictures out and started looking through them. Tears were flowing, of course. The reality was that these were all of the pictures I would ever get of Kevin. My only family pictures. It was only a handful, but I had these. I was going to treasure them. All of Kevin's things became prized possessions to me. I knew I would never part with any of it. I remembered the picture frame I got at one of the baby showers. I went into the nursery and got the collage picture frame. I carefully placed the pictures in the openings. There were just enough pictures for every opening. Fate, I thought. I hung the collage on the hall wall just outside of our master bedroom and gave Kevin a kiss. It was just a picture, but I was used to giving Kevin multiple kisses every day and this seemed to help. Every time I passed the collage in the hall, I kissed Kevin since he wasn't there for me to kiss.

    The rest of the morning was spent sitting and crying. I was trying to put together the pieces of the puzzle so I could figure out how it all went so wrong. The doorbell rang and it was the medical supply company from Hospice. The nurse had called the company and arranged for the driver to retrieve the supplies that we no longer needed. Kennie had placed all of the supplies at the front door from both of the medical supply companies. The driver made a couple of trips to his truck and came back for the oxygen tank. He picked up the one that belonged to him in one hand and then picked up the broken tank in his other hand. I had to stop him because the broken one belonged to the medical company the insurance company sent out, not Hospice. He noticed that it was broken and asked if I had another one. With a face full of tears and trying to wipe them away, I told him that my son had died. We were no longer in need of the tank. With a sincere look on his face he said he was sorry for my loss and said goodbye. I shut the door and stared at the broken oxygen tank. He knew it was broken just by looking at it. This made me wonder about the durability of the tank.

    In less than an hour Kennie was home from his shift. It was obvious he had been crying too. I needed to get out of the house, but where do you go when your face and eyes are so swollen that you can't even cover it up with sunglasses?

Kennie to the rescue, "Do you want to go to the cemetery and see Kevin?"

Perfect! You don't have to worry about people staring at you because you're crying. More than likely they are crying too. What time do they close? Kennie read the pamphlet and it said from sun up to sun down. It was summer and the days were longer. When we arrived at the gates, I started to notice how big this cemetery was. It was huge, very green, well-kept, and Kevin was smack in the middle next to the business office area. This seemed to be a good thing. I had some comfort knowing he wasn't alone with all of the living people walking around. We pulled up to the curb and got out of the car. Kevin was right next to a big palm tree and a memorial bench. Kevin's grave site was easy to spot. The small mound of dirt with no grass on it was an obvious sign. It was small with no marker yet or flower vase. We wouldn't be buying flowers today anyway. All I would want anyway would be baby's breath, little white flowers. Still seemed appropriate to me. Sadness took over. The baby I was holding just a few days ago was now in the ground below me and not breathing. This was a hard reality. I just had to take my mind off of it.

Looking up at the palm tree and sky I said, "I need a sign that everything is going to be okay." Just at the moment I was saying that out loud, a seed from the palm tree hit me on the top of my head. I guess that's when I started to believe in signs or at least started testing the waters. I'm a factual person. I need proof.

I asked Kennie, "Did you see that?" (Kennie heard me ask for a sign.) We both stared up to the tree for the answer. Divine help we thought. It wasn't long until a squirrel came out from its foliage. Either way that squirrel may have been the one delivering the message to my head, but I didn't miss it. We stayed there awhile. We took a walk to the pond, got chased by the aggressive geese and decided it was time to go home.

Another night with no sleep. Kennie was up and off to work again. In some form of comfort, I guess Kennie returned to his normal life. I still had to deal with my empty life. Without needing a television guide, I was starting to figure out what stations were still on at 2:00 a.m. and what was on television at what time. Later that morning was my doctor appointment. I had known this doctor since I was ten. He had been on call for my original doctor for years. He was usually very business driven, good at his practice, but not very emotionally attached, and here I was with emotion written all over my face. The doctor walked in (doctor #11) and listened to my story. At the end I told him I believe I'm going to need some psychiatric help - someone to talk to.

He took a good look at me and said, "You most certainly will." Then he did something totally out of character. He hugged me. He went out to the nurse's station and when he returned, he announced that he had taken the liberty of setting up an appointment today for a psychologist evaluation. The appointment was in just a few hours. Sleep deprived and knowing Kennie would be able to take me I agreed. God knows I needed the help. I had been through so much and I knew I was not acting like my normal self. I had been on a rollercoaster that changed direction over and over, but never ended and I needed to figure out how to get off.

The doctor poked my finger for an instant blood check and it was in normal range. He ordered blood work to confirm that the diabetes was completely gone but could return with future pregnancies. I was also informed that when you have gestational diabetes, more than likely it will return later in life for good. Great. Something else I get to look forward to. This doctor turned out to be very compassionate and understanding to my needs. He was on call for a reason.

I went home, waited for Kennie and we went to the Psychologist's office together. It was about a 30 minute drive. The doctor (doctor #12) brought me back to her office and it was everything you see in the movies. Comfortable looking chairs, a couch, and professionally decorated. It had an ocean fresh scent with water trickling somewhere. Maybe an audio tape.

Once again, I told my story. Her eyes seemed to be holding back a tear for what she really wanted to say, but didn't want to cut me off. Maybe she was coming up with a game plan for my treatment. She did address my concerns of blaming myself. She said that if I hadn't done what I did to help Kevin that day, Kevin wouldn't even have lived to make it to the hospital. It gave me something to think about until the next time I saw her. She took out a sample of Ambien and said it was a medication to help me sleep and it would help me get back on a regular sleeping schedule. She was addressing my symptoms of trauma, grief, depression, insomnia, flashbacks, and recurring memories that were happening every night. She knew sleep was a big part of my recovery. I'm pretty sure she was looking for signs that I was having suicidal thoughts. There were none. There was most definitely depression. There was no impairment to my insight and my judgement. The appointment took an hour and when I returned to the waiting room, I found Kennie on one of the couches sleeping. Much needed and long overdue. I hated to wake him. To delay waking Kennie until the very last minute, I made a follow-up appointment. The plan was twice a week at first, then scale back to twice a month, and then once a month until I didn't need them anymore.

As we walked out, I was telling Kennie about the sample prescription, the conversation with the therapist, and the next appointments. Kennie told me that it would be hard for him to take me every doctor appointment, especially the morning appointments. The afternoon appointments would be okay. I told him that I could make the drive by myself. I needed to start getting my independence back.

When we got home our mailbox was full of sympathy cards. I was touched by how many there were. Some from people I didn't even know who had heard my story from family or friends. I taped them all on the inside of the front door so I could see and read them when I needed to know I wasn't alone. The next thing we checked was the answering machine. More sympathy messages and then there was one very curious message. The insurance company's oxygen tank owners called. They were inquiring about the oxygen tank and wanted to pick it up at my earliest convince. They never acknowledged Kevin's death, just left a strange message. I hadn't called them to come pick up the oxygen tank. Nor did I inform them of Kevin dying.

When the lady left after delivering the oxygen tank, she instructed me to call in an order when it gets low. Not, we will call you soon and check on you. What an odd message. It made us start to think. The message sounded as if someone told them about Kevin dying and their machine falling apart. The only person outside of doctors and family who knew about the faulty oxygen tank was the employee who picked up Hospice's equipment. He must have given them a heads up. This got me thinking and it gave me a distraction from crying. Kennie retrieved the oxygen tank from the front door, brought it in to the family room where it was well lit and began to thoroughly look it over trying to match up the parts that fell off in my hands. The tank seemed to be missing a part. He went over to the recliner where I was sitting that fateful day and moved the recliner. There it was, lying on the floor under the recliner - the missing spring. It apparently had broken off when I went to turn it on. I didn't even realize that it had popped off or that it was missing at all. I'm not mechanically inclined so how would I know? All I knew was the machine broke and I needed to get help for Kevin. Finding the spring under the recliner confirmed right then and there that there was nothing I could have done differently to change Kevin's outcome. The vital oxygen equipment that was there to sustain Kevin's life in the event he needed it malfunctioned. Kevin and I never had a chance.

    The tank was completely full with a broken nozzle that turned it on and off. I was rendered helpless. I was unable to help Kevin. This was proof I needed in order to stop blaming myself. The psychologist words about the CPR I performed added to the relief. Even with logical and physical evidence, I still put the blame on myself. I'm guessing that is a normal reaction and planned to discuss it at my next psychologist appointment. Discovering the faulty part gave me something to do the next day – call an attorney and inquire about the broken spring. I wouldn't have even thought to do if it wasn't for the oxygen company calling.

    I took my pill, went to bed and clutched Kevin's blanket. The pill didn't seem to help much. I kept waking up looking for Kevin every couple of hours, as I had been doing. I finally went into a deeper sleep but in short intervals. I was back to sitting up in bed, watching infomercials commercials, and crying, I caught a glimpse of myself in the mirror across from the bed. I hardly recognized myself.

Looking at myself in the distant mirror I started talking to myself and God. Why? Why did this happen? How am I ever going to lead a normal life? How can young girls who don't want to be pregnant have healthy babies? Then there's me, I desperately want a baby and can't have one of my own? I know Kevin had problems but all were compatible with life and I was willing to do whatever it took. God, I loved him. Why did you take him away? Did I love him too much? I must have or I wouldn't be hurting this much. I looked at myself in the mirror as I put my head down on the bed and more or less collapsed. I felt the deepest of breaths leave my body. It made me think of Kevin's last breath and how he must have felt. I went in and out of sleep and finally got up. I made myself a cup of decaf coffee. I didn't need any help staying awake.

I remembered the phone calls I needed to make. It was still too early to call anyone. I decided to make a list of questions followed by a list of attorneys that I got from the phonebook. Better to be prepared. I made my first call. It was the wrong kind of attorney but at least he was kind enough to refer me to the right kind of attorney. I called the referred attorney but he was not able to take my case due to his current work load. This did however assure me that I had a case. He gave my number to yet another attorney and she returned my call that day. She was really interested and also assured me that I did have a case. Unfortunately, it confirmed that this whole thing could have been avoided and Kevin should still be alive. She asked if I still had the oxygen tank and instructed me to not let anyone have it. She told me not to talk to the oxygen tank company. There should be no reason for them to be calling me. They obviously want the evidence back and now that I have an attorney, they can't have it back until this is settled in court. The attorney had my back and it gave me a sense of comfort, which I desperately needed. Friday afternoon the attorney planned to come to my house to see for herself where I was the day the tank malfunctioned. She was smart, thorough, and creative.

Friday morning came and I had gotten no sleep the night before. I went to the psychologist appointment by myself. Crying the whole time, I managed to tell my story in detail. Telling the story seemed to help me put it in order as if to process the timelines. She asked if I was taking the Ambien and if it was helping me sleep. When I told her that it wasn't helping much, she informed me that it was a low dose and I wouldn't become dependent on it. It should take the edge off. She acknowledged that I never stopped crying throughout the whole appointment and wrote me a prescription for Zoloft to help with depression. I didn't like the idea of taking any pills, but I figured it was worth a try. If it helped, great. I talked to her about the malfunction of the oxygen tank. I told her I was starting to consider that there was nothing in my power I could have done to change the outcome of Kevin's death. I kept choking on the words as I was saying them. Still trying to make myself believe them. The facts were there.

I left the office and got into the elevator. I was joined by a lady with CPR dolls. At first I froze. The idea that I had to perform CPR on Kevin was too fresh. I took a deep breath and decided to start a conversation about the dolls to defuse the anxieties I was having.

"CPR dolls. I learned CPR on one of those."

She responded with, "Oh. You know CPR. You must have trained on an Annie doll."

I said, "Yes. The instructor had two or three of them."

She continued, "Now we have lots of different kinds of dolls. This one you know, it's Annie. That one is our male doll named Buddy and this is our baby, Kevin."

OH, NO! Did she just say that's baby Kevin? I couldn't say another word. Of all the names for a baby including girl names, why did she have to name the little CPR baby Kevin? The doors opened and she had to gather up the dolls. I bolted. I couldn't get out of there quick enough. I cried all the way home. I got home to find Kennie eating lunch. I was crying so hard. I told him what had happened.

He looked at me, smiled and said "That's a good thing."

Shocked I replied, "What? Are you kidding? I'm devastated. How can that be a good thing?"

Still smiling, "Well Kevin is helping save lives." In just a few words he made it better.

Kennie informed me that my boss called and left a message saying I no longer had a job. With the way I am right now would I ever be able to work? How do you resume a normal life? He also said there was yet another call from the oxygen company, inquiring about the machine. They seemed to be getting desperate and really wanted to retrieve the evidence.

I sat down to try and relax while I waited for the attorney to arrive. It wasn't long before the doorbell rang. I opened the door to see two attorneys. We made our introductions and I showed them around the house. I went into detail of the 911 call, showed them the oxygen tank and the spring that malfunctioned. They were impressed that I was able to give them a great amount of detail. They were especially happy about the fact that I was able to save the oxygen tank. I had been called by the oxygen company twice trying to retrieve the oxygen tank and they were still not yet informed that Kevin had died. This was highly suspicious according to the attorney.

Her main question: "Was this a wrongful death or wrongful life, lawsuit?"

I didn't follow. She explained that the wrongful death was something that took Kevin's life and he should still be alive. Wrongful life means the doctor should have caught Kevin's problems while I was still pregnant and you could have terminated life. This was not even a question. Even if I had known about Kevin's problems before his birth, I still would have chosen to have him. He was alive in me. I couldn't imagine terminating his life. Heck the doctors were wrong about the trisomy diagnosis. Without a doubt it was wrongful death. I had given her everything she needed to start a case. She informed Kennie and me that we did, in fact, have a case that she and her team would be happy to handle. She was thorough, compassionate, and answered all of my inquiries. As she was leaving, she gave Kennie and me a hug.

She said, "Think it over and let me know if you want to hire me as your attorney." She said goodbye and I closed the door.

Kennie and I talked about it. There was no need to pursue more attorneys. We found the one we trusted.

The weekend was full of tears, no sleep, Kennie listening and seemingly holding back. Why? I was unloading everything that was on my mind and even though he was a good listener I was amazed that he wasn't feeling the same. I was not willing to go out into public places due to my swollen eyes and face. We started going to the cemetery almost daily. At least it was an outing. It seemed to help and I still didn't have to explain to anyone why I had been crying. Caring for the gravesite and walking around seemed to help, too. The therapist suggested taking lunch to the cemetery and having lunch with Kevin, which we did. It was a little strange at first, but it soon became routine. We brought bread for the ducks and geese. We fed them from the safety of our car. We learned our lesson the first day about the geese.

Sitting on the grass at Kevin's grave, having lunch and crying. I started wondering what purpose I had in life. My baby is gone and the question, was I still a mom, was Kennie still a dad kept coming up. I couldn't see myself being a professional someone. I had always envisioned myself as a mom and having a family to care for. A career woman. I'm smart enough to succeed in whatever I set my mind to do, but what? I never saw myself as anything but a family woman. My life and ideals were changing. I was knowledgeable in caring for someone and had compassion in my heart, but after what I had been through I was no longer confident in my abilities.

The weekend came to an end and I was alone again Monday morning, moping around the house. I looked at the calendar for the next appointment time with the therapist. Not until Thursday. That seemed so far away. I found myself going to the paperwork I dreaded: the support group for people who lost babies. I hated giving into this. Part of me was in denial and didn't want to admit that I needed this group. I looked through the paperwork and noticed the words that addressed the moms and dads that lost their babies. I reread it "Moms and dads that lost their babies". It confirmed that I was still a mom and Kennie was still a dad. I started analyzing my situation. Even though I lost all of my babies, by definition being pregnant meant I was a mom and Kennie was a dad. This was the confirmation, reality check I needed and no one was going to change my mind. If someone only had one child and that child lived for ten years and he or she died they would still be a mom and dad. This was the same thing to me and a game changer in my recovery. Recovery? How do you ever recover from something like this? I don't believe you can. I think you learn how to go on day by day. You can't put a bandage on it and expect to be healed when you pull it off. No this was emotional and a bandage wouldn't do.

Too anxious to wait until Thursday for my appointment, I looked for the time and place for the support group meeting. Call it fate or another sign, but it was that night at 7:00 p.m. All I knew was that I was going.

Kennie came home and I said, "You're taking me to the support group for parents who lost their babies." Kennie looked it up and the meeting was at a local church. The group was not affiliated with the church but the church was generous enough to let them use the facility. It took less than five minutes to get there. We got there early and sat in the parking lot. There were almost no cars in the lot. I was of course crying and trying to come up with the courage to go in. I thought this might be a mistake until I saw car after car pulling into the parking lot and couples getting out and going into the church. By the time I decided to go in the parking lot was almost full. I walked into the hall with Kennie holding my hand. We were greeted by a woman who was, of all things, smiling. How can you smile? I thought for a second I was in the wrong place, until she introduced herself as a parent volunteer and welcomed us to the support group.

We were informed that this was a support group run by parent for parents who have lost a baby through miscarriage, still birth, or infant loss. She added that the support group also provided support to parents who can and choose to go on and have a subsequent pregnancy. She was trying to prepare us for the sight of a pregnant woman here. Again, the smile. I informed her that I buried my baby a week ago. She gave her sympathies, a sincere hug, and showed us around.

They had a newsletter, a call center, a library, refreshments and chairs set up for some kind of introduction with guest speakers. Kennie and I took a seat. The speakers were parents who also lost their babies. They were there to problem solve. They told their stories, addressed holiday situations or whatever the group had on their minds to discuss. After about 45 minutes we broke off into smaller groups of eight to ten in a circle with a facilitator. The facilitator set the ground rules. A loss is a loss, we don't compare stories or downgrade any loss. Do not judge people, no doctor names, no hospital names, or religious preferences. Everyone will get a chance to share their story if they choose to do so. I hadn't thought about speaking, I was just listening.

The facilitator started. What a story she told. Somehow it seemed to compare with my tragic story. Yes, I compared, but never said so. It must be human nature or maybe I needed to know someone else survived this kind of tragedy. She was the one who greeted us with a smile at the door. This at least got my attention. Sitting next to her with Kennie on my right, she looked at me and asked if I wanted to share my story? No, was all I could say. She simply turned to her left and asked the woman sitting next to her if she wanted to share her story. From there they took turns telling their stories. All I could do was sit with my head down, using all of the tissue I could get my hands on. I never made eye contact with anyone in the circle, but I can tell you their stories and what shoes they were wearing. It had finally come full circle. Kennie was next and we were the only ones who hadn't spoken. I made an insecure eye contact with Kennie and he spoke for us.

What he said assured me that he was hurting just as much as I was, but hadn't shared it with me like this. Then he paused and the facilitator asked me how I was doing. She was trying to engage me. It worked. Kennie opened the door and the facilitator invited me in. I told my story starting with the twins, the two other miscarriages, and then the tragic story of Kevin's death. The only time I looked up was when someone asked a question. Every time I looked up there were more mouths dropping open and head shaking. I didn't want to make anyone else's story seem less meaningful than mine. In fact, some seemed to have found comfort that their stories weren't as bad as mine. By the time Kennie and I had finished telling our story the time was up. It was 10:00 p.m. The three hours seemed to move so quickly. Most everyone in our circle gave Kennie and me hugs. Looking around the room as we helped put chairs away, I noticed that there weren't many men in the group as a whole. Our little circle had quite a few dads which I'm sure helped Kennie feel comfortable. We said our goodbyes and got into the car. I felt so much better. Just to know that people can actually smile after something like this gave me hope. Would I smile again? I don't know. I knew one thing for sure; I was coming back to the next meeting.

    When we arrived home, there was a small potted ficus plant on the front porch with a note. A friend that I had known since high school had dropped by for a visit and we weren't home. She left it for us. The note was full of wonderful thoughts and sympathy. The final sentences were, "This is Kevin's tree that you can care for. I know it will get lots of love. I decided to leave it on the front porch so Kevin's tree could greet people who came for a visit."

    I continued to take the prescribed pills and went to my therapist appointments. They helped, but the support group was where I felt most comfortable telling my story to people who had been through a loss of their own - people who walked in my shoes and survived, or were at least trying to survive. Not only was I learning to tell my story, I was actually starting to help people. That's when I realized that telling my story was actually helping me to process what happened while also aiding others in their processing. I still wasn't communicating with Kennie the way I wanted to though. Every time he would start sharing his feelings with me I would start crying. He didn't want to add to my sadness. His answer was to just hug me instead of sharing the way he felt.

    I was talking to my attorney one morning and she wanted me to talk into a little tape recorder and tell my story for her use only. This gave me an idea. I gave Kennie the little tape recorder and asked him when he was alone to talk into it and tape his feelings. Whatever you want to say, all the feelings you're having, I won't be there to stop your thoughts. When you're done you give it to me and I'll listen to it when I'm alone. His feelings were shared with no interruptions. It worked. I couldn't believe what I was hearing. All this time I thought Kennie was not emotionally scarred by what happened, when in reality he had a lot of feelings going on. So much that it took almost two hours of tape. It was reassuring that we were both on the same page of grieving. When Kennie came home I gave him a big, tight hug. He shared with me something special by reaching into his pocket and pulling out a pair of Kevin's little blue knitted booties. He had been carrying them around in his pocket as a way of holding on to Kevin. Both of us were emotionally scarred and walking through the grieving process together.

    I was counting the days until the support group would meet again. When it got here it was October and the topic for the panel of parents was how to survive Halloween. I hadn't even thought about it. The idea was to get us to prepare for the doorbell ringing and kids at the door. It was too soon for me. We broke into little circles. This time it seemed to be a bit easier. My story was more focused, not all over the place like before. More mouths dropped open as they heard my story. One lady who I recognized by her story was there and asked more defined questions. Her questions helped me put more of the story into words. As for Halloween, I used one of the suggestions and we went to my sister's house where Kennie and I didn't have to answer the door. She could deal with the trick or treaters. Kennie and I could sit in the shadows. When we got to her house, I decided that I would walk with the kids as I usually did. I needed the exercise. If I started to cry it was dark and it would be hard to see my tears. I could return to my sister's house or just go home. It worked. The night was over and we went home.

  I couldn't believe it was November 1st. I was going to the cemetery about three times a week, seeing the therapist about twice a month and the support group once a month. While at the therapist's I informed her that the medication I was taking was making my hair fall out. I showed her the bald spots on my head. She changed the Zoloft to Luvox and gave me a lower dose. I was starting to cry less. There was a day or two that I didn't even shed a tear. Insomnia was still a problem and the sleeping pills were still not helping much because I still hadn't slept through a whole night. I was still unable to work because of the spontaneous tears. I wanted to do something productive with my time. I saw on television that the women's shelter needed donations. They said anything would be helpful because some of the women had to leave their homes with their children and only the clothes they were wearing. I pulled out the sewing machine and the leftover material I had from making Kevin's baby blankets. I managed to make a few baby blankets to give away. I gathered up all of the supplies I had, like formula that was going to expire, and took them down to the women's shelter. I figured someone could use them. I delivered all of it, went by the cemetery, told Kevin what I had done, then went home. Somehow this made me feel like I did something productive. It kind of gave me a purpose in life even if it was just for a moment.

    The lawsuit was moving along on its own now. Other than updates I had very little participation in it. My lawyer collected medical records from the many doctors and hospitals where Kevin and I were treated. The records showed that all of my pregnancies were boys. I had five sons. This was a moment of mixed emotions. I had no children with me, but I had a baseball team in heaven waiting for Kennie and me. The attorney we chose was very thorough. She kept everything on track. Confident in her abilities, I never had to worry about what she was doing. I knew she was getting it done.

    November was when I started wondering if there was still a chance for me to have a healthy baby. I remembered the genetic doctor (doctor #10) gave me his card and told me that if I wanted to talk about genetic defects that I could call and he would be more than happy to counsel Kennie and me on the subject. Well it seemed it was time to make that call. It was the first step in answering the curious question: Is it possible for me to have a healthy baby? The receptionist was very nice. She seemed to know all about my case as if she was expecting my call. I was impressed. She made the a few days away which gave me time to write down my questions. I left a pad of paper out and when I thought of a question I would add it to the page. The questions added up quickly.

The appointment came. The doctor's office wasn't far from Kevin's hospital. There wasn't much parking, but behind his modest building were two spots; one was open and just waiting for us. We went in through the back door as instructed and were greeted by the doctor. It was sad but familiar. The room was his personal office, full of books, lots of files, and papers everywhere. We were seated in his office in comfortable leather chairs. He sat down and gave his condolences. We started asking our questions about genetics. He answered by educating us on the X and Y chromosomes and how the fetus develops. The mother's egg is always an X and the father's sperm is the one that decides the sex of the baby. The sperm is either an X or a Y. An X is a girl and a Y is a boy.

He held up his finger, extending his index finger on his right hand and said, "This is the egg and it's an X".

He held up the same finger on his left hand, extended it just the same and said, "This a sperm and it's an X - they are the same. If there is a defective gene from one of them the other will correct the defective problem and the baby girl will be healthy." He used the same example by holding up his extended index finger on his right hand again representing the mother's egg, an X, and changed his left hand's index finger to a bent finger representing the father's Y sperm and said, "If the sperm is a Y it's not the same as the mother's X and has no ability to correct the defective gene. The doctor clarified: There is no way to correct the defective gene because the father's Y is not the same as the mother's X. The chances of a boy coming out with a genetic defect is more likely than a girl."

I told him that all of my miscarriages were boys. Made me wonder how any male gets here without any physical problems. Maybe I missed something, but in a nutshell, we had a 50/50 chance that it would be a healthy girl. The odds got more challenging if it was a boy. The ratio went to 75/25. In the eye of the beholder, the glass was either half empty or half full. I have always been the glass is half full kind of girl. Kevin's problems were more than likely a stroke in utero and not a genetic defect, but there was no way to test for Kevin's kind of genetic defect at the time. We were there for a couple of hours and the doctor never even looked at the time. He seemed genuinely happy to help. He gave us a name of a perinatologist to call if we decided to try to have a baby again. I asked what a perinatologist was. This was a word I had never heard before. He explained that it was an OBGYN doctor who specialized in care of the mother and fetus of a higher than normal at-risk pregnancy. He assured me that he had known this doctor for years, he had a team that included diabetic counseling and he was the best doctor for Kennie and me. Well how do you not take that kind of advice. Here was a doctor who treated Kevin, was counseling us with good intentions and we had nowhere to turn.

    On the way home, we talked about our feelings of trying again. I was not sure, but Kennie said if I was willing to try again, he would be there to support me. My feelings were mixed. Prior to trying to have a baby I was the girl who walked into a room and if there was a baby there, I would be the first to make my way over to pick up the baby and play with it. Now, I noticed, I shy away from them, almost afraid of them and definitely unsure of myself. I would have to give this more thought. Just the idea of trusting another doctor, considering the ones who failed me so far, was a process in itself. I would need more time to decide and then find the right doctor that I could trust. We had one referral.

I made a visit to my sister's house. The kids were getting ready to watch "Casper", a cartoon about a girl and her father who buy a house haunted by a "friendly" ghost. The ghost haunting the house was a boy who died young. This was revealed at the end of the story and the minute it was over I couldn't help but cry. I moved quickly to the bathroom so the kids didn't see me cry. Once I was in there, I couldn't figure out how I was going to hide it from them when I came out. Fortunately, they are kids and didn't even notice.

The support group met and I became more focused on questions I had for a change. It occurred to me during discussion in the little circles that I never knew what became of my miscarried babies' remains. Seeing one of my babies in the butter tub as an embryo was in a weird way comforting because I never got to even see my other boys. This really started to bother me and there was nothing I could do. Someone suggested that I name my babies I lost in miscarriage, since we now know they were all boys. That way I wouldn't have to continue referring to them as just miscarriages, I could refer to them by name. Good suggestion.

One mother in the circle said "I know it sounds crazy, but my arms ached after losing my baby."

The rest of us could relate. We had experienced this too. The facilitator excused herself from the circle and returned with teddy bears that weighed the same as a newborn baby. She handed one to each of us to take home and hold when our arms ached. It worked.

Another thing discussed was the "stupid things people say". This became an open forum, a discussion everyone seemed to have something to add. My personal encounters were people telling me that I shouldn't try again because it was hard on them. If I have the courage to try again then that trumps their feelings.

Something said to Kennie and me came from a family member. He started with, "You're lucky you don't have children/babies. They tie you down. You can't go out. It's hard to find a babysitter."

I know he was trying to be encouraging and find something positive to say, but it was mean and disturbing to me.

My response was, "We are having a baby to share our lives with them. If my baby can't go with us or we can't find a suitable babysitter, it's simple, we don't go out. Our baby is our life. If our baby can't go, we don't go."

Another one that got me was "You're young. You can have more children."

My reply was, "You have several kids. If one of them was to die unexpectedly it wouldn't be a problem, because you have other kids, right?" People just didn't seem to get it, unless they experienced a loss of a baby themselves.

An expected timeline to grieving by others was another misconception. "You should feel better by now." or "Aren't you over it yet?" It's not a cut that heals in a few days. Grieving is a lifetime of work and there is no set time. It was like being on a rollercoaster. Some days you were up and life felt a little normal again. Other days you were down and the tears were nonstop.

Then there were the total opposite people, who would avoid talking about Kevin to me. Yes, I'm going to cry or tear up, but please say his name. Kevin. I want to hear it.

The question came up in the circle, "How do you handle other mothers and their living babies? Baby showers?" I thought about the Lamaze class, the friends I made there and how they never contacted me. I never got any invitations to their baby showers even though we exchanged phone numbers and addresses. It felt as if I had a disease and they didn't want to catch it. Maybe they thought they were protecting their babies from me?

Listening to the moms and dads in the circle, it occurred to me that I hadn't held a baby since Kevin died. "I don't know if I could hold a baby right now." It was as if at that moment, I became intimidated by just the thought of holding another baby. Would it die in my arms like Kevin did? That was not a normal thought. My thought was interrupted by the facilitator's next topic for discussion.

"The holidays are coming up you need to be prepared. Have a plan for doing something nontraditional in case you need the out. It's perfectly okay to change your traditions. Some parents put a teddy bear or an angel in their Christmas card pictures to represent the baby they lost. Anyone close to them will understand the significance of the teddy bear or angel while others will just see a cute teddy bear or angel."

More good advice. The evening came to an end and on the way home I started to pick out names for the boys we lost. Kennie didn't seem to care too much about naming our lost baby boys so I did it. Before we went to bed, I had decided on Alic and Alan for the twins, Mark and Justin for my middle two boys and, of course, Kevin makes my total of five sons.

CHAPTER EIGHT: THE COURAGE TO CONTINUE

Thanksgiving didn't seem to have any problems other than I was still on a rollercoaster of tears. I had no idea when they would hit. Sometimes it was a song, a routine with Kevin that I remembered from the past, or just a random thought. Makeup being a thing of the past was replaced by tissue in my pocket. I came to accept that tears were just a part of me. I could still function, but my life was nothing like it was before Kennie got sick. I obsessed over educating myself over things I didn't understand. Like Kennie's Gillian Barré, why I miscarried my boys, why did Kevin die and how do I get to the perinatologist? Some questions had answers and others didn't. Educating myself on how to get to the perinatologist was going to start soon.

The first Monday in December I sat down with a pen, a pad of paper, and a bunch of phone numbers. I called the insurance company first. I asked about a referral to the perinatologist that doctor #10 suggested to me. The operator told me that the perinatologist was in the system, but not in my part of the zoning.

"Is there a way for me to get to the perinatologist?"

"Yes, but you would have to move to the zone in which the perinatologist is assigned."

Selling our house and moving wasn't much of an option. The operator inquired about my need for this kind of a doctor and informed me that there were other high-risk doctors.

My response was direct and immediate, "NO! The last high-risk doctor was a huge disappointment and my baby died." Silence.

She suggested a perinatologist in my zoning. Why didn't she say that instead of suggesting a high-risk doctor? She informed me I would need a referral from my family practice doctor to an OBGYN, then a referral from the OBGYN to the perinatologist after I was confirmed pregnant.

I quickly responded with, "That's the problem. I need to see the doctor before I achieve a pregnancy. I need to be under his or her care before, during and after the pregnancy. Waiting for conception might put me and my baby at risk for a stroke in utero. Plus, there was no guarantee that I would eventually get to a perinatologist." I think she got tired of listing to me or debating what to do with all of the obstacles the insurance company had. It must have been working in my favor. There was probably a line of calls waiting behind me that she had to take. She suggested to call for a free consultation from the perinatologist in my zoning and gave me the number. I hung up the phone with a page full of notes she and I had discussed. I called the doctor she suggested (doctor #13). He had an opening for after hours that night. I booked the appointment. Funny how the consultation appointments can be fit in quickly, but trying to get an appointment for a routine visit was nearly impossible. I guess because they are always looking for new patients. I remembered that consultations were free. Maybe I should call the perinatologist that I was referred to originally, meet with him and be able to compare the two. If nothing else, get pointers on the protocol of a perinatologist. Wouldn't hurt. Just because I don't live in the zone of his practice doesn't mean I can't seek his advice.

I called and set up an appointment for after hours with

him as well. Turns out free consultations are done Monday through Thursday after hours. The doctors will work late on those days, but want to leave early on Friday. Wow. They are human after all. This was a blessing. I didn't have to come in contact with pregnant women and have that uncomfortable feeling or reminder of my losses.

Kennie came home a bit late and fearing the doctor would lock up the office early, we immediately headed to the doctor's office. We must have gotten there just as the last patient was leaving because they took us right away. This doctor seemed to be in a hurry. He took a glance at the clock on the wall when we walked in. He didn't let us ask any questions at first. Instead he told us how his practice worked.

He said, "Once you're confirmed pregnant and referred to me, I will see and treat you about every third visit with your regular OBGYN."

"Wait, what?" I had to interrupt. Clearly by the look in his eyes he wasn't used to being interrupted. "When I get a referral to see you, I won't be seeing you throughout my entire care?"

"No. I share the regular visits with your OBGYN. In the event that there is something concerning I will treat you as I see fit. The OBGYN will handle the rest of the visits."

"What about delivery, will it be a scheduled C-section delivery?"

"No. We will try to go naturally unless there is a complication that prevents us from doing so." I took the time to fill him in on some details of being pregnant with Kevin, his birth and death since I wasn't allowed to do it at the beginning. During my story, the doctor took a deep breath as if he was annoyed with the length of time he had given us thus far. He finally realized this wasn't going to be a short consultation. I had too many questions for him apparently and my gut feeling was that his protocol was not a perfect fit for me. I asked him what colleagues he had that I could talk to or would deliver my baby if he was on vacation. He informed me that there were plenty of excellent doctors and nurses at the hospital who could deliver my baby in his absence. He then mentioned the hospital name. My body went limp. It was my inferior hospital. I didn't think that I would have to ever go back there. There was so many other hospitals in the area and his privileges were only for that hospital. This meant if I chose to go with him, I had no choice but to make a return visit there. No. Absolutely not! My gut feeling was starting to get louder. He looked at his watch as he had done many times and asked if I had anymore questions? My gut was shouting, "Get out! This is not the place for you!" I thanked him for his time and left with Kennie. On the walk to the car I questioned Kennie about how quiet he was.

He said, "I could tell you weren't going to go with this doctor the minute we sat down. The lack of trust, his shortness with you, and then the name of the hospital. Why bother extending the conversation?" Kennie was right on all counts, even before I told him my decision. I didn't know if I had any other options for a perinatologist with the insurance company. I may have to go with him even though I had serious reservations of the care. Earning my trust was a big deal to me and this was not a good start.

A few days had passed and we were at the consultation of the perinatologist I wanted to go to. Doctor #10's recommendation. It was farther away from home, about 30 minutes more. The office was state of the art compared to other offices I had been in. Parking was close to the front door, plenty of seating, vaulted ceilings, two check in desks, next to several hospitals, one for children, another for women, and another for nonspecific hospital needs. Like before the last of the patients had gone. We were greeted with a smile by a nurse and given a tour. They had large, clean examining rooms, professional looking ultrasound rooms, rooms with doors labeled for specialists, nutritionist, diabetic counseling. I reached up, touched the sign on the door and turned back to smile at Kennie. At the end of the hall was the doctor's office. We were asked to have a seat in his office and offered water. After a minute or two I got nosey. I walked around the room reading about the doctor's accomplishments. Impressive from a glance. At closer look the amount of diplomas that he had on the wall was very impressive. Doing the math, the years of practice were up there too. I was making my way back to my seat when another nurse walked by and I knew her from the support group. She came into the room smiling and gave us both hugs. We had no idea that she worked there. She knew our story inside and out. I informed her that one of the doctors who treated Kevin in his hospital referred us to this perinatologist. We explained that he came highly recommended and we were there only for a consultation. I continued explaining that he wasn't in our zoning, but we wanted his advice so much that we came anyway. She suggested changing our zoning. I told her that it had to do with where we lived and moving was not an option.

    A puzzled look ran across her face. "There must be a way to change that without moving." She suggested calling the front office and asking them about it.

    She hugged us and said, "I hope this all works out for you. He's a very good doctor."

    Not long after that the doctor walked in. Not very tall. Given his accomplishments, he was not very old either. He said hello, shook our hands and offered us something to drink. We were okay, no water for us. Nice offer. To me it meant he wasn't in a hurry. He asked us why we needed a perinatologist? He confessed that his nurse said that she knew us from the support group and added that we had been through a difficult time. We went into detail about our losses, Kennie was even engaging in the conversation. I told him how the insurance had a zoning problem in order for me to be treated there. He agreed with his nurse and encouraged us to call the front office in the morning. He was confident that they could help.

I told him that gestational diabetes was my main concern. He said that I would have to go back on insulin and get my numbers under tight control before I could even think about conceiving, leaving nothing to chance.

He said, "We have a team of diabetic councilors and nutritionist as part of the staff and will help you along the way."

A deep sigh of relief came from me.

I asked, "What hospital do you deliver at?"

He informed me that the hospital he delivers at was right down the street and is a hospital specifically for women. Considering Kevin's need for a high level NICU when he was born, a subsequent pregnancy may need one too. We were informed that there is a tunnel from his hospital to a specialized high level NICU next door.

"What about the delivery? The anesthesiologist had a problem with my back. He couldn't find the place in my back to numb me and I ended up being knocked completely out with several staph infections from poking my back over and over." He assured me that I would have an opportunity to meet with the anesthesiologist before delivery so that he could examine my spine. "Colleagues. Who do you have to assist you if you're on vacation?"

He handed me his card with six or seven other perinatologists on it and said, "These are my colleagues. They work in this office with me." I looked at Kennie and smiled, trying to hold back the tears. It was the moment that I knew this was where I belonged. Kennie and I had been sitting in his office for almost two hours, he answered all of our questions to our satisfaction, and he never once looked at the clock. Trust earned. The walk out to the lobby was dark, everyone had gone home except the doctor. He unlocked the door and said goodnight.

The next morning was somewhat exciting and challenging. I knew the first perinatologist was not for me and I didn't like him. That made me work harder at figuring out how to get to the one we saw last night. Armed with my pen and pad of paper I started calling. The front desk receptionist was kind, but was unable to definitively answer my question about the zoning.

"I'm told that I'm in a different zone than the perinatologist in your office. I want this doctor to treat me for my next pregnancy and for the zoning reason alone I'm being denied a future referral. My question, is there a way to change my zoning without moving and I can be treated by the perinatologist at this office?" She had no idea. However, she did suggest calling the billing department for the perinatologist.

"Why?" I asked.

She explained, "They handle the insurance companies and referrals. They might be able to name doctors who refer to the perinatologists and should have more insight to the insurance company's rules." She gave me their phone number and transferred me to the billing department. Another nice lady answered the phone. I explained what my call was about and told her my story. I'm sure she was busy, but once again she took the time to educate me on the protocol of the referral system and insurance zoning. She gave me names with phone numbers, OBGYNs that refer to them, but again none were in my zone. She suggested that maybe it was just a matter of changing my primary care physician to the zone I want to be in. Wow! The system "worked me" for all of these years. I have played by their rules that I had no control over, but I never thought that there might be a loophole. It's worth the call. I couldn't thank her enough for the idea. I called the billing department of one of the OBGYNs that I was given and spoke to yet another person. She didn't cut me short either. It seemed that everybody I told my story to was willing to listen and help. She gave me names and phone numbers of primary care physicians that referred, confirmed pregnancy to them. My next phone call was back to the insurance company where I started my quest for the doctor of my choice. I kept it a little vague, brief questions, fearing that if I told the whole story I would get denied. I told the insurance company that I wanted to change my primary care doctor to another primary care doctor that was closer to my work. No questions asked. The transfer was done. The only stipulation was that Kennie would have to change to that primary care physician too. I didn't even ask why. I just did it. Success! We were in the zone that I needed to be in to see the perinatologist of my choice. I hung up and it occurred to me that with so many perinatologists at that office, what if I get referred to that office, but not that perinatologist. I called doctor #10 back and told him my dilemma. He solved it by writing me a compelling letter referencing Kevin's life and death. He mailed one to the perinatologist to keep on file for future use and mailed me a copy too. I then called my primary care physician that I had seen most of my life and explained why I was switching physicians. He understood completely and offered up a letter as well with hopes that I would get to the right perinatologist. I also said when I was done having a baby, I would change back to him. Given my track record who knows when that would be?

I figured out how to see the perinatologist. Now I had one more problem to figure out. If the scenario of Kevin having a stroke in utero was correct, his physical problems were caused by my high sugar levels from my out of control undiagnosed diabetes which happens in the first four to six weeks of life as an embryo and the insurance company won't refer you to an OBGYN until you have a confirmed pregnancy. Usually a confirmed pregnancy doesn't happen until at least the eighth week of pregnancy. My baby could be at risk for having a stroke before I even know I'm pregnant. This scared the shit out of me. I placed a call to the perinatologist. The front desk put me through to the diabetic team. The lady there said that she was briefed on my story from the doctor and the nurse who knew my story from the support group and that she was expecting my call. She said that it will be okay this time and she would personally help me. It was almost Christmas, she made an appointment for February of next year and told me to relax and enjoy the holiday. She suggested I take an aerobics class to help get in shape for another pregnancy and added that it would help lower my sugar levels.

"In February with or without your insurance kicking in we will get you what you need to get your diabetes under tight control, syringes, insulin, etc. and when that happens you will get the okay to start trying to conceive again." She told me that they like to see three consecutive months of tight sugar control before the okay to conceive is given.

She said, "Once you get a confirmed pregnancy your

insurance will have to kick in and cover your needs."

I thanked her and said goodbye. I called the billing lady back and thanked her for the idea about moving my primary doctor. Told her it worked.

I took the suggestion of the [nurse] from the diabetic team and started an aerobics class two days a week. It definitely got the blood pumping. Christmas came and went with little to no difference. The only thing that bothered me was not many people mentioned Kevin. I wanted to talk about him to people. I resolved that it was best saved for the support group where people could help me heal and my story could in turn help them.

Just before the New Year I woke up out of a sound sleep. Yes, I was starting to sleep through the night with an occasional bad night. This night I sat right up and I was wide awake. What if our insurance changes at the first of the year as it always does? All of the preparation I did to get to the perinatologist would be a waste of time and I would have to start over. I woke Kennie up to discuss it. We decided that he would talk to his boss and find out if he knew of any changes. It was almost time for Kennie to go to work anyway. He promised me he would look into it for me today. Kennie went to work and I fell back to sleep feeling assured that Kennie would handle it. When he got home, he had good news. The insurance group that we were with was not changing. One more sign that I was where I was supposed to be.

January was a start to a new year. I was going to aerobic classes twice a week and losing weight. My therapist appointments were down to twice a month and changing to once a month starting February. I informed them that I was seeing a perinatologist for a future pregnancy. In return I was informed that when I do start trying to conceive, I need to come off of the pills they prescribed because the pills were not compatible with a pregnancy.

The support group was still only once a month, but I was asked to share my story with different hospitals around town, volunteering as a liaison for the support group. I jumped at the chance to educate the medical professionals on the do's and don'ts. I could defiantly be the voice of the moms and dads of our group. The first time speaking I was at a hospital's NICU. The group was less than 20 people and I was still intimidated. The lead opened with who we were, what we offered, and how we functioned as a nonprofit group. She gave the staff positive suggestions for their patients: hugs, be sincere. She also suggested keeping memorabilia: name tags from the incubator, wristbands, hats, booties, blankets, pictures if possible. We told our individual stories.

The lead suggested things that medical professional shouldn't do: "Don't say you know what we are going through if you haven't ever lost a baby. It's okay to cry with us. Just make sure you tell us why you're crying so we don't feel like we made a mistake.

"Men and women grieve differently and that's okay. Men are more task oriented and tend to not say much. Women cry out loud, want to open up and tell anyone who will listen. We also read a lot."

She ended with, "Keep in mind, when a pregnant woman goes into a hospital to deliver her baby, she is planning for life not death. You are the privileged few who get to meet our babies. Try to keep things positive because we will never forget you and what you did during a very trying time in our lives. Don't make a bad situation worse." The session opened up for questions and somehow I received the most questions. Maybe it was my numerous losses. They varied from miscarriage questions to losing Kevin. People remembered his name from my story. This assured me that I wanted to continue being the voice of the support group. Scared as I was at first, I found it to be therapeutic at the end. I was invited to more in-servicing of hospital NICU, labor and delivery nursing schools and anyone who might come in contact with us and our special needs. I was eventually handed the books to run the hospital liaison part of the support group.

    The first thing I did was look at the calendar for the hospitals that had, at any time, committed to an in-servicing. The inferior hospital I delivered Kevin at was not on the list, but Kevin's hospital was. I figured Kevin's hospital was compassionate and mine needed some help. Seeing this as an opportunity, I reached out by making a phone call to talk to someone at the inferior hospital who needed an education. I was given to the director for their in-servicing. I introduced myself and told her who I represented. I explained how I could help them, help their patients. She flat out refused. I told her about my personal experience there and pleaded with her to change her mind for the sake of future parents. I got a more adamant refusal. In fact, she became incredibly rude. It was a lost cause trying to help them. After hanging up I looked through the previous calendars and their name never appeared on the schedule. Now I understood why I was mistreated. They never fixed or even attempted to change things for the better. I focused on the way I could help and I felt like I was making a difference, getting our name out there, reaching moms and dads in their time of need. There was a growing number of parents coming to the free meetings. They told us when they walked through the doors that the hospitals were referring them to us. I finally found something good that came out of something bad in my life. Kevin had given me a purpose.

Before I knew it my scheduled appointment with the diabetic counselor had come. Kennie and I went together, signed in and had a seat. The room was cool, probably for the pregnant woman. The chairs were comfortable and oversized. Magazines were mostly woman oriented - not much for Kennie.

The door opened "Carol Johnson." My name was called. Excited, nervous, even scared of what to expect. Am I really doing this again? A question that was rattling around in my head. I got up and went to the lady who called my name. She introduced herself as the diabetic counselor and reminded me that she was the one I spoke to on the phone. She led me down the hall to the room that said "Diabetic Counseling" on the door, opened the door and asked me to have a seat. She stepped out of the room to retrieve something she forgot. The room was small, but big enough for a round kitchen like table with fake food on it. There was a credenza along one wall with plastic body parts on it that helped explain how the digestive system worked. Directly across from the kitchen table where we were sitting was her desk with personal stuff on it like pictures of kids and positive messages.

Kennie and I looked at all of the stuff she had for educating us on diabetes. Kennie liked the plastic food that looked real. Just as he was pretending to eat it, she walked in and he was caught. Fortunately for him she had a sense of humor.

She started by giving me a hug and said, "I know what you're going through. I had trouble with having a baby too. I now have twins and they are healthy. I help people with diabetes go through pregnancies and have diabetic moms who have healthy babies all the time. That's my job and I love it."

I could tell she was sincere. She looked me strait in the

eye and never looked away while she said it. My emotions were starting to get the better of me and my spontaneous tears were starting to emerge. She assured me that diabetics can have healthy babies if they are monitored closely. She then leaned over to her desk and grabbed the brown paper grocery bag on it and placed it on the table in front of me. She reached in and pulled out syringes and asked if I have been on insulin before?

"Yes" was my reply. I briefed her on my story and told her that I had been seen by an endocrinologist the last two months of my pregnancy.

She said, "They probably had you pulling your insulin out of a 70/30 bottle of insulin. You can't get your diabetes under control with that kind of guessing. How can you tell what is going into the syringe? The 70 or the 30? It works for people who are diabetics who are not pregnant. We want better control for you." She pulled out two insulin bottles; one bottle represented the 70% and the other represented the 30%.

She said, "We will talk everyday if you need too. I never have done this before but here is my home phone number on the back of my card. You can call me day or night if you have questions." She continued with, "I want you to poke your finger to check your sugar levels before breakfast, an hour after breakfast, an hour after lunch, and an hour after dinner. Write it down in this book." She handed me a book that looked like a check register. "Then I want you to call me first thing every day and tell me what your numbers are and I will instruct you on what insulin you need. As the numbers get in control and you stabilize them, you'll only have to call me once a week. After three months we will take your blood for an A1C count and if they are in tight control you can try to conceive. The A1C test tells us how your sugars have been doing for the past three months."

I told her that getting pregnant wasn't the problem anymore, it was having a healthy living baby.

She said, "If the A1C comes back in tight control, the baby and you are no more at risk than a normal mom without diabetes." She continued showing me the rest of the supplies: the meter to test my blood, lancets, test strips, alcohol pads that go with the machine, more syringes, and insulin. She reminded me that the insulin has to stay refrigerated and to use a small insulated lunch box for travel. It was all overwhelming.

I asked, "How much is this going to cost me? I don't have insurance covering this yet."

She told me that I owed her nothing. It was a pay it forward kind of thing. I understood that when I finished having my baby and no longer needed my new unopened supplies, I would just drop it off to her and the next in need mother would benefit from it. This did make me shed a tear. She was the first person who touched me in a caring way. She really wanted to help me get through a difficult pregnancy to a healthy baby. I had never met anyone like her in the medical field and I had met a lot of people. Kennie carried the supplies and we left. I was crying all the way home, but for the first time in a long time they were happy tears.

I started the next day. I took my blood and called her with the number. She in turn gave me the amounts to pull from each bottle. One was fast acting to bring down the sugars from what I ate and the other was long lasting in the body to control the overall sugars for the day. I called her every day for two weeks. I didn't understand how the carbs and protein worked in the body.

One day I ate a half of an English muffin and my sugar levels spiked. I was instructed to eat a whole English muffin, egg and cheese. The numbers never moved with the same amount of insulin injected and I ate more. I really didn't get it, but as boring as it was, if it's what kept the levels down that's what I will eat until I have a healthy baby. Lunches were small portions of carbs, but I still ate lunch. Example: a half of a small potato, a quarter cup of noodles with spaghetti sauce, small amount of rice, but always include protein to help balance the levels. Exercise and building muscle helped too. I didn't understand how that worked either, but it helped burn off the sugars in the blood stream. As the sugars got in tighter control, I didn't need to call the diabetic counselor as much. Out of respect, even though she offered it, I never wanted to call her at home. I felt privileged that she gave me her home number and didn't want to abuse it. I saved it for only in an actual emergency, which I prayed would never happen.

Just about a little over a month into it, after mastering a routine with the insulin twice a day, poking my finger four times a day and reporting regular levels of sugar levels, I was asked to go have an A1C blood test at the end of March. The levels were below normal. I was told that I was in better control with my numbers than a person without diabetes. I was told that less than a month to go and we could start trying to have a baby.

April marked our ten-year wedding anniversary. We managed to pay for a trip to Hawaii. We were encouraged by all of the doctors to go because it would be a relaxing trip and an opportunity for me to stop focusing on having a baby. "Go have fun" was the sentiment. We did. When we got back, we were given the okay to conceive. It was safe now to carry a baby, the diabetes was under tight control.

"What if it takes over a year to get pregnant?"

Answer, "We will be here as long as it takes."

Comforting words I needed to hear from the diabetic counselor.

My next appointment with the physiologist/therapist was at the end of April. I informed her of the "okay" to conceive because of the sugar levels being in control. She reminded me that I needed to stop taking the pills that were prescribed. I think at that moment and not a minute sooner I was finally ready to try it on my own. Without pills. Maybe I had the confidence because everything seemed to be going well.

May was and always is a busy month for us. It felt like Christmas all over again. Six birthdays, Mother's Day, and to boot Father's Day is just around the corner in June. Mother's Day didn't seem to bother me. Probably because there was so much time between Kevin's death and the Mother's Day celebration. Father's Day would probably be the same for Kennie too. We were busy in May. I couldn't remember when my last period was and started thinking maybe I should go have a test done. I went in on the first Monday in June. No appointment necessary, no co-payment, a urine test and I was confirmed pregnant. Here we go again. Only this time I had a team of people helping me go through it. Kennie and I were not alone. A blood "pregnancy" test was ordered *stat*. No taking any chances here. The sooner it was confirmed with the blood work, the sooner I could become an official patient of the perinatologist.

The blood work came back promptly from the primary care physician (doctor #14) and a referral was made to the OBGYN. It was a little difficult at first explaining to the primary care physician why I wanted an OBGYN that was far away, but after I told my story the papers were signed and I was on my way. I called the OBGYN and couldn't get an appointment for two weeks. This burst my bubble. I had no choice but to wait it out. I called the perinatologist and the front desk receptionist assured me that I would still be seen with or without a referral. She assured me that with a confirmed pregnancy test the insurance can't deny you the necessary care. Problem solved. I realized that not only were the perinatologist group going to have to treat my pregnancy, but they were also going to have to treat my mental state. Everything that set me off was going to have to be addressed and taken care of.

    I had a moment to sit back and realize that what I had been through had changed my life and how I would handle being pregnant again. In the past I couldn't wait to tell everyone in my path that I was pregnant. Now my first response was to call the doctors, arrange appointments, make sure everything is taken care of. At my next therapist appointment, I shared the news of being pregnant. Eventually our moms and dads were told. They understood it was going to be like walking on eggshells, but they tried to be positive.

    The night of the support group was in June. I had mixed emotions. I was now pregnant and was able to join the subsequent pregnancy group in the back room. Usually this was the group that had sudden outbursts of laughter mostly driven by anxious nerves. The circle groups I was currently in had a lot of crying and running out of tissue. Secretly we all wanted to be in the subsequent pregnancy group because it gave hope of moving on from the tragedy we were all dealing with. Another part of me felt like I was leaving Kevin and this was hard for me. I knew the best place for me to get in the right frame of mind was the subsequent pregnancy group.

    We went into a room full of expecting mothers who didn't know me or my story. The doors closed behind me and we had a seat at a large table. This was obviously some kind of conference room for the church. We shared our stories briefly and with a new group of people there were once again mouths dropping open. I told them that I just found out I was pregnant again. I was seeing a perinatologist and I was on insulin. Almost everyone at the table didn't have a clue what a perinatologist was.

One lady asked, "When are you due?"

I answered, "February seventh." I hadn't thought about the due date much. I guess the fear or figuring that the chances of carrying full term wasn't gonna happen anyway. What's in a due date? Was it self-protection or denial? In either case I was having a difficult time bonding with the baby I was carrying. I loved the baby, every one of us love the child we carry, but attachment was another subject. The topic that night was whatever was on your mind. Everything from doctor appointments, sleeping positions, emotions and of course problem solving. I found almost everybody including myself was carrying baggage full of fear. The "what ifs" were the big ones. The unknowns. We all had hurdles to jump - milestones/hurdles of dates. Dates where we lost our babies or something terrible happened. We all seemed to have our own days flagged and as you passed them, you jumped the hurdle and you seemed to breathe easier. It was as if there was some kind of guarantee that after you jumped the last hurdle you would finally win. Unfortunately, if you did just jump the last hurdle and something happened to you again, now you have a new hurdle to add to your jumping in the future. For me that meant six weeks after I give birth, I would be able to breathe easier. It meant I had the farthest to run. This got everyone's attention.

Someone brought up baby showers. I had mixed emotions. I'd never been much for superstition prior to my first loss, but I felt the baby showers jinxed me.

I said, "I'll wait to have a "welcome home baby shower", that way I don't have to be upset if I don't have a baby. I won't feel obligated to return the gifts either." I added a comment a little off of the baby shower topic just to see who at the table agreed with me and how they would handle the problem.

"Have you ever been in a circle of friends or ladies, usually at baby showers and they start telling their stories about their births? "I was in labor 36 hours." "They had to cut me to get the baby out. He got stuck." and they make it sound horrible. I'm sure it is very traumatic for them, but after what we all have been through, I sometimes just want to say, "At least your baby lived and you got to take him/her home.

"The other situation is when you add to the conversation and start telling your story, everyone shuts up. It's like they don't want to hear it. They don't want to hear about your dead baby. If it is at a baby shower it's like you're an omen and a reminder that things can go wrong. I got to a point that I stopped telling my story because it made people uncomfortable. I deny myself of telling my traumatic story and it's sad because we need to tell our stories to help us process what we went through. Yes, the normal births need to be told too and they have a place to still share the stories. We don't. Anybody else have this kind of problem come up?" The nodding of heads told me they agreed. Some chimed in and basically resolved it the same way. We just don't participate in birthing stories any more.

That week was the OBGYN appointment (doctor #15). We went in. Followed protocol: big waiting room, little waiting room, told our story, doctor's notes written on my behalf and then the referral to the perinatologist I wanted was in my hand. I shed a tear and hardly noticed it running down my face.

I looked at Kennie as he whipped it away and said, "It's official." I had just jumped a big hurdle considering what it took to get there.

I called the perinatologist and let them know I had an official referral (doctor #16). I was seen immediately by the perinatologist and his staff to get things officially on record. I received more supplies and prescriptions to fill as needed. I had appointments set up about every two weeks with the perinatologist, diabetic counselor and nutritionist. All were important in my care. Brochures on baby stuff, magazines, advertisements for state-of-the-art baby supplies, free formula, and diaper coupons were all placed in a free diaper bag and given to me.

I went home and went through the goodies I was given at the perinatologist office and one of the papers that stood out was a list of classes. I was not interested in taking another Lamaze class. Tour of the hospital, yes. Maybe this one will be more than just a pretty place to have your baby. It will actually care for me and my baby. I signed up for a CPR class later that month. After Kevin's 911 call I needed my confidence restored. I signed Kennie up too.

The following Monday was the July meeting for the support group. Even though the due date wasn't significant, the counting of the weeks was. I was ten weeks along. Almost at the first trimester, another hurdle. We discussed "A life is a life no matter how long it is" and mine was ten weeks in utero. I couldn't get over the rollercoaster of emotions that were starting to creep up. Some days I was normal, but lately I was wigging out on everything. Controlling, aggressive and trying like hell to keep things in order. I figured it was hormones from being pregnant. Someone remembered my dates in my story of Kevin and reminded me that Kevin's birthday was next week. How could I forget something that important? The facilitator at the table said that it was normal when the dates get close. She starts to get snippy too and her loss was years ago. It's just what happens. The therapist said something like that the other day. We were talking about Kennie's Guillain Barré, she said that when you live through something so traumatic that you instinctively mark the date and when the date comes around it will throw you off whether you remember the date or not. Sometimes you start marking time by the date it happened. Example: When was the last time we went to Disneyland? It was a few days before Kennie was diagnosed with Guillain Barré. She said that living through this kind of terrifying situation is something you store in your subconscious. When you have a situation that triggers the emotion you felt that day, it will feel like that day is happening all over again. It's a different day, but the surge of feeling is the same. You just have to acknowledge it's happening.

    The CPR class came quickly. I had taken a class like this before, but I wasn't sure Kennie had. We walked in and there were the CPR dolls – it was a bit disturbing, but I got through it. Luckily for me the instructor forgot the baby CPR doll at home. He gave a verbal explanation of the difference between a baby and an adult. Done. We were certified in CPR. Kevin's Birthday. What do you do when your child should be one year old today and you don't have the child? We were supposed to have a three-day celebration of birthdays, my sister's on the 24th, Kevin's on the 25th, and my father-law's on the 26th. We celebrated on the 24th and had plans for dinner on the 26th, but what about the 25th? I went to a party supply place and bought balloons and a pin to wear for Kevin that said "Birthday Boy". The people who we came in contact with me looked at me strange because I'm a girl wearing a "Birthday Boy" pin. Some asked and I got to talk briefly about Kevin. Needless to say, this was going to be a tradition on his birthday. We went to the cemetery with the balloons. We parked on the little road and walked up to Kevin.

I said "Hello Kevin. I love you." I took a marker out of my car and wrote a note to Kevin on the balloons. "Happy Birthday, Kevin! Love you. Miss you. I'll see you one day." Then I handed Kennie the marker and he wrote his message, we sang Happy Birthday and let them go into the sky. It was a clear blue sky. We watched them go for a long time. We saw a commercial plane fly by on its way to the airport and wondered if the balloons could be a hazard for the plane. It was only going to be once a year and what were the chances of something happening? Another new tradition for Kevin's birthday. It didn't take away the pain, but it did give us something to do for his birthday and a place where if we cry no one will look twice at us. The other thing that was significant about that day was it marked the end of my first trimester, another hurdle.

The following Wednesday I felt the baby kick. I thought it was early, but Kevin was so small I didn't feel his kicks until much later than in usual pregnancies. I took this as a good sign. I also noticed that I didn't have any morning sickness. Some people don't get sick, some start later in their pregnancy, and some are sick the whole time. I was counting my blessings. My sugar levels were still in tight control. Injections were still not easy, but I got through it. Same routine of sticks to my body. Three insulin injections, four poking my fingers for results, and still calling them in once a week. Even though things seemed to be going better I couldn't get my hopes up and this kept me from enjoying being pregnant.

I was still going to the cemetery but only once or twice a week. My weekly schedule was packed with a doctor appointment, therapist appointment, support group meeting or in-servicing at a hospital, attorney calls, or visiting family. The busy schedule kept me from dwelling on the things that scared me. I was sad because I wasn't getting to the cemetery like I did in the beginning. I felt guilty.

The time came to do the blood work for down syndrome. I kind of figured that if something was going to go wrong it would be at this time. To my surprise it came back fine. Yep, another hurdle.

At 18 weeks I went in for an ultrasound. I was told that I could bring a video tape to record it and share it with family. I was thinking that I could watch it over and over to check for problems. Why do I think like this?

I was at the perinatologist office and of course I was early because Kennie drove. I was asked by the nurses how things were going. I said that I could feel the baby kicking regularly. Nothing like before. Kevin was only three and a half pounds and this one I think will be much bigger. My name was called. This was exciting and frightening all at the same time. I went back, they had me lie down on the exam table and pull my shirt up to expose my baby bump. This sparked the memory of my bumpkins. She put the tape into the machine, squirted the cold jell on my belly and shut off the light. She put the wand on my belly and my baby's image came up. I could hardly see it from the tears coming out of my eyes. Kennie was in awe of the image. He squeezed my hand. She scrolled around, taking measurements. Not knowing our story, she assumed this was the first time we had this procedure done.

She explained everything as she went. "This is the baby's head, face, spine, belly, arms, hands, legs, feet, the umbilical cord. Then she said, no wait, that's a boy." Then looked up at us with a surprise look on her face and said, "Oh gosh I hope you wanted to know the sex of your baby." Kennie squeezed my hand again while we assured her that it wasn't a problem. I kinda figured I was caring a boy, but it also meant the glass is half full and there wasn't an extra "Y" to fix any chromosomal problems. If that was Kevin's problem. If it was a stroke, the sugars are under control and the baby boy I'm caring is safe. Based on what we were seeing he looked like a whole baby. His face looked like it was intact, his feet were going in the right direction, his hands seem to be waving at us almost as if he was saying "Hi" and trying to assure me that he was fine. I had to stop thinking this way. I'm only going to get upset later. Deep down I was starting to allow myself to relax after seeing his little face. We took the tape and showed it to the grandparents. Our moms and dads were happy for us.

While at Kennie's parents' house we were pointing out the baby's head, spine and boy part.

Ruth got excited and said, "I see him."

My father-in-law smiled, nodded his head and acted like he understood it. He then confessed, "I don't know what the heck you're all looking at. The only things I see are waves and snow." We all laughed.

Something happened that I had to figure out how to handle. A stranger asked about the pregnancy. The questions that got me were: Is this your first baby? How many children do you have? I problem solved this in the support group and decided to answer the questions on a "need to know" basis: If the stranger was, let's say in the grocery store. My answer was: Yes, this is my first baby. Chances are I'm never going to see this person again. I felt like I was depriving my boys of their existence, but I was self-preserving by avoiding judgment. If the stranger was someone I was being introduced to and will see them again my answer was: No, and I would go into more detail. I got used to the jaws dropping open. Amazing what you can get used to.

Late October I jumped another hurdle. I was officially in my last trimester. I was in the perinatologist office and the nurse from the support group was checking for the baby's heartbeat with a machine that had audio but no video. The machine never made a sound no matter where she placed it on my abdomen. A scary chill went through me. Did he die? We just saw him. My anxious thoughts seemed to be talking to me, "It's okay. At least I got to see him and I at least have that memory." This is why I was trying hard not to get attached. It was as if the rollercoaster was on a very fast track headed downwards. The nurse understood the panic I was experiencing because she had experienced a loss, too. She said it was probably a dead battery. Wrong choice of words and she knew it when she said it.

She asked, "Can you feel the baby moving?"

I answered, "Yes." That was comforting and my feet were back on the ground. She told me to focus on that and ran to get the perinatologist. He instructed the nurse to go get the ultrasound machine. The minute he placed the wand on my abdomen you could hear the baby's heartbeat and see the baby on the monitor. He showed me that the heart was still beating. He assured me that it was just the audio machine that was not working. You could see the panic leave my body as my muscles relaxed. They never used that audio machine on me again, it was always an ultrasound.

The following Sunday was the tour at the new hospital. The parking lot was secure and had cameras. It was a short walk across a valet drive and in through sliding doors. The facility was a state of the art and totally designed for women, which comforted me. We signed in with the front desk. The security guards present gave me a secure feeling that they protected the moms and their babies. There was a big open waiting room with couches and comfortable chairs. I could smell and hear a coffee stand, but couldn't see one.

"Can I help you?"

"Yes. I'm here for the tour of the hospital." She instructed Kennie and me to sign in and gave us bright green guest stickers to wear. We were directed to the elevators and given the floor number with the assurance that the nurses would help us when we arrived on the floor.

Sure enough we were asked, "Can I help you?" when the doors opened. Nothing was left to chance. There weren't many people on the tour with us. It felt like a private tour. Nice. We were shown the rooms and how they convert to a birthing room. Much smaller than my inferior hospital where I delivered Kevin. Maybe this was a sign that they put their money towards patient care. There seemed to be only one vacant room on the floor, all the rest seemed to be filled.

We passed a nursery where they were taking a newborn's picture. We then received confirmation of what we had already noticed: the safety, protection of the newborns was top priority. The babies were fitted with a wristband that matched the mom's and dad's wristbands. It was mandatory that the dads wear the wristbands or they could not walk out of the birthing room holding their baby. In fact, if you were a guest you could not walk out of the birthing room with the baby at all. A few short days, no one should complain.

There was a large waiting room on each floor which was good considering the family, friends, and following we had. Each one of my losses acquired more and more people. The

OR was pointed out down the hall for C-section babies. The nurse told us that we were next to a hospital for children with a level three NICU. We were also told that the underground tunnel that led to the children's hospital NICU omitted the need for an ambulance taking the baby far away from the mother. Oh, how I wished this is where I had given birth to Kevin. I quickly dismissed the thought. I couldn't change the past anyway. The reassurance that it gave me for the future was comforting. The tour ended with questions and answers. Kennie and I went down to the lobby and went into what we thought was just a gift shop. It turned out to be a lactation education center. Books, videos, supplies and a table set up like a class participation room.

Once again, "Do you have any questions?"

"Yes. What is this all about?"

She said it was support for breast feeding. Maybe this time I might get a chance to breastfeed.

Halloween. I did okay last year. This year I would do the same, the only difference was we went to a party. I made mummy costumes out of bedsheets and thermals. I was much smaller when I started it. This baby boy was going to be a big baby boy. I sewed a few adjustments and the costumes were a hit. Kennie was a mummy and I was a mommy-mummy.

In the beginning of December, we had another ultrasound scheduled. This was the kind that we could video tape. In the dark sonography room, the wand went over my belly and there he was. I was attached with reservations. The support group was very helpful, but listening to everyone else's stories and tragedies I acquired more than just my hurdles. Then the technician asked if we wanted to know the sex of the baby, we told her we knew he was a boy.

She said, "And there is your proof," as she slid the wand

on my belly and focused in on that area. It was as if he heard us in the womb and had to see for himself. The baby reached down in that area and it appeared that he grabbed himself, because at that moment he jumped and so did my belly.

Kennie, who's usually quiet, asked, "Did he just pull a Michael Jackson?" It sure looked like it. We needed the relief that the burst of laughter gave us. One of the things discussed with the doctor that day was an NST. I had them with Kevin. The tests were to start the next week, earlier than with Kevin. Two times a week at the new hospital. He complimented me for keeping my sugar levels under control the whole pregnancy. He even pointed out that my A1C was at 5.0 - better than a non-diabetic. He made it clear that it meant there would be no complications that I would contribute to the diabetes. He smiled and I returned the smile.

The NST appointments were in the hospital in the morning hours and Kennie couldn't attend any of them. I parked the car, waddled into the lobby, signed in, and was shown to the NST room. The ladies were very sweet. Without delay I was listening to the heartbeat. The technicians were good and found the heartbeat the first time. Of course, he was bigger than Kevin and there was nowhere to hide. He stretched out my belly pretty good. One time he had his foot pressed up against my skin so hard you could see the impression of his foot and toes. I was told the NST would continue until the baby was born, for the baby's safety. That meant through the first of February. I suggested exchanging addresses so I could send them all Christmas cards, halfway joking. I was scheduled for 14 NSTs and was informed that the normal number of NSTs was considerably less than that. I figured that after what I'd been through, this was owed to me. The perinatologist wasn't taking any chances. Treating the mother's thoughts and emotions by extra assurance from NST. Smart.

Christmas came and went. I asked family and friends to hold off on giving gifts for the baby and they did. Another superstition - didn't want to jinx it. The New Year came and went.

January was full of all the normal appointments with the NST appointments added. I was a busy pregnant woman. One day I noticed I was leaking fluid. Panicked I called the perinatologist. I was instructed to go to triage (another kind of emergency room) at the women's hospital.

The doctor added that any time I had a problem and wasn't sure what the problem was, to go to triage. "You don't have to ask just go. That's what it's there for. You're high risk and we don't want to take any chances." Fortunately, Kennie was there to take me. Kennie dropped me off in the valet and I signed us in. A wheelchair arrived at the same time Kennie did and I was wheeled up to triage. I was called back quickly and shown to a room that was more of a supply room, but there was an examining table in it. Great, flashbacks. They apologized for the room and I was given a gown to change into. After changing I made my way on to the table. After a few minutes the doctor arrived and introduced himself as one of the perinatologists at the hospital. He asked a few questions and tried to start the exam but then realized I was on a broken exam table. The stirrups were missing. He lowered the back of the table to where I was in a flat position and asked if I could put my feet up on the table.

He said, "I know there isn't much room for a pregnant lady in her 35th week but it's the only way I can continue the exam." With a little help sliding up and then down again I was finally in the position, except he needed my bottom raised to be able to see. A stack of towels did the trick. The next obstacle was no proper lighting and the nurse suggested using a flashlight.

The doctor chuckled and said, "We're a top-rated hospital and this is how I have to perform an exam?" As the doctor finally started, holding the flashlight in his mouth in lieu of a proper light he said, "This exam reminds me of a plumber looking for a leak under a sink." What he said was muffled by the flashlight in his mouth, but it showed us he had a sense of humor. At the end of the exam he had found nothing. He said that sometimes the baby pushes on the bladder and the mom can't hold the urine and you leak. Kevin wasn't big enough and couldn't have done that to me. Better safe than sorry, he assured me we did the right thing by coming down there.

"Any future concerns don't hesitate come straight to triage and we will check it out."

Feeling relieved and a bit embarrassed at the same time we said goodbye. It was a false alarm, but I didn't care. My baby was the most important thing here not my embarrassment.

I was starting to worry about the toxemia coming back with this pregnancy. There were some red flags but no bedrest was recommended. My weight was up there, but the sugars were under tight control. The weight was never frowned upon. The goal and the only thing that mattered was getting this baby into the world healthy. While at an appointment with the perinatologist my blood pressure was slightly raised so he had me lie down on my left side for a few minutes and rechecked it. It was normal. I was told that the left side is where the heart pumps the blood to first. Lying on your left side helps the heart function better. I was also told that lying on the right side helps the stomach empty into the intestines better. If you have an upset stomach drink lots of water, turn on your right side and let it drain. Good to know.

I felt like I was going into labor a couple of times and one was during an exam at the perinatologists. He said they were Braxton Hicks - not real labor pains and they would go away. I never experienced labor pains with Kevin.

One day the pain didn't go away and was getting worse. We had talked about normal vaginal delivery and the pros and cons but it was a wait and see thing. I was just into my 36th week and back to triage we went. Same formalities and we were now in a normal exam room, not a storage room. Much nicer and had all of the equipment needed.

The doctor came in, did his exam and announced "You're in labor! Looks like you're going to have your baby early. These are in fact real labor pains." Kennie, the nurse, and I filled him on my story. He excused himself and called my perinatologist. He returned with a new game plan.

"Babies born to mothers with diabetes take longer to develop their lungs. There is a shot that we give the mothers that will help mature the baby's lungs but the best thing is to try to keep the baby in the mother as long as possible." Normally 36 weeks in utero is an okay time to deliver a baby, but caution flags go up with the diabetes. The test that doctor #7 did in his office on Kevin was repeated on this baby to check lung maturity. This time I knew what was going to happen. The only difference was they numbed the spot before puncturing my belly. It helped a bit or maybe I was more prepared. The test still hurt and within minutes amniotic fluid was drawn from the womb. The lab results showed that the lungs needed more time to develop. I was given terbutaline, a medication injected under the skin that would stop the contractions. I asked if it would hurt the baby. They assured me that it wouldn't.

The terbutaline was worse than the contractions I was having. It made me shake uncontrollably and made my heart race so fast I felt like it was going to jump out of my chest. It made me break into a sweat and I wanted to throw up. I just hoped this wouldn't affect my baby even though they told me it wouldn't. I had a trust issue and I double checked everything. I had no choice but to go through with it. After hours of lying there and enduring the medicine's side effects, the contractions stopped and I was released. I was told during the release instructions that the goal was to keep the baby in utero until at least the 38th week. My heart was racing like I had run a marathon and I was exhausted. Home we went. To bed I went. To sleep I went and this time I went out. No insomnia tonight. This was a reminder that it was time to pack for the hospital. With babies you never know.

      Saturday morning, January 25th I felt like I was having back labor. It started in the center of my back and wrapped around my side to the front. It felt like I pulled something at first and then it became more and more intense. I didn't inform Kennie. My due date was still two weeks out. The perinatologist told me that once I cleared my 38th week the baby's lungs would be compatible with life and yesterday was the day that marked my 38th week. This could be false labor and why panic Kennie again? I'll tell him when I feel more confident that it is really happening.

The pains became more intense and somewhere around 3:00 p.m. I told Kennie, "I believe I've been in labor since 8:00 or 9:00 a.m. The pains are getting stronger and I need to go have it checked out." He reacted the way I expected. He jumped up, ran around the house like a chicken with its head cut off, and was getting nothing accomplished. It was kinda funny. I took over, locked up the house and told him to get the bag that was next to the door heading into the garage. I was starting to doubt if he could drive us there, but he managed. He dropped me off out front of the hospital and I went in and told the security desk that I believed I was in labor. A wheelchair was brought to me. Kennie walked in and proceeded to push me to triage where we were greeted by the nurse who immediately took me back. Between the labor scares and the NST they got to know me and my story. The nurse had me change into a hospital gown that said "angelic" all over it. This helped me know I wasn't alone. Lying on the examination table the nurse hooked a makeshift NST machine up to listen to the baby's heart. There was another machine to check and confirm the contractions. They were real. I was in labor again, only this time I was being admitted into the hospital to have my baby. No stopping the labor with terbutaline. I had heard of back labor, but now I understand what it was first hand. It was a bit of time before they were able to move me to a room - enough time for Kennie to make some phone calls to the family and inform them that I was being admitted. I was moved to a gurney and wheeled me to my room. This one was bigger than the rooms we saw in the tour. I was moved to the labor and delivery bed which broke apart to effectively support the legs and spread the body for the birth when the time comes. I still had a way to go before this happened. The contractions seemed like they were progressing slowly. The perinatologist on call suggested Cervidil, a medicine that was placed like a tampon in the vagina with an extremely long string to retrieve it. The hope was that it would dilate the cervix and the labor would progress. A little uncomfortable, but nothing I couldn't handle. Looking around the room I saw there was an uncomfortable chair or two. I guess they didn't want many visitors and they most definitely didn't want them staying long. I wondered where Kennie was going to sleep or if he would have to go home. Good question that we forgot to ask during the tour. Oops! The room was basic beige and soft light blues, well lit, large bathroom, and curtains to draw for privacy throughout the room.

The nurse came in with a makeshift dinner. "I'm guessing you're hungry?" and handed me the tray as she went to retrieve a portable table from another room. She was right I was hungry. It was diabetic friendly and she gave me my required insulin shot. I had the opportunity to ask about a bed for Kennie. She said that unfortunately this room was not equipped for the dads, but she did have a mat that she could put on the floor under the window. He would have to make do because I needed him here for support. The mat arrived with a pillow and a blanket. I couldn't help but laugh when the time came to for him to use it. He looked like a dog curled up on the mat. Unfortunately, as uncomfortable as it was, I made him get up all night and help me to the bathroom. No catheter for my urine was placed, the IV in my arm was dripping fast enough to fill my bladder and I needed to go. The nurse was called every time to disconnect the monitors for the baby's heartbeat. I dragged my IV pole and Kennie helped me to the bathroom. I had no underwear, but the Cervidil's string was so long that I had to hold it or it would hit the toilet water. I went back to bed and tried to get the contractions to progress. Some were good and seemed to give promise. Our moms and dads came stayed for a while then went home as it got late.

The next morning was Super Bowl Sunday. Well this would give him a theme for a birthday party every year. The perinatologist on call came in and checked to see if I progressed. Not much. She removed the Cervidil and placed another one. She talked about Pitocin and said I had to be farther along before they could use the medicine in my IV drip. Our family started making an appearance and then leaving. The Super Bowl came on and at one point I think people forgot that I was in labor. I really didn't care. The contractions disappeared anyway. After the game was over and most everyone had left, I noticed that I could hear the babies being born around me. I could hear the nurses calling for the doctors when they got close. One baby was born in the hall with the mom on a gurney. I could hear the baby cry with its first breath. Success. This made me smile.

I rubbed my belly while speaking to my baby, "See? That's how it's done. It will be your turn soon."

Night came and Kennie was on the mat again. Before we knew it, Monday morning had come. I was in labor, but it wasn't progressing. The contractions went from intense and then back to tolerable. I couldn't understand why the staff wasn't doing anything like breaking my water. Or discharging me. I got it, I was too high risk to send home. The perinatologist came in and did her examination. She told me that my perinatologist would be in on Tuesday and if nothing happened on its own by then he would be able to decide what to do next.

I had been there for three days and no baby yet. I knew that if there was an emergency I was in the right place.

My insulin and eating needs were being taken care of except for one afternoon. I was given an injection and was told my lunch was on its way, but it never made it to the room. Babies were dropping left and right. Doctors were called and had to handle two and three births at a time. I could hear a nurse yelling for a doctor, a baby was born and the doctor moved to the next room.

I noticed my sugar levels were dropping. The room was closing in on me. Kennie asked about my lunch. He was told that it was on its way. We waited again, but the clock was ticking and my sugar levels were not going to last. Trying to help me out Kennie went to the cafeteria to get me something to eat. Considering how busy the staff was we figured I was forgotten. Kennie managed to get me a deviled egg sandwich and I ate half without even tasting it. I waited to make sure that my sugars settled before I ate the second half. They did and I ate the other half. It was good. After about an hour a nurse came in the room. I would have thought that she would have brought me something to eat. She didn't know Kennie bought me lunch. Her records showed I had been given an insulin injection hours ago. I told her what had happened. I knew they were incredibly busy because I could hear everything. She asked if I hit the call button. Of course I did, but it was either not picked up or empty promises were made. No one showed.

"That's unacceptable", she said. "I'll make sure it never happens again." Another night ended and I was almost in tears. I had been there for three days and it was evident that I was going to be there another day.

Tuesday January 28th. The first thing in the morning my perinatologist walks in.

He's smiled and said, "I read your chart. How about a repeat C-section?"

"Yes." I was so relieved. I asked him if he could do a tummy tuck while he was cutting into me. He laughed. It was worth a try.

He said, "That baby is not going to come out on his own." He described it as if the baby was hitting his head on a brick wall. His head would give out before the wall would.

He removed the last Cervidil and said, "You never progressed far enough for the Pitocin drip." It wasn't long before a team came in and started prepping me for surgery: the cocktail to prevent vomiting, a vitamin K shot for the bleeding issues that Kennie has that the baby might inherit, and shaving prep for surgery.

The anesthesiologist came in and asked me if I had any last minute questions. None that I could think of. He said, "I'll see you in there then."

They were all in scrubs, booties, and blue hats to cover their hair. There was one nurse who had a different hat then the others. It had teddy bears on it. It didn't take me long to bond with her. I told her that I need someone who could keep my head in the game and told her the details of Kevin's birth - how I was knocked out and Kennie wasn't allowed in. There was so much I wanted to tell her and I had a limited amount of time before I was being wheeled out and family was giving me kisses on the cheek. Kennie was dressed and waiting in the OR hall once again. The teddy bear hat nurse assured him that she would come get him in a few minutes. They wheeled me into the room in a wheelchair and I managed to get my big body onto the OR table.

There was a big male nurse with lots of gold earrings curling around his ears. He was someone I would never forget. He kept talking to me and I needed it. For a big man he had a soft voice. I asked him if he was going to be there with me the whole time. He said yes and informed me that he was going to be counting the supplies in the room to make sure they were all accounted for before they sewed me back up. I asked him if he would make sure that he had all of his earrings accounted for too before they sewed me up. He laughed and assured me he would. He then asked me if I had ever had a saddle block before? Yes, but it went terribly wrong and I explained briefly.

He said, "The anesthesiologist is going to do his job and then I'm going to slam you like a hockey puck on the table and get you lying straight out on the table to prevent the anesthetics from settling in one spot. You will be numb by then and unable to move from your chest down. Your arms will still be functioning."

I told him that I weighted a lot and he was going to need help to move me if I'm paralyzed from the chest down.

He said, "I have moved bigger moms to be than you."

Just then I noticed the anesthesiologist setting up his table. Here we go I thought. The big nurse had me lean forward toward him, he braced me and the anesthesiologist poked my spine. He got it in the first shot. He taped it to my back and like the big male nurse promised I was slammed like a hockey puck onto the table. Actually, he was very gentle and I never once did I think I was going to fall off onto the floor. He winked at me as if to say we did it. Someone said to invite the dad in. A tear of joy rolled down my face. Everything was going like it was supposed to. I was waiting for a hiccup, for something to happen. Kennie walked into the room with his deer in the head lights look and a Polaroid camera hanging and swinging from his neck.

I looked at the anesthesiologist and said, "I think he's going to need a chair, preferably one without wheels. No doctor stools, please."

With a slight chuckle he pulled a chair over. His job was mostly done unless there was a problem. I asked him if he could talk to me as the C-section was going. I told him I was better off knowing what was going on than letting my imagination take over in the silence. He said he was better than a sports announcer and I smiled.

Kennie came over to the stool and sat down looking at me. I asked him to make sure to take pictures of the baby when he is born.

Kennie stood up and announced, "Oh no I left the camera out in the waiting area."

I had to laugh. I said, "It's around your neck." It was even swinging back and forth on his neck. Clearly this whole thing made him nervous, but he was there. The anesthesiologist asked Kennie if he was going to be able to take the picture and if he wasn't up for the task the anesthesiologist volunteered for playing photographer.

He said, "We don't need two patients in this room."

I don't think Kennie got it. Kennie agreed to let him take the photos. Everything was moving quickly. A three-foot blue screen was put up at my chest to block my view of the perinatologist basically cutting me open. I could feel tugging on my body but I couldn't feel any touching of my body. I heard music playing in the room. Creedence Clearwater Revival (CCR) rendition of Proud Mary was on. One of my favorites.

As if out of nowhere the perinatologist was suddenly standing next to me.

He said, "Hello. Let's get started." He disappeared around the blue screen wasting no time.

I could hear the perinatologist say, "I'm going to do a test to see if you are numb? Can you feel that?"

"No. Nothing."

He said, "Good because if you could you would have gone through the roof."

I figured he had started cutting into me. Kennie sat there quietly. True to his word, the anesthesiologist was giving me a full description of what was happening in laymen's terms. The perinatologist took over telling me what was going on the other side of the screen and asked me if I was okay.

"Yes."

He told me he had already cut through to the amniotic sac where the baby was and announced he was cutting into the amniotic sac next.

I replied, "When I hear the vacuum I know you're in where the baby is."

He complimented me with my knowledge and then I heard the vacuum. I could hear the perinatologist suctioning and then he announced, "He's here Carol! Your baby boy is here and he's breathing on his own."

Actually, screaming at the top of his lungs. Tears were flowing down my face. Only this time they were happy tears. The anesthesiologist asked me if I was okay.

"Yes. These are good tears." I said.

He then stood up and took pictures. Kennie stood up, took a look, and then sat back down. I was still open and all of my internal organs were exposed. It was obvious that Kennie wasn't cutting the umbilical cord.

The perinatologist said "I'm glad you sat back down. We don't need two patients here."

Gee I heard that before, except this time Kennie got it. The doctor then handed the baby off to the nurse and went back to closing me up. He said that I would feel some tugging and if anything was uncomfortable let him know. I said, that I didn't mind how long it took to close me up, I was preoccupied with my baby. The nurses were asking for guesses on his weight. After most gave a guess, she asked me for a guess.

I said, "Eight pounds, twelve ounces," and that is exactly what he weighed.

Her remark was, "Mom knew what she was carrying. What are you going to name him?"

My answer, "Cameron"

I know the surgery had to be quick for the baby and my safety, but Creedence's Proud Mary was still playing after Cameron was born. My son was born to Proud Mary playing in the OR. That was cool. The nurse sat the baby in the incubator where it was warm and he peed all over the nurse. Nothing wrong with his kidneys. Kennie got up and went over to the incubator to look at him. Big boy was true. He was healthy. That was what mattered to me. He didn't have any cleft lip, cleft palate, or club feet and his hands worked great. It didn't take him long to find his fingers to suck on. Another proof of Cameron being healthy - he could suck. They checked his blood and found his sugars were low. Apparently, the baby gets used to having higher blood sugars fed to him by the diabetic mother's blood. Their little pancreas work to control the sugars flowing through their little bodies and they produce insulin to accommodate it. When the baby is born the sugar supply is not there anymore, but the baby's body is producing insulin and Cameron had too much. The remedy is to feed the baby. He sucked down a remarkable two ounces in no time and the nurse had Kennie take a picture. The nurse had him sitting up in the incubator with the empty bottle in her other hand and Cameron had a full belly, like a puppy. As quickly as the team set up for surgery it was equally fast for the cleanup. The next thing I knew I was being wheeled out. I didn't get a chance to thank everyone individually, but I was truly grateful of their skills. They all succeeded at something that so many other doctors that treated me failed to do. They brought me through a tough, stressful pregnancy, kept my mind in the game, and delivered a healthy baby with no major complications.

  While in recovery I was very aware of my body being numb. My arms could move, but I couldn't move my legs or even scoot my body at all. Kennie brought me Cameron and put him in my arms. He was all bundled up tight and had a little hat on. All you could see was his little pudgy face and puffy red lips. Oh, what a sweet moment. I hadn't held a baby since Kevin died and now I was holding his younger brother. He made it and he was healthy. His face and head were perfectly round. He didn't have to go down the birth canal, he was just lifted out of his womb, no stress. As much as I wanted to never let him go, I felt the urge to throw up. I asked Kennie to take Cameron and hand me a pink tub to throw up in. I didn't know it was possible to vomit lying flat on your back, but it was. Once I was done, I was given Cameron back. Cameron was a healthy 8 lbs. 12 oz, 20 inches long and able to scream at the top of his lungs. Music to my ears. After almost losing Kennie, 16 doctors, seven years of trying, losing five sons, I finally got one I could keep.

The feeling in my legs came back slowly and it was time to move me up to a room. The normal baby tests, blood work, etc. needed to be done on Cameron. Kennie went with Cameron to have tests done. I was being moved to my room from the OR recovery.

As I was being pushed down the hall on a gurney, I heard someone say, "There's Carol." As if I was a celebrity. I could hear a cheer like at a football game. Unable to sit up yet, I raised my hand to acknowledge the praise. The gurney was backed into the elevator and the doors closed.

The orderly said. "You have quite a fan club."

"Yes, I do." The amount of people who had been following Kennie's and my quest to have a family had been growing for years.

We finally arrived at the room where Kennie and Cameron were waiting. Cameron was sleeping in the incubator with a full belly. I was moved into the real bed and in walked the perinatologist. Congratulations was said and then he smirked. He usually was more serious and got straight to work. This was uncommon for him.

I asked, "What was the grin for?"

He said, "I went to the waiting room as I always do to announce the baby was born. I walked in. Saw a bunch of people there and asked who was here for the Johnson baby. To my surprise the whole room stood up. There must have been over 40 people, every chair was filled with someone waiting for news about the Johnson baby, even on the payphone. Then I announced that Cameron was here and everything went well. To my surprise I got a standing ovation. All my years of practice I never got a standing ovation." Then he smiled and went to work on my chart.

Lying in bed to my left was Cameron in the incubator. At the far wall a door leading into the bathroom, a tv, and a closet. To the right of me was a mommy chair, changing table and my portable table for food. Kennie reached into the incubator and handed Cameron to me. Even though I was a bit out of it from the pain medication I wanted to see Cameron. I just had to be reassured that he was fine. I took his hat off to see he had a head full of dark hair shaped in a pointy mohawk. His face was round and perfect. He had a tiny perfect nose and plump lips. His tiny neck seemed too small to ever hold his head up. It's going to take some time to get enough muscles to support his head. Why stop there? I needed to see for myself he was healthy. The room was warm. I opened up the receiving blanket and he had a little perfect body. Kennie was looking him over too. Just then he yawned one of those yawns that the whole face yawns. I got a good look into his mouth. His palate was intact all the way back. Even though I know what I saw, but I couldn't wait for his next yawn so I could see it again. His chest was just as broad as Kevin's was, only bigger. Five pounds made a difference. I stretched his little arms out and counted his fingers on both hands. I then exposed his feet and counted his toes. Little and perfect too. I measured Cameron's foot up to my little finger. They were the same size. I pointed it out to Kennie.

I heard from the door, "His foot won't be that size for long." The grandparents came in with smiles and all took turns holding Cameron. I was a bit out of it from the medicine when I heard Cameron crying nonstop. Kennie, Ruth and my mom all tried to calm him down to no avail.

Unable to focus and uncomfortable with Cameron crying, I stuck out my arms and said, "Give him to me, let me try."

Kennie walked over to me with Cameron in his arms. I could hear the crying getting closer to me. Kennie placed him into my arms and I cradled Cameron close. I didn't jiggle or rock him. I just sang to him. Cameron's eyes seemed to try to focus on me just like Kevin's did. Cameron never uttered another cry and went to sleep. I guess he knew his mommy. Someone put a pillow under my arm to help support him. The C-section incision was starting to remind me I had been cut open and there was pain to accompany it.

This time I knew I was going to breastfeed and was concerned about the medicines in me going into Cameron through the breastmilk. I was told that it would be okay, Cameron had already had two ounces of formula in the Or and probably won't need to be fed for a while. Two ounces, wow! I had seen the empty bottle. He drank it all. Little by little everyone made it into the room to see Cameron and to congratulate Kennie and me. A totally different experience than last time. This is how it was supposed to go. No surprises.

Food arrived for me and that's when I noticed I didn't have a catheter and I had to go. Everyone in the room left and with Kennie and the nurse's help, I made it to the bathroom. I was in a smaller room and didn't have far to walk. There was not as much pain urinating like last time. Made me wonder if something else went wrong in the OR last time. I was hungry and the food went down quickly.

Time passed. I was enjoying watching everyone holding Cameron. The pride I was feeling was something I never felt before. Last time there were questions. I never had the luxury of just being a mom. The lactation nurse entered the room asked everyone to wait in the waiting room because it was time to breastfeed Cameron.

"Well hello baby Cameron" she said, as she picked him up and handed him to me, but not to hold the normal way across my stomach. Instead a pillow was placed under my right arm and I was to place Cameron on the pillow and hold him like a football. Holding him across my stomach would have put too much pressure on my incision. Supporting Cameron's head with my right hand and holding my breast with my left, Cameron latched on and had his second meal.

The nurse said, "You got this. I'll be back to check on you in a few minutes."

Ten minutes later she returned and said, "You can let go of your breast, he's good." I let go and all I saw was Cameron's little pointy mohawk, his little arms and hands flailing. I thought I was suffocating him. I quickly pulled him off and saw that he was okay. Great, after all I went through to have him and I suffocate him with his first feeding.

Things quieted down. Family and friends went home. The lights were dimmed and all was quiet. Cameron was in the incubator in the room with us because I wouldn't allow the nurses to take him to the nursery. I was starting to become very protective of him. I needed to see him to know he was all right.

I started to get an intense abdominal pain, but not from then incision. I called the nurse. She explained that during surgery the doctors opened me up and let air into my abdomen. It would eventually make its way out, but without much movement, like me not walking much, the pain would intensify. I was thinking that I didn't have this kind of pain last time. Last time I was at another hospital getting up and down, walking, making trips to the bathroom and not in bed like now. Last time I didn't allow myself the privilege of acknowledging my pain. The nurse left and returned to the room with a warm blanket which she put directly on my stomach and covered it up. She saw that my chart said diabetic and handed me a cup of warm diet seven up to drink. She said both would help to move the excess gas trapped in my body. She turned down the lights and left. I drank the diet seven-up and it wasn't long and the gas was starting to move. A small relief. A few more diet seven-ups and the pain was gone.

    Breastfeeding quickly became a normal thing. I wanted to try walking down the hall knowing what I was able to accomplish last time. I didn't seem as strong as I was with Kevin. The staff was so caring. Food arrived on time, nurses answered when I called them, and family was welcome. I was relaxed. I did continue to take short walks at first, pushing the incubator with Cameron in it and a wheelchair behind me just in case. Before long I was walking around the floor very slowly, but I was walking and proudly pushing Cameron.

    It was day three. I had spent two nights at the hospital. The doctor made his rounds and removed my staples. Everything was textbook. I was told that I could get Cameron's baby picture taken down the hall at the nursery. After the doctor left, I decided to go check out the nursery and get the picture taken. It gave me something to do. On our way there with Kennie and Cameron, I passed a room that was full of family members and the grandma asked me if I had a C-section. I told her yes, three days ago. She asked when did I first get up and start walking? When I had to go to the bathroom the first time, a few hours after surgery. She then explained that her daughter had a C-section on the 28th too and hadn't gotten out of bed except to go to the bathroom. For some reason she was scared that the staples would pop open and cause more pain. I went into the room and explained to the new mom that walking was the best thing she could do, that it moves the gas, gets the blood flowing, and when she gets home her baby is going to depend on her.

"You need to try moving here where if you have any problems someone will be here to help you." I told her congratulations, got a wink and a thank you from the grandma and left for the nursery.

The nursery window blinds were shut. I had to knock to get someone to open the door. The door opened and I told the lady I was there with Cameron for newborn pictures. She rolled Cameron into the room, but asked us to wait outside. All the incubators were full. She opened the window so Kennie and I could watch. The picture was done and we walked back to my room, but before going in I noticed down the hall the new mom had gotten out of bed for a walk. I smiled thinking maybe I said something that made a difference.

That night was our last night in the hospital. Dinner came for both Kennie and me. This hospital had a first family meal together too. I almost started to cry. It was something we waited a long time for.

January 31st, Cameron was three days old. His due date was two weeks away and he was safe in my arms, not my belly. The pediatrician made his rounds first. He congratulated us and examined Cameron. Cameron had a slight touch of jaundice, nothing to worry about. The doctor released Cameron to go home. He told us to make an appointment within the next week for Cameron's first well baby check and left. This protocol was new to me. The next doctor was my perinatologist. He came in with a smile and announced that it was going home day with Cameron. It seemed he was genuinely happy for us. I couldn't thank him and his staff enough. Given what Kennie and I had been through, I could never have imagined that we would have such a perfect outcome. He performed a quick exam and signed the release papers. I gave him a hug and Kennie shook his hand. He too asked me to make an appointment for two weeks out and left.

    I ate breakfast and Kennie went to get the car when I was done. A wheelchair was brought to my room by a nurse who helped me gather Cameron and my gifts, courtesy of the hospital. Going home gifts - another thing Kevin missed out on. I had to stop comparing my inferior hospital to the new hospital. I was mistreated and nothing will change what happened. I sat down in the wheelchair and was wheeled down to the valet where Kennie was parked. He opened the door for the nurse to inspect that the car seat was fastened correctly. Hospital policy. Cameron was put in the car seat and then I got in the car. I was unable to crawl into the backseat with him and I had a hard time with Cameron facing backwards. I couldn't see him. Kennie assured me he would be okay. Cameron fit better in the car seat than Kevin did. I just held my breath all the way home with anxieties racing. We made it home without any problems. I held Cameron as I walked into the house. Home. We were home and safe. I made my way into the family room where Kennie had prepared the house for Cameron's arrival with all of the baby stuff left over from big brother Kevin, including the Kenny Loggins music playing.

I looked at Cameron and said "We are home Cameron."

When we went to bed, I had no intention of putting Cameron in his crib. I just could not be that far away from Cameron. We used the little bed that Kevin used between us and it worked just fine. We put Cameron on the little mat connecting the stuffed rollers and placed it in between Kennie and me. Cameron fell fast asleep. We got ready for bed and turned out the light. In the middle of the night I had a flashback from when Kevin was alive. It took me a minute to realize that it wasn't Kevin. Kevin made a lot of noise when he slept. It was one of the ways I knew he was still breathing. Cameron on the other hand was a sound quiet sleeper and was not making a sound. I was told you can see if a baby is still breathing by holding a small mirror under their nose and you'll see it fog up. In a panic and knowing it would take too long to turn on a light, I shook Cameron's shoulder just enough to wake him. I got the reaction I wanted. He let out a scream and started to cry.

I picked him up and told him, "Mommy is here. It's okay."

Kennie turned on the light and asked what happened?

"I don't know. He just started crying." Knowing very well I caused the whole thing.

My insomnia, which was all but gone, was replaced by Cameron's feedings. I had a new reason for being awake in the middle of the night and I enjoyed every minute. The only problem was guilt. I was holding Cameron and not Kevin. I had an enormous amount of guilt. I should be holding Kevin too. Hormones were particularly to blame. Some of the girls in the support group, who had successful babies before me, were talking about guilt after their losses. I knew now what they were talking about. One morning I was walking by Kevin's pictures holding Cameron. As usual I kissed Kevin's picture. At that moment I vowed to Kevin that every time I kiss Cameron it would be the same as kissing Kevin. This helped me deal with this problem.

That weekend we had lots of visitors. My mom took the opportunity to start planning the "Welcome Home Baby Shower". The date was set for the middle of March

Cameron's first pediatrician appoint came and Cameron was at the top of all of the charts. I made an appointment to have Cameron circumcised. Cameron still had a touch of jaundice. My breastmilk was not really flowing the way it needed to be. The doctor suggested bottle feeding to get Cameron's kidneys working the way they should and the jaundice would go away. He also suggested using a high wattage light at home to help get rid of the jaundice, which of course we did, day and night. Cameron liked his bottle. It was less work and he would finish it quickly. The jaundice went away and needless to say, so did the breastfeeding. Someone forgot to tell my breasts though. The milk finally came in full blast. Back to the cabbage in the bra.

Cameron wasn't even holding up his own head and I was what we call "Cameronizing". It was recommended to child proof your home for safety. Cameronizing. They suggested that you crawl around on the floor and see for yourself all of the dangers. Kennie did this. We plugged, locked and put everything unsafe up high. It was also suggested to do this again at the baby's crawling stage. More Cameronizing.

The day came for the circumcision. I told Kennie this was one I didn't want to do by myself just in case Cameron was upset and I needed to ride home in the back seat with him. Kennie took us down to the doctor's for the appointment. The place was hard to find. We were the first appointment. Cameron was called back right away.

Kennie last minute said, "I'll wait for you right here." I guess it's a guy thing. Mixed emotions that this was going to be painful for Cameron, but knowing we were making the right decision. I brought him into this world and I wasn't going to let him go through this alone. Small room, typical cupboards, first aid materials, chairs, doctor stool on wheels and a desk with something that resembled a gingerbread mold. I handed Cameron to the nurse who placed him in the gingerbread mold and removed his diaper. The doctor came in and took his place on the stool. He looked at Cameron and sized him up for his bell cap. Apparently after removing the skin a bell cap is placed to protect the area from infection. The doctor told the nurse he needed a size five cap.

Joking, I said, "I'll tell his dad you used the biggest cap you had available."

The doctor and nurse got a chuckle. The nurse soaked a gauze in a fluid and gave it to Cameron to suck on. I asked, "What was that?" The nurse said it was sugar water to keep the baby pacified while the doctor did the procedure. A needle to numb the area was injected and he immediately peed. The doctor almost got wet. He informed me that always happens. Cameron continued to suck on the sugar water, while I held his little hand, the doctor continued and finished with no surprises. I was given instructions for care. The bell cap should fall off slightly after the umbilical cord. I went out to see Kennie. Hesitation at first, then Kennie coddled Cameron as if he was sorry for what just happened. When we got to the car, I told Kennie what it was like during the procedure. I told him the doctor had to use the biggest bell cap on Cameron. Kennie's reply was, "That's my boy."

My checkup time arrived after two weeks and as I promised I gathered up all of my unopened diabetic supplies and happily gave them to the diabetic counselor. I shared with her that Cameron has her name as his middle name and told her that we would never forget her. She played a key role in getting Cameron here and healthy. I was and will be forever grateful for what they all did for me.

"Welcome Home Baby Shower." The day was here. The celebration we had been waiting for. Cameron was a little over five weeks old. Both the belly button and circumcision had healed. He had a little outfit with pockets. Why would they give a baby pockets in their pants? So he could put his car keys in them? Or maybe for putting his hands in them and looking cool? Whatever the reason he did look adorable. My mom and dad had decorated their two-story house with blue and white balloons, piano music was playing and people were already there when we arrived. Finger sandwiches, drinks, and cake for dessert. I walked in with the guest of honor in my arms and within minutes he was taken by a grandma. In fact, it was some time before I saw Cameron again. No doubt he was being taken good care of. The house was full of people. There was a book to sign in on and write a message. The house had a grand staircase which we sat on and opened gifts. There were so many of them that it took over an hour with both Kennie and me opening them. By the time we were done we had one of everything you could think of that a baby would need. We were blessed by a loving family, friends, and a healthy baby. At the end of the day the question of how many people were at the "Welcome Home Baby Shower" came up. Ninety plus. Ninety people signed the book and left messages, but not everyone signed in. It took a few truck loads to get everything home. Every gift was put to use.

Cameron continued to grow at a normal rate and every day was precious. I was still volunteering at the support group. It was a way to honor Kevin. The lawsuit was almost over in our favor. I was fortunate enough to stay home with Cameron. I didn't care what adjustments we had to make. It took me too long to have Cameron and there was no way I was going to hand him over and let someone else raise him with their values while I went to work.

Another thing that came full circle was kissing Kevin's picture. Cameron saw me kissing Kevin's picture once and started kissing it too. In the morning when we would get up, both of us would kiss Kevin.

I started asking Cameron, "Do you know what time it is?"

He would smile and wait for me to say, "Time to kiss Cameron." Then I would kiss his entire face and he would giggle.

Cameron had learned to walk and we went to the park with friends. Most of the friends were from the support group and understood when I pulled out binoculars when Cameron went over to the baby swing set. I watched him like a hawk and when I couldn't see him, I would panic. The binoculars were a way for me to see him get into the tube to slide down and appear again. Silly maybe to most, but it worked for me. The grocery store was a bit of a challenge when he started walking, because he would disappear as a lot of kids do. The panic was scary for me. I was told once that the fear I had was a normal fear. Everyone panics when they lose their child in a store. No. My panic was different. Normal parents would franticly look for their child. I would franticly look for Cameron too but I would also say to myself: I've lost babies before. I've buried one child I'm strong enough to do it again. This was NOT normal! I tried not to be over protective. I even reminded myself from time to time that it would be okay. If Kennie was present when this would occur, I would tell Kennie to take over so I wouldn't continue to panic. It was obvious that it was me. I knew nothing was going to happen, but there was something in me that wouldn't buy into logic.

Cameron was about two when Kennie and I started talking about a second child. We decided on one more try with conditions: If I made it to delivery, I would get my tubes tied. If I couldn't conceive or I miscarried Kennie would go in for a vasectomy. I called the perinatologist and started the ball rolling again. I went in and got the supplies for the diabetes. The diabetic counselor was just as awesome as before. Knowing the insurance still wouldn't kick in until I was confirmed pregnant, she gave me all of the supplies I needed. I was almost a month into the routine of insulin when my numbers were nowhere close to being regulated. The numbers were constantly too low to support a pregnancy and adjustments were made to correct it. The diabetic counselor was confident she could regulate the sugars to safe levels. She also reminded me that I had a beautiful baby and it was okay to not try anymore. She must have known before me that I was ready to throw in the towel.

I was sitting in the family room one evening and I felt the room closing in on me. I could hardly focus on the television. I called for Kennie who was watching television in the master bedroom with Cameron. I had him get my monitor and I checked my sugar level. Forty-five. I knew at that moment that I was done. I had been trying to have a child for so long it consumed me. Trying to have a family seemed to be the only thing that I was trying to do in life. I looked at Cameron who was playing on the floor. Cameron had completed my family. I smiled at him and a tear fell from my eye. Kennie seemed to know instinctively too. It was over. My family was complete. I'm the mother of six but I have only one living son.

The only thing left to do was a vasectomy. I was thinking I was going to get some back peddling from Kennie, but he was willing to go through with the vasectomy considering all of my efforts.

We went into our primary doctor's office. This was the doctor who had treated me since I was nine. He said he was trained and certified in the procedure if Kennie was okay with him doing the vasectomy. It was set for Friday morning 7:00 a.m. in his office before the office opened to the general public. Having the procedure on Friday gave Kennie the weekend to recuperate. He gave Kennie a prescription for pain and inflammation. The doctor suggested filling the prescriptions the night before the procedure. The instructions Kennie was given for after the vasectomy was to go home, stretch out and not move much for the first 24 hours to keep the swelling down. He told us stories and it didn't take much to convince us how serious this was. He also suggested that Cameron and I leave Kennie alone to sleep through it. You don't want a two-year-old who doesn't understand jumping on you. Enough said.

  Early Friday morning we dropped Cameron off at my mom and dad's while he was still sleeping and went to the doctor's office. It was a bit strange being there that early with no one in the parking lot. The doors were locked. Kennie was probably thinking the doors are locked, oh well we'll have to go home. The doctor must have been waiting for us. Within a minute he was on the other side of the doors to unlock them and let us in. It was a dark office with a dim light in the hall to show us the way. It became obvious that we were the only ones there. The doctor handed Kennie a gown and asked him to disrobe from the waist down and told him he could leave his socks on. I started to giggle suspecting what was going to happen and it wasn't the vasectomy that was making me giggle. Kennie changed and sat down on the exam table. The doctor came in and had Kennie lie down on the exam table and gave him a pillow which Kennie put behind his head, leaving Kennie's long legs dangling off the table. He rolled the chair around in front of the exam table. He moved the table with the instruments he needed for the procedure close to the chair.

  The doctor looked at me and asked, "Carol will you be my assistant? I know you have been through a lot and you have an interest in this kind of stuff." He then said that he really didn't need an assistant, but I was welcome to stay and watch. My answer either way was yes. Then the doctor pulled the stirrups out of the table for Kennie to put his feet in. I started to giggle, my suspicions were correct. Kennie was going to experience the OBGYN examination table. He told Kennie to scoot down. Kennie scooted down. Not enough. Scoot down a little more please, until you feel like you're going to fall off. That's when I had to openly laugh. Kennie finally got to experience what I went through with all of the OBGYN exams. The doctor was good and explained what he was doing as he was doing it. I watched everything. The injection for numbing the area. The incision, cutting the tubes, removing a section so they can't grow back together, tying off the remaining part and finally closing the incision. Kennie was a good patient. The doctor even jokingly offered him a sticker. I helped Kennie get dressed and we went home. He felt every bump in the road even though I was driving slowly. I had him get comfortable on the couch, handed him the remote and the house phone. I put an ice chest filled with food and drinks next to the couch loaded and loaded it with bags of ice to put on the incision. I handed him his pills to take and left the rest on the floor next to the ice chest for his next dose. Once I knew he was going to be okay I left him alone to sleep.

 I went to my mom and dad's so they wouldn't have to watch Cameron all day by themselves. When I got there it was lunch time and my mom was telling Cameron that when he got home today take it easy around daddy, because daddy was going to have a big owie.

 Cameron asked, "Why?"

 Mom answered with, "Daddy went to the doctors so they could help him. They had to cut him a little bit and place a bandage on him."

 Of course, Cameron doesn't stop until he truly understands.

 The next question was inevitable. "Where did the doctor

cut him?"

I had to look away to keep from laughing, because this was very serious to Cameron.

Mom said, "On his private parts."

"Oh." was Cameron's response with a very concerning look on his face. I hung out for a bit with mom and dad. I called to check on Kennie to see how he was doing. A little while later we said goodbye to mom and dad, got into the car and headed home. I took the time to remind Cameron about daddy's owie and how quiet he was going to have to be. We pulled into the garage. I helped Cameron out, walked to the back door and noticed Cameron tiptoeing behind me. We entered the house and the television was the only light on. Cameron was still tiptoeing behind me down the long entry.

When we went into the family room Cameron went up to Kennie and gently touched his forehead and said, "Aww daddy. Are you okay?" Kennie assured him he was. Cameron noticed the big bag of ice on the area that had the incision. Cameron tiptoed again to get a closer look at Kennie's owie. After getting a good look at the bag of ice Cameron turned to me and announced he needed a bag of ice too. He tiptoed his way over to the other six-foot couch, crawled up on it very slowly and stretched out like his daddy. I was laughing a bit at Cameron's shenanigans and the fact that he remembered how important it was to tiptoe around daddy. I went into the kitchen and got a snack baggie, put two ice cubes in it and went over to where Cameron was laying down acting like he was in pain too. I placed the little ice pack on Cameron's diaper in the same location as his daddy's owie and Cameron let out a sigh of relief.

THE END

"THE FAMILY PORTRAIT"

Made in the USA
San Bernardino, CA
20 December 2018